HEROES OF JADOTVILLE

Rose Doyle is a writer and journalist. Her novels, nineteen in all, include *Fate and Tomorrow* (set in the Congo in 1902) and *Shadows Will Fall*—both international bestsellers—as well as three books for children. *Trade Names: Traditional Traders and Shopkeepers of Dublin*, the book of her long-running series in *The Irish Times*, was published by New Island in 2004. Comdt Patrick Quinlan, who led the Irish UN troops at Jadotville, was her uncle.

Heroes

of

Jadotville

THE SOLDIERS' STORY

ROSE DOYLE

Exclusive material provided by Leo Quinlan

NEW ISLAND

HEROES OF JADOTVILLE: THE SOLDIERS' STORY
First edition published in 2006
Second edition published in 2016
by
New Island Books,
16 Priory Hall Office Park,
Stillorgan,
County Dublin,
Republic of Ireland.

www.newisland.ie

PRINT ISBN: 978-1-84840-488-5
EPUB ISBN: 978-1-84840-489-2
MOBI ISBN: 978-1-84840-490-8

British Library Cataloguing Data.
A CIP catalogue record for this book is available from the British Library.

Typeset by JVR Creative India
Cover design by Mariel Deegan
Printed by ScandBook AB, Sweden

 New Island is a member of Publishing Ireland, the Irish book publishers' association.

New Island received financial assistance from The Arts Council (*An Chomhairle Ealaíon*), 70 Merrion Square, Dublin 2, Ireland.

10 9 8 7 6 5 4 3 2 1

CONTENTS

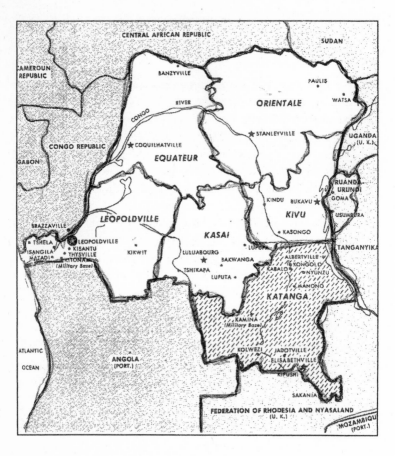

Above: Map of the Congo as it was in 1961. The province of Katanga, in the south-east, seceded from the rest when the Congo attained independence from Belgium in 1960.
© *Irish Defence Forces*

FOREWORD

Rose Doyle's important work, *Heroes of Jadotville*, is a vivid account and vindication of the heroic battle fought by A Company of the 35th Irish Battalion at Jadotville in the Congo in September 1961.

Heroes of Jadotville is a story of two parts. The first part comprises a forensic account of an extraordinary battle fought over a number of days by besieged Irish troops at Jadotville, a predominantly Belgian mining town in the province of Katanga in the searing African heat of September 1961. Under the command of Commandant Pat Quinlan, fewer than 200 Irish soldiers, many of whom were on their first deployment overseas, held approximately 4,000 heavily armed Katangan Gendarmerie and European mercenaries at bay for several days.

Rose Doyle weaves a compelling account of the siege at Jadotville through personal diary entries of those engaged in the combat, alongside dramatic and at times poignant entries from A Company's radio log and interviews with survivors of the battle. One is left with the indelible impression of a unit whose survival was a direct result of the leadership of Commandant Quinlan and his dogged insistence on fire control, iron discipline and the retention of the initiative in the face of overwhelming odds. One is also left in no doubt that A Company's survival was in defiance of the apparent and almost incredible indifference to their precarious situation of the Irish military authorities, both in the Congo and at home in Ireland.

Eventually, when water and ammunition supplies ran out, the Irish commander agreed to a ceasefire and to truce negotiations. Seemingly abandoned to their fate by the UN and the general staff of the Irish Army, Commandant Quinlan and his troops were subsequently taken into captivity by the Gendarmerie and mercenaries in Jadotville, who reneged on their truce agreement. Abused physically and psychologically by their captors, their treatment as prisoners, whilst harsh and unnerving, would pale into insignificance by comparison with their subsequent treatment by the Irish military authorities on their eventual release and return to Ireland.

The second part of Rose Doyle's story describes the shameful treatment meted out to Commandant Quinlan and the soldiers of A Company by the Irish general staff, who refused to acknowledge their heroism on their repatriation to Ireland, and allowed those who fought for their lives at Jadotville to become unjustifiably stigmatised as cowards and isolated within the Irish Army.

The treatment of Commandant Quinlan by his superiors subsequent to the battle is described in detail by Rose Doyle in this book. It describes a process of character assassination and dirty dealings by a cosy coterie of senior Irish officers intent on saving their own reputations and career prospects at the cost of Commandant Quinlan and A Company's collective reputation. According to Doyle's comprehensive and lucid account of Jadotville and its aftermath, the explanation for the despicable behaviour of the Irish military authorities is clear and unmistakable. If they had acknowledged Commandant Quinlan's bravery and leadership, if they had acknowledged A Company's true predicament at Jadotville, they would also have had to acknowledge their own incompetence, culpability and contributory negligence, which resulted in the desperate battle for survival that took place there.

In summary, *Heroes of Jadotville* is an important and detailed record of the experiences of Irish troops in combat on a UN mission far from home. Sadly, much of Ireland's military experience abroad remains untold. Apart from sanitised and heavily redacted archive material, there are only a few books that speak of the combat experience of Irish peacekeepers in the raw vernacular of Irish soldiers. Rose Doyle's work stands out in this regard, and combines a variety of sources to tell one of the greatest stories never told of the role of Irish citizenship in global conflict.

– Tom Clonan

INTRODUCTION

It is a pity that we, who never believed in the use of force, must suffer for the blunders of little dictators and stupid military leaders ... We did not come here to shoot Africans, we came to help them ... I was not prepared to let my brave men die for nothing.

Comdt Patrick Quinlan, Jadotville, September 1961

This is the true story of a battle fought by Irish United Nations peacekeeping soldiers in Africa in 1961. Like all good stories, it is about life, and about death. Because it's an Irish story, it is also about silence, denial and the art of letting sleeping dogs lie.

The story is not over, yet.

The battle was fought in Jadotville, a wealthy, Belgian-controlled, mining town in the province of Katanga, Congo, Central Africa, over the five days from Wednesday, 13 September to Sunday, 17 September 1961. The soldiers belonged to A Company, 35th Irish Battalion. There were 156 of them and they were attacked by more than 3,000 heavily armed members of the Gendarmerie, the mercenary-led Katangan Army.

Isolated, ill equipped, without water, food or reinforcements, the Irish soldiers defended themselves in what became a remorselessly brutal and bloody encounter. None were killed. Hundreds of Katangans died.

Lies, betrayal, hunger, thirst, the failure of reinforcements to reach them and of communications to make contact—all made surrender inevitable.

On Sunday, 17 September, the soldiers' commanding officer, Comdt Patrick Quinlan, agreed terms with Godefroid Munongo, Katanga's Minister for the Interior. The same day, UN Secretary

General Dag Hammarskjöld, on a mission to bring peace between UN and Katangan troops, died in a Congo plane crash.

A Company was taken prisoner, hostages to be bargained with in the Katangan/Belgian power struggle with the United Nations. Freed in late October, they resumed their tour of duty.

These, then, are the bare and pitiless bones of what became known as 'The Jadotville Affair', outline details of the longest protracted action of an Irish unit in the Congo during the period, a summary of a battle unacknowledged for 44 years, with the courage of the men who fought it still unrecognised.

> *With no hope of more help my only concern was for the lives of my men. Before God and their Irish mothers and wives and fathers I am satisfied that I have done my duty. Further fighting would have achieved nothing except useless slaughter.*
>
> Comdt P. Quinlan, September 1961

The soldiers were honoured, finally, in November 2005, in a plaque unveiled by Minister for Defence Willie O'Dea TD in Athlone's Custume Barracks, from where they had left in the early summer of 1961 for Elisabethville and Katanga, Congo. A portrait of Comdt (later Colonel) Quinlan hangs in the Congo Room in the United Nations Training School in the Curragh. However, recommended medals were not awarded and for all concerned there was a sadness that, even now, commendations for bravery were withheld.

Acknowledgement came only after campaigning and exposure of the facts on several fronts.

In the beginning, in 1996, there was Liam Donnelly. A Captain in Jadotville, Donnelly gathered facts and intelligence together in a masterly submission made to Chief of Staff, Lieutenant General G. McMahon, in 1996. Tireless and fair minded, Donnelly sought to 'rectify an outstanding injustice' by having the bravery both of the unit and of its commanding officer, Comdt Quinlan, recognised and by having recommendations for awards for bravery re-examined. His submission was ignored.

In the years that followed, Colonel (retired) Terence O'Neill had prestigious articles on Jadotville published internationally and, in an Ireland aspiring to transparency, broadcaster Tom Maguire's award-winning documentary, 'The Siege of Jadotville', was transmitted by RTÉ Radio 1. Through it all, John Gorman, who had been a 17-year-old private in Jadotville, campaigned tirelessly in Athlone, ensuring that Jadotville would not be forgotten by either politicians or the media.

In 2004, Liam Donnelly re-submitted his document to Lieutenant General Jim Sreenan when that soldier became Chief of Staff. 'I trust,' Donnelly noted in his submission, 'that time will prove to be once again the only judge in matters of love and history and truth.'

Dáil questions were asked, and debated, and time proved itself. Liam Donnelly's submission was acted upon and the company and its commander were at last acknowledged, albeit without the awarding of the recommended medals. For many, including the by now deceased OC, Pat Quinlan, recognition came far, far too late.

For all involved, there is a sadness that, even now, the awards and commendations for bravery continue to be withheld. As do the answers to myriad questions surrounding events in Jadotville in September 1961.

Why, for instance, were the soldiers of A Company sent 80 miles from their base in Elisabethville to defend a town whose population didn't want them there? And why were they then abandoned to certain attack? Why was Comdt Pat Quinlan not given written orders? Why, given their vulnerable and surrounded situation, were they not told of Operation Morthor, a major UN offensive planned for Elisabethville, the Katangan capital? Why, when he asked permission to take his men out of the besieged and cut-off mining town, so as to return to base in Elisabethville, was Comdt Quinlan told to remain in Jadotville? Why were reinforcements recalled by Battalion HQ when they were part of a Brigade Task Force mission, the Brigade having the superior authority? Why were the Ethiopian jets requested and scheduled for their aid refused permission to refuel in Uganda? And why did a radio message, from their Elisabethville HQ, demand of Comdt Quinlan when the battle was all but over if he was 'deserting the men'?

This last remained a particularly sore and bitter point with Pat Quinlan and the men of A Company.

Heroes of Jadotville: The Soldiers' Story looks at all of these questions, and gives answers. This book also reveals what is without doubt one of the most important pieces of evidence about what really happened. Colonel Jonas Waern was Commander of the Swedish Battalion in Katanga. He was also a United Nations intelligence officer. On Friday, 15 September 1961, two days after A Company was attacked and twelve days after the Katangan Gendarmerie first began to surround it, Waern submitted an estimate of the situation to General Kas Raja, Senior United Nations military officer in Katanga, requesting a relief force for Jadotville.

What is interesting is that this document comes from the Swedish commander and not from the Irish Battalion Commander, Lieutenant Colonel Hugh McNamee. A thorough search of A Company's archival documents and the History/Original Record of 35th Infantry Battalion in the Congo 1961 failed to unearth anything similar emanating from Irish Battalion HQ at the time.

The document is especially revealing because, with Waern doubling as UN Intelligence Officer, it is at once an operation order requesting permission to get relief to A Company, a situation report and an estimate of the likely existing and future situations regarding Jadotville.

The document displays throughout an acute awareness of the terrible danger facing the besieged A Company, of the consequences attaching to the very real probability that the Irish soldiers could be 'wiped out', as well as a recognition on the part of every officer in UN Katanga Command that both strategic and tactical intelligence were shockingly lacking.

Waern was strongly of the view that the 'Gendarmerie are capable of pitting more troops against Company in Jadotville than against all UN forces in Elisabethville'. He states baldly that 'if they [A Company] are not resupplied or relieved they may be wiped out'. Such a risk was then, 'considered against possible losses in Elisabethville with reduced strength.' Waern said further that 'success of this operation [getting a relief patrol to A Company] would be a great boost to UN ops. Failure to retrieve this company would be a crippling blow to the UN.'

A Company's survival had to do with tactics, great courage and, everyone involved afterwards agreed, divine intervention or a miracle of some sort.

> *The people of Ireland will pass judgement on whoever was responsible for the callous disregard of 156 Irish lives.*
>
> Comdt P. Quinlan, September 1961

Maybe they will, too.

Jadotville memories are long. *Heroes of Jadotville: The Soldiers' Story* tells what happened in the words of some and in the deeds of all of those who fought in the mining town during those five unforgiving days in September 1961.

Mostly the words are those of the man who led the garrison. Comdt Patrick Quinlan, 42 years old and a native of Reeneraugh, Waterville, Co. Kerry, well knew the danger they were in, and the reason why. Loudly vocal at the time, he recorded what he had to say in letters home, in a private journal, tactical notes intended for the better future training of Irish soldiers, reports and documentation on the battle.

Intended for a book he never wrote and as an accurate recording of what happened, his writings make for a compelling, insightful and passionate account of the politics and personalities dictating events in the newly independent Congo.

> *The UN made a complete mess of things. Organised by the Belgian government we were lured to Jadotville ... and ended up as hostages.*
>
> Comdt P. Quinlan, September 1961

From Kerry's savagely beautiful Iveragh peninsula, bred of an Irish-speaking culture steeped in notions of truth and obligation, Quinlan was irredeemably exacting and scrupulous, as quick to forgive as to anger, a warm-hearted, intelligent man of acknowledged courage. His sharp wit and blunt directness gained him respect but little kudos from those in authority. He could not and did not accept that the men in his charge should fight and die for a cause which was not theirs and, having led them into a battle they fought and survived and won, he could not accept that they should be forgotten. Before, during and after the battle, he asked questions and demanded answers that he was never given.

He died in 1997, his frustration at A Company's denial by the army, government and the United Nations a furious part of him still.

This, his book, is shared by others who served and fought with him. Men for whom Jadotville, in the words of Noel Carey, the company's youngest officer, 'became a living sore, there all the time.' Survivors who, as they became fewer, were, according to Liam Donnelly, 'more vocal and aggressive regarding their need to have the Defence Forces acknowledge their brave contribution to UN service.'

Others who speak for Jadotville include John Gorman, who has never allowed Jadotville be forgotten, and Paddy Neville, Quartermaster Sergeant with the company, brave beyond measure and memory acute.

The account by Sergeant (retired) Walter Hegarty, one of the five wounded, is full of a wry humour, while Colonel (retired) Joe Clune recalls things from his perspective as medical officer. Leo Boland speaks from the perspective of a 19-year-old private in Jadotville. Billy Ready was 20 in 1961, a fitter/private attached to A Company and the first to be wounded. Sean Foley was also 20 years old, an Irish-speaking, bagpipe-playing corporal in the Congo. Bobby Allan was the company's cook/corporal, famous for both his courage and a concoction called Jadotville Stew. Lars Fröberg, the Swedish Army lieutenant who was Comdt Quinlan's interpreter, tells how he found himself part of something that was far, far more than he'd bargained for, and Colonel (retired) Michael Shannon gives the view from the bridge, as it were. He was twice part of the relief force which tried to cross the 18-miles distant Lufira Bridge to get to the beleaguered troops.

Mrs Lola Leech, widow of Joe Leech, a young lieutenant in Jadotville, tells of the waiting and nightmare times for the families, and Mary Manning-Lattimore remembers for her brother, 19-year-old Private John Manning.

> *It's the old Irish thing. If it's a problem, bury it, let it die and it'll die. The Congo died in all of us. We moved on, because you do move on, but it was a living sore there all the time.*
>
> Noel Carey, 2005

Joseph Conrad's *Heart of Darkness* has given the Congo a grip like no other African country on the Western imagination. The Jadotville Affair's deep, many tentacled roots found purchase in the soil of the Congo's decades of colonialism, in the activities of those Conrad described as 'tearing the treasure out of the bowels of the land'. The treasure seekers in this instance were Belgium, America and Britain, all fearful for their vast investments in the copper, gold, cobalt, diamond and zinc riches of Katanga.

The roots were there too in American and Belgian involvement in the 1961 murder of Patrice Lumumba, the Congo's first democratically elected Prime Minister, the subsequent political manoeuvring for control of mineral-rich Katanga, and the UNs' confusion about the role of its peacekeeping forces.

The resulting turmoil, intrigue, civil war, havoc, political ambition and lack of communication allowed A Company to be used by Belgium, abandoned by the United Nations and its own army and, subsequently, ignored by successive governments through the years.

But in the burial of the Jadotville Affair there lies the wider question and bigger story of how, as well as why, 156 Irish peacekeeping soldiers became pawns in the international politics for control of Katanga and its vast mineral wealth.

> *The evidence is indeed very strong to suggest that A Company was used to justify the illegal use of military force in the furtherance of political and personal objectives....*
>
> Capt. Liam Donnelly

Belgium's 80-year rule of the Congo ended, abruptly, on 30 June 1960. King Baudouin of Belgium, in an Independence Day speech, displayed a patronising paternalism shocking even for the early 1960s. 'The independence of the Congo,' he announced, 'is the crowning of the work conceived by the genius of King Leopold II, undertaken by him with courage and continued by Belgium with perseverance....'

King Leopold II's ownership of the Congo had overseen the murder of an estimated 10 million of its people between 1885 and 1908. It was the Irish patriot, Roger Casement, who, after diligent and dangerous research in the Congo's jungles and along its river, famously denounced Leopold's Congo Free State in a report to the British Parliament in 1904. Calling it an 'infamous, infamous, shameful system' of exploitation, he detailed the horrors of severed hands, decimated villages, torture and genocide of the 'poor unhappy souls' who were the people of the Congo. The country, as a result, moved from Leopold's personal ownership to become a Belgian colony.

This lasted until the Congo was given its independence in 1960, by which time Belgian misrule had created a seriously underdeveloped state. The Congo is five times bigger than France, has 60 million inhabitants and over 200 African ethnic groups. Katanga is one of the largest provinces. The Congo at independence had no Congolese officers in its army, no Congolese doctors, agronomists or engineers, only three African managers in the entire civil service and only thirty African university graduates.

Prime Minister Lumumba made an unscheduled, and compelling, speech in reply to that made by the King of the Belgians on Independence Day. He passionately denounced the brutalities and indignities suffered by the Congolese people under Belgian rule, said that the land of the Republic of the Congo was 'now in the hands of its own children' and called for 'a noble struggle that will bring our country to peace, prosperity and greatness.'

This, and his further call for an Africa free of its colonial past and role as an economic colony of Europe, caused huge concern among European powers with stakes in the Congo.

It also ensured that Patrice Lumumba got no Western help with his country's rocky transition to independence. Turning to the Soviet Union for help, he was inevitably branded a Communist sympathiser, by America and Belgium, and thus sealed his own personal fate.

Katanga was the wealthiest of the Congo's provinces. Jadotville was in Katanga and Union Minière de Haut-Katanga, the all-powerful mining company crucial to Belgium's interest in the Congo, was based in Jadotville.

When Katanga, within weeks of independence and with Belgian backing, declared itself a separate state, Lumumba looked for, and was given, United Nations peacekeeping help.

However, by the time the 35th Irish Battalion and A Company arrived in the Congo, Lumumba was dead—murdered with the now-proven connivance of the American CIA and Belgium. Following a commission of enquiry in 2002, Belgium offered the Congolese people 'its profound and sincere regrets and apologies' for its role in the assassination of Patrice Lumumba. In the US, declassified documents have revealed that the CIA plotted to assassinate Lumumba, and in December 2013 the US State Department admitted that President Eisenhower authorised his murder.

The outcry following Lumumba's murder led the UN Security Council to draw up a resolution urging the UN to 'take immediately all appropriate measures to prevent the occurrence of civil war in the Congo' and authorising 'the use of force if necessary in the last resort.' The resolution called too for the withdrawal and evacuation of all Belgian and other foreign military and paramilitary personnel and political advisers not under UN command, including mercenaries—of whom there were many.

The Irish diplomat, Dr Conor Cruise O'Brien, was appointed UN Secretary Dag Hammarskjöld's Special Representative in Elisabethville, capital of Katanga. Irish Army man General Sean McKeown was appointed Force Commander for UN troops in the Congo.

Together with UN officials both in New York and the Congo, they proceeded to preside over a situation that was truly chaotic, and not a little volatile.

We wanted to see things, all the bloody things under the sun! There was the money and the excitement; it completed our love of soldering. Nearly completed us altogether!
Paddy Neville, Quartermaster Sergeant, A Company

In Ireland, in the springtime of 1961, those volunteering for peacekeeping in Africa were mostly untravelled, mainly in their teens and twenties and variously filled with an urge to find adventure, bring peace and escape economic misery. Decent and upright, they were quintessentially of their time.

They left for the heat of Africa in uniforms of Bulls' wool, with, as Paddy Neville puts it, 'butty leggings and brown studded boots that could be heard coming a mile off.'

A 26-county census that year revealed a population of almost three million; a general election returned a minority Fianna Fáil government under Seán Lemass; the last of the Liffey Steamers was taken out of service; and RTÉ television began broadcasting. In the United States, John Fitzgerald Kennedy became President and Gary Cooper died. In Russia, the nation's space hero, Yuri Gagarin, returned to earth.

The troubled and newly independent Congo was known in Ireland as the place in Africa where nine Irish soldiers had been ambushed and killed in Niemba by Baluba tribesmen. Some 300,000 members of a shocked nation had turned out to mourn their returning bodies in November 1960.

The peacekeepers of the 35th Battalion were undeterred. Extraordinary men in an extraordinary generation, they were of a time before Ireland changed, joined the EU, spun the progress wheel and moved on. They believed implicitly in handed-down values, in God and family, church and state.

They believed in the United Nations too, until they got to Africa. And they believed in their army.

> *The average age of the NCOs was 25 and of the privates 19 or 20. We had no previous overseas military experience and most of the Battalion's senior officers were over 50 years of age. We knew nothing about the Congo and the army knew less.*
>
> Lieut Noel Carey

Michael Shannon, Chairman and CEO of the Irish Peace Institute in Limerick, went to the Congo as a young lieutenant with the 35th Battalion's B Company. Recalling the culture of the time, he says: 'We had God on our side—how could we fail? Our cause was to establish peace in darkest Africa. A very noble aspiration. You were imbued with the ethos that your superior would look after you, God would look after you and the guys at the top after everyone else. The autocracy in the country was enormous.'

> *We walked innocently into the jaws of a trap which snapped shut as soon as we arrived in Jadotville ... Pat Quinlan was the one went*

out to the Congo with a realistic view and expectations. He was a
great soldier, a very brave man.

Lieut Noel Carey

Pat Quinlan was also an angry man, railing with a fury similar to that of his compatriot, Roger Casement, half a century earlier, at the system of misrule in the Congo, at puppet rulers and Belgian control. He railed too at United Nations 'bungling'.

The whole UN is the greatest racket of all time. Some people are
making fortunes and the soldiers are suffering. It is sickening.

Comdt P. Quinlan, July 1961

He found no reason to change his mind. Casement, in 1904, had called his British Foreign Office superiors 'a gang of stupidities' and 'a wretched set of incompetent noodles'. Pat Quinlan, in November 1961, as A Company's tour of duty came to an end, wrote: 'There is no more disorganised or incompetent body in the world today than our U.N. It is sinful for our Irish Government to commit our Irish soldiers to the whims and fancies of that crowd of parasites.'

In November 1961, Quinlan noted too that, 'the Belgian officer who shot Lumumba was second in command of operations against us (in Jadotville)'. The world knows now what Comdt Quinlan knew then. Belgium, 41 years after the event and on foot of definitive proof, apologised (in 2002) for its role in the murder of Patrice Lumumba.

Belgium might also consider apologising for its role in endangering the lives of 156 Irish peacekeeping soldiers.

Brigadier Inda Jit Rikhye, the UN Secretary General's military representative in the Congo, has long confirmed UN reports that Belgian civilian personnel made it impossible for UN civilian experts to work properly.

An apology to the soldiers of Jadotville is long overdue too from a United Nations which issued the order for Jadotville from New York, then left them there.

Comdt Quinlan, almost as Jadotville ended, saw the cover-up coming. 'Too many big shots are involved and too many heads would roll … the whole thing stinks before heaven.'

Liam Donnelly, whose family served with distinction in the army for generations, was 33 years old in Jadotville. He makes the same point: 'Had the United Nations force in Jadotville been annihilated or suffered major casualties, the Belgian consul would have been justified in his ruse and Conor Cruise O'Brien would have had justification for his failed Operation Morthor. Afterwards medals would have been awarded posthumously and the dust would have settled … the major problem which arises from the survival of A Company is the fact that the near total incompetence at higher levels, both political and military, could and would unfold.'

The long, silent denial of Jadotville also rejected, and continues to reject, a group of heroic people who helped A Company. There was the elderly Madame Lamonfagne, who literally put herself in mortal danger when she refused to leave the battle area, giving A Company every help possible.

And it rejects Monsieur Louis Christiaens who risked his life to help A Company by going into Jadotville during the fighting, to gather information.

There has never been recognition of the heroism of the volunteer helicopter crew of Norwegian pilot Bjerne Hovden and Swedish co-pilot Eric Thors, who flew a mechanically dubious helicopter on a rescue mission to Jadotville, landed in what Quinlan described as 'an inferno with all hell let loose' and remained to fight .

There are others too who helped, putting themselves at risk of life and livelihood: Belgian Mark Pierre, Luxembourger Major Guertz, Wexfordman Charles Kearney, and the young Baluba, Emmanuel Kamujeki, were all essential to the outcome at Jadotville.

Requests from Comdt Quinlan that their help be acknowledged, even commended, went unheeded.

Silence has other consequences. What happened in Jadotville has long been recognised by those who have cared to study it as a battle fought with tactical brilliance, one offering life-saving lessons. The silence to date has denied its lessons to a wider audience of student soldiers and peacekeepers.

Colonel (retired) Terence O'Neill, who served in the Congo, Lebanon and Angola and has studied the UN's peacekeeping role, says that what happened in Jadotville highlights the failure of the UN to 'determine from the outset whether peacekeepers are symbols of the UN's moral authority or soldiers, members of a military force capable if required of imposing the UN's will.'

O'Neill says too that 'failure to learn the lessons [of Jadotville] led to many of the problems encountered by UN troops at Srebrenica and in Rwanda and Sierra Leone' and points out that 'literature on UN peacekeeping makes little or no reference to the events at Jadotville ... remarkable given the numbers killed—almost 200 Katangese—and its impact on Operation Morthor and subsequent developments.'

Silence has denied the soldiers who fought in Jadotville and, as a consequence of silence, they have lived feeling ostracised, and with shame and anger. They soldiered on, because that is what they know and how they are.

> *God, my men were fine ... Ireland never reared better sons. They would have died to a man if I had decided to continue. They never wavered ... No man ever got the loyalty I did from those boys. When things were darkest they were always smiling.*
>
> Comdt P. Quinlan, October 1961

Patrice Lumumba, just weeks before he was murdered, said that Africa would write its own glorious and dignified history. There is much that is glorious and dignified in the history of the men who fought in his country in the town of Jadotville. There is great courage, too, and drama, and, through it all, there is humour.

Heroes of Jadotville tells that story.

It is the story, too, of what happened afterwards, of how good soldiers and principled men suffered the humiliation of imprisonment and, for all of the years since, the more corrosive humiliation of the silent denial of their action, their betrayal by the army to which they pledged their loyalty, the country they loved, the peacekeeping organisation they trusted.

Theirs is an honourable story. A moral tale indeed.

Nine years have passed since Heroes of Jadotville: The Soldiers' Story *was first published by New Island. Some of Jadotville's heroes, interviewed in this book, have since died. RIP.*
Those who have died are:

Joseph (Joe) Clune (Doctor/Commandant)
W. (Bobby) Allan (Corporal)
Patrick (Paddy) Prendergast (Company Sergeant)

ACKNOWLEDGEMENTS

That this book has at last seen the light of day is a tribute to the memories, writings and help, so generously and courteously given, of many of the men who fought in Jadotville in September 1961. It could not, literally, have been put together but for Leo Quinlan, first born son of the heroic commander of Jadotville's A Company who, diligently and patiently, gathered together his dead father's letters, journals, reports and anything else of relevance to the story of events. It was Leo who transcribed the handwriting which, like the man, filled pages with urgency and impatience. No one else could have done it. But then Leo Quinlan was for years determined that the story of Jadotville would be told from the viewpoint of his father and the men who fought there with him. It was Leo who rallied the troops, so to speak, and made the way possible for this writer to come to know and speak with Jadotville survivors.

It is an even more literal truth to say that I could never have got their book together without the selfless help, so magnanimously, unsparingly and thoughtfully given, of the following: thank you Liam Donnelly, Noel Carey, John Gorman and Walter Hegarty, to whom I went in the first, and last, instance. And for their memories, time, photographs and hospitality, thanks to Paddy Neville, Joe Clune, Bobby Allan, Sean Foley, Billy Ready, Leo Boland, Mary Manning-Lattimore, Lars Fröberg and Lola Leech.

To Michael Shannon, so helpful and painstaking with the detail of his account of how things were for the reinforcements, my sincere thanks. Thanks too to Coleman Goggin, psychologist and soldier, for sharing his knowledge of the growing awareness in the army of psychological damage suffered by soldiers in battle situations.

And there were others: Eamonn Russell M. Phil. gave of his time and considerable learning to carefully translate the radio messages sent, and received, during battle by Comdt Pat Quinlan. My great thanks,

Eamonn, for this and many other kindnesses. And my thanks to Fr Pat Hudson OFM, both for the encouragement and useful contacts.

We all of us owe thanks to Edwin Higel of New Island who, without hesitation and with enthusiasm, knew from the beginning that this was a book he wanted to publish, knew its importance. Everyone at New Island has believed, everyone has been enthusiastic and encouraging. Deirdre Nolan, Editorial Manager, was a joy to work with—and a woman who knows how to have great, rambling conversations without ever losing sight of the ball. Fidelma Slattery, with a designing eye like none I know, came up with the perfect layout and look for the book, and Tom Cooney and Ronan Gallagher, with their acute knowledge of the business, encouraged and brought a hopeful reality to things.

Dublin City Library Archive, Pearse Street, and the staff there were, as always, of immense help, giving me access to the wealth of newspaper coverage of Jadotville, the Congo and more.

I am grateful to Tom Clonan for his foreword to this new updated and expanded edition.

The following works were of background help:

William G. Donnelly (Comdt ret'd), Submission to the Chief of Staff (and later additions), December 1996.

John Terence O'Neill (Col ret'd), 'The Irish Company at Jadotville, Congo, 1961', *International Peacekeeping*, Winter 2002.

Students of the 50th Command and Staff Course, 'The Battle of Jadotville, 1961: A UN Case Study', Curragh Camp, Co. Kildare, 1993.

Adam Hochschild, *King Leopold's Ghost*, London: Pan Macmillan, 2002.

Ludo De Witte, *The Assassination of Lumumba*, London: Verso Books, 2002.

Conor Cruise O'Brien, *To Katanga and Back*, London: Hutchinson, 1962.

Brian Urquhart, *Hammarskjold*, London: Random House, 1972.

Indar Jit Rikhye, *Military Advisor to the Secretary General: U.N. Peacekeeping and the Congo Crisis*, London: C. Hurst & Co, 1993.

'Upside Down – The United Nations at 60', *New Internationalist*, January/February 2005.

PART ONE

PROLOGUE

The Katangese are good soldiers, and brave, and this is their country.
I don't blame them for attacking us.

Comdt P. Quinlan, September 1961

The trenches, five feet deep in the dry, African soil, were what saved them. The trenches and the defensive tactics of their commanding officer and their own bloody-minded courage.

God helped too. They agreed on that afterwards. God had been on their side in the trenches.

They were parched, filthy, exhausted, fly-encrusted and dug in when the enemy Fouga jet fighter, piloted by the Belgian Major Jose Denlin, appeared out of the sun on the second day of battle. Dark in the scalding sky, its whine incessant above machine-gun and mortar fire, it came in over the valley below Jadotville, circled their position several times and disappeared in the direction of Kolwezi.

A Company of the 35th Irish Battalion, UN peacekeeping force, 156 in number and commanded by Patrick Quinlan, was made up of three platoons, a special Support Platoon, cavalry section of two armoured cars and Swedish Interpreter Lieutenant Lars Fröberg. The soldiers of A Company, to a man, had come to the Congo believing they could help restore peace.

The Congo, newly independent after 80 years' rule from Brussels, was in turmoil following mineral-rich Katanga's secession from the new state with the backing of Belgium.

Comdt Quinlan, 42 years old and reared in the savage grandeur of the Iveragh peninsula's Atlantic coastline, was less than inspired by the Katangan landscape.

'The whole of Katanga,' he wrote, 'is on a plateau—flat as a table for hundreds of miles around with small stunted trees and elephant grass 5–6 feet high. Slow moving, twisting dark green muddy rivers wind their way to God knows where. It's a featureless, uninteresting sun-baked land with clouds of red dust from the hard red earth. It is now mid-winter, sometimes very hot, sometimes cold enough, especially at night....'

But then Pat Quinlan, according to those who fought with him and to Noel Carey, from Limerick and at 24 the youngest of the company's officers in Jadotville, '...was the one went out to the Congo with a realistic view and expectations.'

Quinlan's expectations didn't include Jadotville. No one expected Jadotville.

A Company arrived in the Katangan mining town, which was dominated by mining giant Union Minière and had the third largest concentration of Europeans in the Congo, ten days before the battle. The men had been made immediately unwelcome, hostility and the sour air of potential trouble all pervasive. They were in a state of boycott; their water and electricity had been cut off and shopkeepers and hoteliers refused to serve them. Gendarmerie patrols drove through their position; the exit roads to Elisabethville and the rest of the Irish Battalion had been blocked; and enemy reinforcements were converging on Jadotville. Quinlan had started digging trenches at once.

Liam Donnelly, a Dubliner, 33 years old in Jadotville and a captain with charge of the Special Support Platoon, remembers Quinlan saying: '"We've a problem here. We'd better be prepared." Then he got us dug in and got us positioned. There were complaints from some of the men but he was right.'

Everyone has trench memories. Quartermaster Sergeant Paddy Neville recalls:

> There were patrols of Gendarmerie up the road every hour, on the hour, watching us. Pat Quinlan said, 'every man in this company will dig trenches.' We were dug in at night, nice and easy. A lot of the company would have been in their teens, only schoolboys.

Corporal Sean Foley was 20 years old. Digging the trenches was, he says, 'like digging concrete; the red earth was so dry it had a formulation like cinder–clinker in some parts. We found the trenches safe though; you could protect yourself inside them.'

Cook/Corporal Bobby Allan is absolutely convinced about their live-saving qualities: 'We'd have been slaughtered if it wasn't for them.'

Quinlan's positioning meant pinpointing areas the enemy was likely to attack and deciding on potential targets for the company's mortars and machine guns. No.1 and the Support Platoon were positioned nearest Jadotville with a gap of 200 yards between them and the area occupied by HQ and Numbers 2 and 3 platoons.

When they found themselves surrounded and all exit routes cut off by Katangan Gendarmerie, they dug further trenches, by night.

Their position, on the edge of Jadotville, was exposed, unsuitable and chosen for them by UN Procurement officers. The trio of villas (bungalow-style houses) they had been allocated, along with HQ rooms over a garage called Purfina, were enclosed by dense bush, elephant grass, low buildings, ant hills and, now, some 3,000 heavily armed Katangan Gendarmerie soldiers and an unknown number of Jadotville's male civilians. The Gendarmerie soldiers were led by mercenary officers, most of them ex-French paratrooper commandos, others ex-Belgian Army.

Katangan reinforcements to hand in surrounding villages included men of the Beyeke, tribal brothers of Katanga's Interior Minister, Godefroid Munongo. Backup included the Fouga jet.

The UN had no fighter aircraft and no anti-aircraft guns.

A Company had small arm weapons, 60mm mortars, four WWI Vickers machine guns, a few 84mm anti-tank guns. They were supported by two 1940s vintage cavalry armoured cars with Vickers machine guns mounted on them. They had no flak jackets, no functioning internal communication system and they wore plastic UN helmets. They had requested, but had not been given, barbed wire and flares. Lack of transport had prevented them from bringing their 81mm mortars and ten-day stock of emergency rations.

Their limited rations were now all but gone, their ammunition running low, their water contaminated and the supply from the town cut off.

They were cut off too from their main HQ base in Elisabethville, 80 miles away, and the support of their colleagues in the Battalion. This was against every military principle.

Reinforcements, small in number and inadequately equipped, had so far failed to cross the strategic Lufira Bridge, 18 miles distant.

Jadotville's white population, 5,000 strong and allegedly in need of A Company's protection, adamantly did not want the UN in the town. The 75,000-strong Congolese population had not been consulted. The threat of attack, the gathering strength of the enemy surrounding, the very real danger of annihilation, had been apparent for days.

Group Mide, consisting of the Swedish APC Company under Major Mide and B Company of the 35th Irish Battalion, had been sent on an abortive mission to Jadotville a week before A Company's arrival. Their orders were to protect the white population in the event of rioting. Ordered out of town by the Burgermeister, Mide withdrew, followed by B Company. As they crossed Lufira Bridge, A Company passed them on their way to Jadotville.

A Company had been sent to Jadotville by order of HQ, Dr Conor Cruise O'Brien of the UN, and at the very specific request of Belgium's Foreign Minister, Paul Henri Spaak. Although Quinlan and his officers had repeatedly made clear the danger of their situation, they had been told to stay where they were.

So it was that Quinlan, unwilling to allow his men to die, planned a defence and dug them in.

He would not be silent either. Sending A Company to Jadotville was, he declared, 'a well-thought-out Belgian plan to take us prisoner and use us as hostages in negotiations for Katanga. As for our army and Battalion HQ ... all their military training was forgotten, every principle of war violated.'

Liam Donnelly agreed: 'It's my belief we were meant to have been cut off in Jadotville. The Belgians wanted us as bargaining power with the UN.'

Belgian mining interests were hugely vested in Katanga; an independent Katanga was very much in Belgium's interests. Providing the Katanganese with hostages would frustrate UN efforts to bring an end to Katanga's defiance.

Quinlan reassured the men under his command that God on their side and five-foot trenches offered 'protection against almost anything. Except thirst.'

And hunger. And dust. And the humid, unmoving air and the parasites that settled quickly into broken, unwashed skin. And disease.

And bombs from the air.

The night before the attack, when a big gun (French 75mm) was discovered trained on their position, Quinlan ordered more digging. A Company finished the last of the trenches just hours before the battle began.

The men were consulting with God when they were attacked.

CHAPTER 1

I was left in the lurch. Only for our own alertness we would have been wiped out that morning.

Comdt P. Quinlan, September 1961

DAY ONE
Jadotville. Wednesday, 13 September 1961

The Congolese say that the sting of a fly can launch the end of the world. In the case of the Jadotville Affair, the stinging fly had been busy long before the battle. Comdt Patrick Quinlan had had intimations of this, seen writing on walls from the moment he and his troops arrived in the Congo. 'Small things,' he believed, 'alter world events.'

So it would prove, for A Company, the UN and the Congo.

A Company *could* have been caught off guard when the attack came. They had been spied on and they had been betrayed. But their defences were well prepared.

None of them, however, from commanding officer down, was prepared for the radio messages: one before the attack, one near the end of the battle. Nothing in their military training had prepared them for betrayal by their own army.

When the first message came, at 7.25 on Wednesday, 13 September, most of A Company was assembling for a daily, open-air Mass. They carried loaded weapons. Others manned the fortified villas. All of them, for days, had slept in their clothes, with their boots on and fully loaded weapons beside them. More than a third remained, constantly, in the trenches.

Quinlan was in the Company's HQ rooms over the Purfina Garage. He was shaving when Lieutenant Noel Carey brought him the radio word from Battalion HQ that Operation Morthor, a major UN offensive against Katangan separatists, had started in Elisabethville more than three hours earlier.

A Company, cut off and vulnerable in Jadotville, had been given no warning that it would take place.

0725 HRS. ELISABETHVILLE: OPERATION MORTHOR. SUSPENSION OF KAT GOVERNMENT. ARREST OF CERTAIN CABINET MINISTERS AND OF WHITE OFFICERS OF SURETE OF POLICE. SEIZURE OF RADIO STATION AND ALL COMMUNICATIONS COMMENCED 0400 HOURS TODAY. OPERATION HAS BEEN COMPLETED SUCCESSFULLY.

Operation Morthor was, in fact, a shambles.

The UN forces involved had been fiercely resisted and had failed to occupy the Katangan HQ at Camp Massard in Elisabethville. A full-scale military operation, it had been put into effect on the orders of Dr Conor Cruise O'Brien, the UN Civilian Representative in Katanga, and supported by Brigadier Kas Raja, Senior Military UN Commander in Katanga—but *without* the knowledge of either the UN's Secretary General, Dag Hammarskjöld in New York, or the UN Force Commander in the Congo, General Sean McKeown.

Quinlan was incensed by the radio message:

This was the first indication I had of any action planned for Elisabethville. I'd smelled something in the air the night before and asked Battalion HQ [where the commanding officer was Lieutenant Colonel Hugh McNamee] three times for information. The only reply I got was 'Níl aon scéal'—there is no news. The enemy knew all the plans for Elisabethville but we knew nothing. I knew this meant trouble for us and shouted out the window to stand to and pulled on my clothes.

But the shooting started at the same time. A group of Gendarmerie, about 30 strong, rushed our forward positions in jeeps and on foot. Our men attending Mass carried loaded weapons and were in action almost immediately.

He ordered Noel Carey to alert all troops, radioed Elisabethville HQ about the situation and was told to, 'defend yourself with maximum force'.

The early minutes of battle, for A Company and for Quinlan, were telling as they were short, and confusing. According to Quinlan:

> It was difficult to establish whether it was the gunner in the first enemy jeep or one of the Gendarmerie in the bush who fired first. It may have been an accidental shot from one of the men in the bush but the gunner in the first jeep opened up prematurely when Private Albert Dell, on guard on a sandbagged veranda outside the villa nearest Jadotville and alerted by the attitude of the men in the first jeep, brought his Gustav to his shoulder and returned fire. The jeep swung around on the road less than 100 yards from where the men were at Mass.
>
> Sgt John Monaghan, on guard at the villa, grabbed a mounted machine gun from one of the A Company jeeps and opened fire on the enemy infantry approaching through the bush. All the other men of the guard in that villa were in action immediately and immediately after them those attending Mass, who'd had loaded weapons slung on their shoulders, were at their posts.

Noel Carey was alerted when he saw Katangan Gendarmerie troops dismounting from trucks across the road from the area occupied by the Special Support Platoon. He 'roared at the lads to occupy the trenches' then alerted No. 1 Platoon area, commanded by 27-year-old Dubliner Lieutenant Joe Leech.

Driving back to HQ in the Purfina Garage, Carey heard the first burst of fire, grabbed his weapon and equipment and, together with Lieutenant Tom Quinlan (in charge of No. 2 Platoon), reported to commanding officer Quinlan on the roadway. Small arms fire continued from Liam Donnelly's Support Platoon and from No. 1 Platoon area.

Comdt Quinlan ordered a roadblock to be set up and ordered Private Kieran Lynch to cover it from his trench with an 84mm anti-tank gun.

While Tom Quinlan's platoon took on Gendarmerie coming across the scrub ground, Carey rushed to his trench, abandoned his Gustav, and,

> after getting directions from my driver Pte Leo Boland, I began to engage the Katangans with a Bren gun. There was absolutely no doubt in my mind that we were under fire, under unprovoked attack, and were fully justified in defending ourselves. At the same time, I heard the crump of mortar fire towards our comrades in No.1 Platoon and Support Platoon positions and could clearly hear the rattle of machine-gun fire.
>
> Then the firing began to slacken and, apart from small arms fire, we felt we had repulsed their efforts.

All of this initial attack went on for some 10-15 minutes before, according to Pat Quinlan, 'the Gendarmerie broke and fled. Many went to cover in the bush and remained there all day.'

The Katangan plan of attack, now foiled, had been drawn up based on intelligence about A Company's movements. With light machine guns mounted on jeeps, they had planned to drive through the company's position, firing on the men as they attended Mass. In the ensuing confusion, Gendarmerie creeping through the bush would rush forward and capture the rest of the troops.

As plans went, it was feasible. It could have succeeded too, if A Company had not been prepared, alert and in trenches.

The lull that followed lasted about three hours. It would be the only one in a battle which would become bloodier and more brutal until it was described by Quinlan as 'an inferno with all hell let loose'.

Radio messages from Battalion HQ in Elisabethville continued to give false reassurance:

0850 HRS. ELISABETHVILLE: ELISABETHVILLE IS IN OUR HANDS.

0915 HRS. JADOTVILLE: ALL QUIET—WAITING. HOPE YOU ARE ALL SAFE WITHOUT CASUALTIES.

Contact, after that, was intermittent. A Company breakfasted in the trenches, the sun climbed higher, Chaplain Fr Joe Fagan gave all the men a precautionary general absolution by way of last rites, and Pat Quinlan prepared for what was to come.

CHAPTER 2

Pray that your loneliness may spur you into finding something to live for, great enough to die for.

Dag Hammarskjöld, Diaries, 1951

UN Secretary General Dag Hammarskjöld was in Accra, en route from New York to the Congo, when he first heard about Operation Morthor. That a major UN Offensive should take place just before his arrival in the Congo was both a surprise and a shock.

He had not authorised it, nor even known it was taking place. General Sean McKeown, UN Force Commander in the Congo, had not known until late the night before.

Aimed at maintaining order in the Elisabethville area by 'seizing, holding and controlling radio installations and the post office and by taking into custody personnel who are responsible for disturbances of the peace in Katanga', Operation Morthor was ordered by Dr Conor Cruise O'Brien, UN Representative in Katanga, and supported by Brigadier Kas Raja, Senior UN Military Officer in Katanga. Dr Cruise O'Brien knew exactly the sort of military action he had in mind. '*Morthor* is a Hindi word,' he wrote. 'It does not mean "Sound the alarm; there is arson in the garage" or "Let us now assist the provincial authorities to maintain order". It means "Smash".'

When the UN Secretary General arrived in Leopoldville on the afternoon of 13 September, he was shocked, too, to learn about the Jadotville attack on A Company.

Invited by Cyrille Adoula, Prime Minister of Congo's Central Government, Hammarskjöld hoped to bring Adoula and Katanga's

President Moise Tshombe together for talks aimed at resolving the growing turmoil in the breakaway province.

Operation Morthor made for further chaos in an already volatile situation, seriously compromising Hammarskjöld's objective. Katangan fighter-jet superiority, a successful propaganda war waged by mercenaries using Katangan and Rhodesian radio, and UN ineptitude did not help.

It was clear, too, that the Gendarmerie had known about Operation Morthor and been well prepared. The earlier Operation Rumpunch, on 28 August, had succeeded because it had been a surprise. A Company had, as per orders at the time and without difficulty, placed Katanga's Interior Minister Godefroid Munungo under house arrest. A Company left Elisabethville on 3 September.

On 13 September, when UN troops went to get Munungo, he was gone.

In the time between Rumpunch and Morthor, a highly inflammatory propaganda campaign had been waged by Katanga against the UN on the radio, in the press and on posters. Irish troops were targeted particularly when the Katangan cause was cleverly likened to Ireland's in the past.

The UN had hugely underestimated the strength of Katangan resistance and there was bloodshed and chaos throughout Katanga as Hammarskjöld's 3 p.m. flight landed at Ndjili Airport, Leopoldville. He was met by Cyrille Adoula and members of the Central Government, among them Colonel Joseph Mobutu.

It was some hours later that Stüre Linner, the UN Officer in Charge in Leopoldville, gave him full details of the situation in Elisabethville. Operation Morthor had been intended as a short, non-violent offensive. The plan had been to occupy strategic locations so as to neutralise the Katanga regime and, vitally, apprehend and evacuate foreign military and paramilitary personnel. It had quickly turned into a bloody war between UN forces and the mercenary-led Katangese Gendarmerie.

President Tshombe had disappeared. There were still more than 100 Katangan mercenary officers at large, including the most active and dangerous.

A reportedly preoccupied Secretary General Hammarskjöld attended a dinner in his honour on the evening of 13 September. Guests included Adoula, General Sean McKeown and Mahmoud Khiari, the UN's Tunisian-born Chief of Civilian Operations in the Congo.

The much-stretched Irish Battalion in Elisabethville had a rough and terrible time on this first day of Operation Morthor. Private Gaffney and Cavalry Trooper Patrick Mullins were killed, and Private French wounded, in an armoured car ambush. Despite great effort, Mullins's body was never recovered. Others of the Irish UN peacekeeping force were taken prisoner.

CHAPTER 3

*Enemy intelligence was very good and ours was non-existent. From
the beginning it was known what we were doing.*

Comdt (retired) Liam Donnelly

Jadotville. Wednesday, 13 September

God might well be on the side of A Company but the enemy had
the balance of things—air superiority, an intelligence system and a
Madame Van Habost—on their side.

Van Habost was Belgian, the wife of the owner of both a bus
depot and second garage close to A Company's position. The home of
the violently anti-UN couple overlooked the spot where A Company
routinely gathered in the mornings for Mass.

Before the attack, Van Habost has been spotted on the phone near
a window. That she'd been giving a signal was clear.

Quinlan wasted no time when the shooting stopped:

> I took Company Sergeant Jack Prendergast and four men
> and seized the nearby bus depot and the private house
> of Van Habost. The Van Habost family, including five
> children, had all their personal belongings packed in a
> station wagon and were driving out the gate when we
> stopped them. We found two telephones in the house, at
> windows overlooking our positions, and one telephone in
> the garage.

Quinlan, in the tense days before the attack and knowing that A
Company's meagre transport fleet of a couple of jeeps, an ambulance,
a saloon car and a mechanically unreliable Bedford truck wouldn't

get them far, had planned to seize the buses and 'make a breakout if necessary'.

But the four buses found in the depot that morning were of no use to anyone.

> Two were out of action with engines removed and undergoing repairs. The other two had been put out of action with parts removed. Our fitters, Cpls John McEntee and James Lucey, got them repaired and we took possession of them.

They had reckoned without the Fouga. The buses would not survive the bombs to come.

A French 75mm gun was trained on the company's position and the besieging Katangans continued to encroach. Quinlan wrote:

> During this time, a large number of Gendarmerie, between 60 and 100, were observed in very close formation approaching the nearby Golf Links at a range of about 1000 yards. We had one armoured mounted machine gun and two mortars trained on them and ready to fire....

Captain Liam Donnelly and Lieutenant Kevin Knightly were two of those training Bren guns, ground Vickers, armoured car mounted Vickers and 60mm mortars. Donnelly (whose backup plan was to stalk through bush with a 60mm mortar to within range if the 75mm gun opened fire and he failed to silence it) had started to give the fire orders to the mortars when Quinlan made a tactical decision:

> We could have inflicted heavy casualties at this stage but I ordered mounted machine guns and mortars to hold fire as the news from Elisabethville was good and there was a chance that the attack of the morning was the action of some hot heads. There had been no firing since that first attack and if it had been carried out by some extremists then further action by me might precipitate a full-scale battle. All was now quiet and might well be over.

Nevertheless, he took precautions.

> We collected all telephones from private houses within our
> position and advised the occupants to leave. We found two
> houses evacuated: one owned by the Vice President of Union
> Minière, the other occupied by the Governor of the jail, an
> African. The previous night he'd driven in furiously and left
> again a short time later, almost crashing his car. We'd thought
> him drunk....

Not drunk at all. The governor had been aware of Operation Morthor
and the consequent attack planned on A Company.

Quinlan issued a stern warning to his troops, ordering that
'not even a souvenir' was to be taken from the empty houses. Any
kind of looting would, he said, 'be summarily dealt with'.

Weighing up the situation, he considered a 'quick move' into the
city to capture key points.

> I expected that if the action continued the water would be
> cut off. Such a move would secure the water supply vital to
> our survival. It would also cut off reinforcements coming in
> from Shinkolobwe, ten miles west and where we knew there
> was a force of 1600 Gendarmerie.

The heavily guarded uranite mines at Shinkolobwe had been the
source of more than 80% of the uranium for the American atomic
bombs dropped on the Japanese cities of Hiroshima and Nagasaki
in 1945. Katanga's mineral wealth, which included gold, cobalt,
copper and diamonds, was the reason A Company had been sent to
Jadotville. Quinlan knew it. His officers knew it. Most of the rank-
and-file soldiers knew it now too.

But the encouraging radio reports from Elisabethville decided Quinlan
against going into Jadotville. Even in the worst of circumstances he felt he
could, 'hold out for two or three days until UN reinforcements reached us.
By doing this I would tie down large forces of Gendarmerie that would
otherwise be used against the UN in Elisabethville. This, I knew, would
accelerate a decision in favour of the UN there.'

Then, too, an attack on the town was bound to result in casualties.

Unless attended by quick success it would leave me in a most vulnerable position where the Company would be so badly cut up as to render it incapable of further action. Serious casualties without hospital facilities were a risk that could not be justified in the prevailing circumstances, except as a last resort.

As an immediate resort, he ordered that every available container be filled with water. Medical Officer Commandant Joe Clune and Fr Joe Fagan, together with the cooks and medical orderlies, had just finished doing this when the water supply was cut off.

But the collected water, stored in baths and buckets and left standing, of necessity, in the heat, dust and debris from shelling and bombing, would turn putrid within two days.

It was while the water was being collected that Emmanuel Kamujeki, Quinlan's Baluba houseboy (terrified after a journey by stealth in and out of Jadotville) returned with the news that there were about 1,000 troops in the town.

And it was about now too that a Belgian friend, Louis Christiaens, brought a report which made all the difference.

Christiaens was an aspect of Quinlan's earlier, and more unique, preparatory tactics. Allying his Kerryman's instinct for friendship to an acute, soldierly analysis of the chilly animosity to the UN presence in Jadotville, he had gone regularly into town in the days before the attack, hoping to foster good relations.

He had failed dismally with 'the all-powerful white man in Jadotville', the President of Union Minière, who had given him a 'very cold and formal reception'. He had failed too with the African CO of Gendarmerie in Jadotville, Major Makito, described by Quinlan as 'most suspicious and hostile, scowling and twisting in his chair, an impossible person, a witch doctor I was told, who still practised his trade. He certainly looked the part.'

Appearances can be deceptive and the Gendarmerie Captain Tschipolo who 'appeared to be more genial' was, as they discovered later, 'an even more dangerous character.'

But there were those, like Louis Christiaens, who felt differently about the UN presence. Disgusted with Belgium's duplicity and with the murderous, international greed behind Katangan politics, Christiaens and a small, disparate group of others risked their lives, jobs and way of life for the sake of the 156 Irish peacekeeping soldiers.

Pierre Marc was one such. A Belgian who had been an observer in the RAF during the Second World War, he had driven through A Company's position in the days before the attack, thrown a map to one of the men and asked him to bring it to Quinlan.

The map indicated Gendarmerie surrounding positions as well as the location of a 'heavy gun—French 785—I think trained on your HQ.' Donnelly, verifying this with field glasses, had picked up the gun and estimated the range at 1,000 yards. Nothing in Jadotville, not even family relationships, was what it seemed; Pierre Marc was also the son-in-law of the anti-UN Van Habosts.

Marc had warned Quinlan that his father-in-law was reporting A Company's moves and defence positions to the Gendarmerie, and had told him, too, how the buses were being driven away from the depot on the evening before the attack and parked for safety at a school in the town and how other buses, as they finished their regular runs throughout the day, had also been parked in the school.

All of which made it 'quite obvious' to Quinlan, once the attack happened, 'that the Katangan authorities had had prior intelligence of UN intentions in Elisabethville.'

Then there was Major Guertz.

A Luxembourger, lawyer and estate agent in Jadotville, Guertz had been a major in the British Army in East Africa. He had also been the first to warn A Company about hostilities in the town and the one who had arranged meetings between Quinlan, Jadotville's Mayor Amisi and Union Minière's President.

And there was Charles Kearney. From Wexford, a civilian technician working in Katanga, he repeatedly reported Katangan moves to Quinlan in the days before the attack.

Madame Lamonfagne was arguably the most courageous of the group, literally risking life, limb and home for A Company.

Elderly and Belgian, she lived alone near the Purfina Garage. She treated A Company to the home-baked honeycomb pastries she made for sale, spoke English badly and kept a cockatoo which spoke only French—much to the disgust of Quartermaster Sergeant Paddy Neville who wanted to know what the bird was saying.

Sickened by the duplicity of her countrymen, by what she perceived as the trap set for A Company, Mme Lamonfagne refused to leave when the attack happened.

'She was a very brave woman,' according to Platoon Sergeant Walter (Wally) Hegarty.

> She refused to leave even though the C/O offered to arrange her departure, encouraging us all even though she spoke no English. She sent the company several consignments of cakes and chips ... Once we knew she was still baking we were not going to give in.
>
> It was her phone the interpreter, Lieutenant Lars Fröberg, who was Swedish, used and she was always there to tell him who was speaking on the other end and what kind of man he was, friend or foe.

Mme Lamonfagne's home became a defence position, her furniture and mattresses cover for riflemen. Quinlan used her phone throughout the battle to relay and receive messages from Jadotville. She was tirelessly helpful and stubbornly brave. According to Quinlan:

> Her nieces rang a number of times, imploring her in tears to leave, saying they would arrange for her safe conduct through the Gendarmerie. She refused, saying that she would be well protected by the Irish who were the finest gentlemen she'd ever met. I also urged her to go but she said no, that she felt she could help us with the people telephoning from Jadotville. She got no sleep during the whole five days and nights.

And then there was Louis Christiaens, the Belgian proprietor of the Purfina Garage over which A Company's officers had their HQ.

When the lull came, Christiaens went into Jadotville and, at great risk to his life, obtained detailed information about the situation in the town. He was the one who told Quinlan that reinforcements of approximately 1,000 were on their way from Shinkolobwe and that a full-scale attack with mortars and artillery was planned for some time after 11.30 a.m. All of which proved correct.

While he was in Jadotville, Louis Christiaens was asked to get Quinlan's permission for a truckload of workers to pass through A Company's position to one of the Union Minière quarries. Quinlan recalled:

> This truck load turned back when within sight of our position, but Christiaens came on and told me about the reinforcements and planned large-scale attack. He also told me that the town was well fortified with dug-in guns and that the white population was assisting the Gendarmerie.
>
> This was not good news but at least I was prepared for what was to come and it relieved me of any anxiety I still had regarding my mission to protect the white population!

Before the lull ended, Quinlan used Mme Lamonfagne's phone to call Jadotville's African Burgermeister/Mayor Amisi, a man he had already met and found to be resentful and suspicious of the UN. He demanded an explanation for the attack.

Mayor Amisi replied that the UN had attacked the Katanga government in Elisabethville and that many Katangan troops and civilians had been killed. He said we were at war and that all my troops would be killed unless we surrendered. He also said that a mob of thousands would attack us. I told him very firmly that surrender was out of the question and that as Elisabethville was now in UN hands, any attack on us in Jadotville was futile.

> I further warned him that we would cut down any attackers mercilessly and with all the force at our disposal and that I would hold him personally responsible for any loss of life or destruction of property that would result.
>
> I appealed to him to use his office to avoid unnecessary bloodshed. He sounded as if he was impressed and said that he was already trying to stop it. I suggested that we talk it

over. He asked me not to cut the telephone and said that he would get in touch with me again as he himself was doing his best and did not want any fighting.

I agreed to leave the telephone intact and it remained intact throughout the battle. It was used as a channel on which to wage psychological warfare as time went on but as there was only my courageous Swedish interpreter, Lieut Lars Fröberg, and myself at the receiving end this did not achieve its purpose.

Fröberg became an integral part of the company despite his initial doubts about his ability to understand Quinlan's robust Kerry accent. He was reassured when Lieutenant Joe Leech cheerfully told him, 'We don't understand him either.'

Quinlan brought some psychological analysis of his own to bear on Mayor Amisi:

I believe he was genuinely doing his best to prevent fighting. In fact I have reason to believe that he was not a follower of Katanga's chief minister Moise Tshombe, who was a puppet of the Belgian mining interests, and that he secretly believed in the reunification of the Congo. He was in a very difficult position and I don't blame him for anything.

Using the initials FCA as a code for Gendarmerie (from Fórsa Cosanta Áitiúil, Ireland's reserve defence force) he radioed Elisabethville.

1100 HRS. JADOTVILLE: BIG REINFORCEMENTS TO FCA EXPECTED 1130 HOURS. LARGE SCALE ATTACK EXPECTED ON MY POSITION SOON AFTER. CAN YOU SEND ME REINFORCEMENTS?

There was no reply to this. When the second attack came, far more savagely determined than the first had been, he radioed again.

1140 HRS. JADOTVILLE: WE ARE UNDER FIRE.

1140 HRS. ELISABETHVILLE: SO ARE WE.

1150 HRS. ELISABETHVILLE: GIVE ANY INFO. YOU CAN.

1156 HRS. JADOTVILLE: HAVE BEEN FIRED ON AND RETURNED FIRE. FIRING STILL IN PROGRESS. STRENGTH OF OPPOSITION UNKNOWN.

1225 HRS. JADOTVILLE: ENEMY MORTAR AND SMALL ARTILLERY FIRE. FIRE RETURNED WITH GOOD RESULTS. BATTLE STILL IN PROGRESS. HOW ARE YOU DOING? GOOD LUCK AND GOD BLESS.

1258 HRS. JADOTVILLE: FIRE CONTINUING.

Their radio equipment, faulty and unreliable at all times, was sorely pressed during this and every exchange for the days to come. That it worked half as well as it did was thanks to the company's signal corps, as Quinlan acknowledged:

Corporal Frank Williams, my excellent wireless operator, had three men, also wireless operators, in his signal section. Cpl Williams manned the set continuously day and night from Saturday 9th September until Monday morning 18th September when he put it out of action after sending message regarding our capture. He got no sleep as far as I could see.

It was impossible to move our wireless mast and cables more than a few feet during battle. After the first attack we moved the wireless set the short distance to a coal house adjacent to HQ in the Purfina Garage where we hoped it would be a less likely target. Williams maintained a position in a trench just outside the coal house until the evening of 16th September with the wireless balanced on his knees. I saw him with his face covered with flies and he could scarcely wipe them off....

The Katangans' second attack, that first morning, 'opened somewhat unexpectedly with a mortar bombardment and mounted machine-gun fire.'

Our whole position came under automatic fire from all sides with heavy mortar bombardment and ground attack on No. 1 Platoon position and on the villa position nearest Jadotville, held by elements of Support Platoon and Company HQ. The men in the forward positions facing the attack put down a withering fire.

The area rocked and shuddered and Liam Donnelly went into action, opening fire on the heavy gun position with his mortars.

He hit it with the first four rounds. The ammo dump must have been hit as it burned all day and into the night. Before it was hit the heavy shell which we thought came from it screamed over our heads and exploded harmlessly in the valley beyond us. The enemy continued with heavy mortar bombardment from 4.2 and 81mm mortars. Our mortars knocked out at least two enemy mortars during this time. Our mounted machine guns broke up enemy attacks and cut down mortar crews who ran out of their positions from our counter bombardments.

The screaming, piercing sound of mortars was followed, as they exploded, by the terrifying sound of shrapnel cutting through the air.

Quinlan, constantly assessing the situation and tactics, gave a graphically detailed description of their far-from-ideal position:

The ground in our forward location sloped away from our right flank (facing Jadotville and north of town) for about 400 yards, then rose to a crest approx 1700 yards distant. Most of this area was thickly covered by bush and observation close to our position was difficult. We had fairly good observation however on the slope at distances of 600–100 yards and in some places up to 1700 yards. Some of the enemy succeeded in infiltrating the bush close to our position before the attack was broken up. Others succeeded in gaining a foothold in two or three villas on the main Jadotville road and brought heavy fire on our forward positions.

Donnelly says that at this point, and for the rest of that day, 'all enemy movement was stopped or interfered with at ranges of between 400 and 800 yards.'

Quinlan got back on the radio to Battalion HQ in Elisabethville.

1310 HRS. JADOTVILLE: WHAT IS POSITION IN ELISABETHVILLE?

1313 HRS. ELISABETHVILLE: WE ARE DOING WELL BUT NOT DECIDED.

By then, A Company, finding itself dealing with a renewed, larger-scale attack, was, as Quinlan described, doing decidedly well. The company also had its first casualty.

> Some infantry got into the bush close to our position. They appeared to join up with some of the force that attacked us in the early morning who had gone to ground in this area. Our forward positions came under rifle and light artillery fire from this dense bush area from very close range. Private Billy Ready was wounded when a bullet passed through his thigh and grazed his stomach. He was with two other men in an isolated position and, owing to the intensity of fire, could not be evacuated. Corporal Patrick Duffy, Medical Orderly, dodged out to him and applied a tourniquet. We evacuated him in an armoured car about four hours later.

Billy Ready himself well remembers, too, how Corporal Jimmy Lucey and Kevin Knightly 'also rescued me from the line of fire':

> The battle was horrific—I never dreamed it would happen to me like that, that I would be in a battle. I always wondered, as you do, how I'd react. But I was absolutely happy about how I reacted and delivered when it did happen. It's true I

went out of it pretty quickly; I wasn't even able to stand up when they got to me. Dr Joe Clune was great, a good and nice man. I was put under the stairs in the Purfina Garage building with mattresses and blankets to protect me should the jet bomb there.

I can still hear the jet coming in—a terrible sound. It used fly very low over our position. It was a miracle we weren't all killed. It just doesn't add up. We were under fire for so long and in such conditions. Someone was looking after us—I suppose our number wasn't up.

Quinlan was determined that their number would be anything but up:

The situation was very serious now and I realised that if the enemy attacks were pressed home our present position would be untenable as the platoons were not mutually supporting and my force could be split by infiltration between platoon positions. I realised also that I was greatly outnumbered, by perhaps 20 to 1, and that the enemy had heavy mortars with which they could reduce my position from outside the range of my weapons. I signalled Battalion HQ....

1315 HRS. JADOTVILLE: SEND ME REINFORCEMENTS AS SOON AS POSSIBLE. URGENT.

...and decided to withdraw my forward platoons later, under cover of darkness, and to organise a compact company position in the vicinity of the Purfina Garage where Company HQ was located.

I ordered more trenches to be dug and the new position to be prepared for occupation at last light. Each platoon supplied a few men for this task. The danger was that the forward platoons might not be able to hold out until darkness and it would be most difficult to disengage in daylight, certainly it could not be done without suffering casualties.

Frank Williams, diligently working to keep radio contact, intercepted a message, at 1335 hours, which was heard giving the order in Elisabethville to 'have Support Platoon and another platoon ready to proceed to A Company immediately.'

This being very good news, Quinlan responded quickly.

1347 HRS. JADOTVILLE: GIVE ME ESTIMATED TIME ARRIVAL OF REINFORCEMENTS.

1355 HRS. ELISABETHVILLE: NO ESTIMATED TIME ARRIVAL AVAILABLE AT MOMENT.

1401 HRS. JADOTVILLE: INCLUDE SECTION 81MM WITH REINFORCEMENTS.

1405 HRS. ELISABETHVILLE: WHAT AMMO DO YOU WANT?

1412 HRS. JADOTVILLE: AMMO SATISFACTORY SO FAR. SEND 81MM'S AND AMMO FOR 81'S. HOW IS YOUR POSITION? BE CAREFUL OF LUFIRA.

And so the Lufira Bridge became part of the Battle of Jadotville, heavily stressed and vital even in its first mention.

Some 18 miles distant, control of the Lufira Bridge gave entry, exit and de facto control of Jadotville. A UN force on the Jadotville side of the bridge (as A Company) would be in territory hostile to the UN, territory in which towns and villages were filled with men and trained soldiers willing to join the Gendarmerie in the fight for Katangan independence. The Lufira Bridge, in Quinlan's view, was where a wrongly made decision helped alter the future for Katanga. A Company would be living, embattled proof of the consequences.

The road between Elisabethville and Jadotville was metalled and straight, unique and vital in a land where most were no more than winding tracks. What was also a reality, in the existing war situation, was that anyone using the road would be vulnerable to both ambush on the ground and attack from the air.

The Lufira Bridge, Quinlan had maintained from the outset, 'was the key to the whole of Katanga—it and another bridge near Kolwezi.'

> On Saturday 9th, when we were surrounded, I got on the wireless [voice] to Mac [Lieutenant Colonel Hugh McNamee, in charge at HQ in Elisabethville] and told him of the situation. I begged him to send a company to take the Lufira Bridge. I had no transport, only two jeeps, two armoured cars, a saloon car, an ambulance and a broken-down truck. If we were to take the bridge, we would have to walk and leave all our equipment behind. Transport was always a problem; we never had any.
>
> He [Mac] agreed to this at first but after consultation with Raja [Military UN Officer in Katanga] and Conor Cruise O'Brien the idea was abandoned and I was told not to use any force. On Sunday evening and on Monday morning, I begged again for the taking of the bridge and to be given permission to force the barriers.
>
> Eventually I got a small party together which I was going to lead myself as a test case to force one barrier—shooting them off if necessary—but Capt. Dermot Byrne and Fr Joe Fagan prevailed on me not to do this without permission.
>
> I'm sorry now I did not go ahead as I would have forced their hands.
>
> If I had known [about Operation Morthor] I would have taken Lufira that morning and all would have been over in Katanga because they had 90% of their forces on my side of the bridge....

Lufira, and the failure to take it, became for Quinlan the stinging bee, one of those 'small things which alter world events'. It prevented what he believed would have been 'a tremendous Irish victory'. It also, and he was adamant, 'had far-reaching repercussions on UN and Congo affairs.'

Sean Foley and many in A Company agreed with him. According to Foley:

> The bridge over the Lufira river should have been taken. We should have been allowed take it. We'd have had a hold on it and they could have got reinforcements to there from Elisabethville. We would have had a holding ground and it would have changed everything. Katangan troops couldn't then have got to Elisabethville when Operation Morthor was going on.

About half an hour after his Lufira Bridge warning, Quinlan again radioed HQ:

> 1450 HRS. JADOTVILLE: CAN ESTIMATED TIME ARRIVAL REINFORCEMENTS BE GIVEN NOW? CAN SPARE C12 (RADIO) SET BE BROUGHT WITH REINFORCEMENTS?

> 1455 HRS. ELISABETHVILLE: C12 WILL PROBABLY BE GOING WITH REINFORCEMENTS.

And the battle went on:

> ...the forward sector came under very heavy mortar fire from a concealed mortar position. After some time, Private Thomas Larkin of No 1 Platoon located the enemy mortars and shouted a fire order to Sgt Martin McCabe 150 yards away. He picked it up and passed it on to Sgt Tom Kelly at our mortar position. Sgt Kelly engaged the enemy position and put it out of action.

God and tactics and A Company's luck came into play.

> One shell from this enemy mortar glanced off the roof of a villa and landed right between two men who were beside the villa. It did not explode. It's worth recording too that after the first bombardment that morning Capt. Donnelly

had moved his mortars to a new position. He thought his first position too vulnerable. In this new attack a salvo of enemy shells landed right on his old mortar position.

I shudder to think what would have happened if our mortars had been knocked out so early in the action. There was some stronger force than simple good luck on our side from the start ... Someone greater than any human who got us out.

But reflective thought was short-lived and followed, very quickly, by the reality of combat, and of killing, again.

Several white civilians were seen moving about, openly.

Perhaps because of the apparent casualness of their movements we did not realise they were taking an active part in the operations. We took them for bold men who wanted to have a grandstand view of the battle. One man in a white shirt who was very conspicuous became somewhat too bold. He was clearly seen signalling with his hand in a wide sweep as if directing the advance of infantry. He was cut down with a burst of machine-gun fire.

Not all decisions to fire were as easily made. To A Company's left front, at about 1,100 yards' range, a group of Gendarmerie and white civilians gathered around a large school building.

They had very good observation of our position but because of the residential, built-up area around the school, and the fact that children might be in the school, we used great restraint in not firing for a long time. They probably felt outside our range and quite safe. I was forced to take action after some time. The concentrated fire of two Bren guns, one armoured car and one mortar cleared the area in quick time.

It also ended open movement by white civilians. They donned their camouflage uniforms thereafter.

Three of this group had earlier moved forward and at 800 yards were cut down by a light automatic [ie a Bren gun] from Purfina Garage. This brought retaliatory M6 fire on the garage as our fire had been observed. At the time Capt. Dermot Byrne, Sgt Frank Gilsenan and myself were at an open window. A burst of fire passed between our heads and shattered the walls and ceiling.

Paddy Neville, in common with others new to the killing realities of battle, found that a military response took over:

When you saw the first fellow bleeding, poor divil, you cancelled all thought. But when one of your own was shot, you didn't feel anything, you just fought back. In battle you don't think. If things don't go one way, they'll go the other....

He is echoed by Donnelly:

While the battle was going on, our thoughts were solely military, as to what were we going to do without arms and ammunition? Pat Quinlan tried to make assessment of how things would last ... we were counting shots fired, we'd no water. You had people under you and you were wondering what was going to happen....

At 1610 hours, Quinlan again radioed to know when he might expect reinforcements.

The reply came in Irish, a futile attempt at concealment from the enemy since (unknown to either A Company or Battalion HQ in Elisabethville) a couple of Connemara-born, Rhodesian-based Irish-speaking miners were being paid to expose their compatriots and translate intercepted messages for the Katangans.

Quinlan, himself a native Irish speaker, would later, and furiously, see this as a treacherous betrayal.

1621 HRS. ELISABETHVILLE: ESTIMATED TIME ARRIVAL NAOI UAIR DÉAG. [1900 HOURS]

1622 HRS. JADOTVILLE: WHAT REINFORCEMENTS ARE YOU SENDING?

1622 HRS. ELISABETHVILLE: SUBSTANTIAL.

1635 HRS. JADOTVILLE: WE ARE UNDER HEAVY ATTACK. SEND REINFORCEMENTS IMMEDIATELY.

At 1657 hours, Quinlan was reassured that the reinforcements had left some 40 minutes earlier, at 1615 hours. Quinlan fully expected, because of the fighting in Elisabethville, that they would be delayed. It was now dusk. In less than an hour, it would be pitch dark, night falling as suddenly, Neville recalls, 'as turning off a light'.

CHAPTER 4

If I'd taken the bridge, and with a river to my front, I would have held them [Katangans] for the next year and all would be over in Katanga.

Comdt P. Quinlan

Lufira Bridge. 13 September 1961

The Lufira river, from where it rose on a plateau south of Jadotville, travelled a circuitous 600-odd kilometres to meet the Lualaba river. Eighteen miles outside Jadotville, at a deep, fast-flowing point, it was crossed by both the sturdily structured Lufira Bridge and, a little further along, a railway bridge.

On the Elisabethville/Jadotville road, the Lufira Bridge controlled exit and entry to Jadotville. It was strategic even to the excellent cover given by the high savannah covering the low hills on either side.

In Elisabethville, as Operation Morthor raged, the relief patrol for Jadotville was put together from troops withdrawn from the fighting. The assembled force consisted of Numbers 5 and 6 Rifle Platoons, B Company's Support Platoon and sections from the Cavalry Group, Swedish Armoured Personnel Carrier and medics.

In the charge of Commandant John Kane, it was called Force Kane.

For transport, Force Kane was given two Irish and two Swedish armoured cars, five trucks and one passenger minibus. The average age of troop members was between 18 and 23 years and, since they'd been fighting in Operation Morthor from early dawn, everyone was already tired as they left Elisabethville at 4.15 p.m.

The omens, from the beginning, were not good.

Even as they set out, along Elisabethville's Avenue De Saio,

Force Kane's armoured cars were attacked. They returned fire, then continued on a journey plagued by the thick red dust swirling about them as they went, blinding and smothering.

When they came to a halt a few kilometres before the Lufira Bridge, Kane, in the absence of maps with which to make a recce of the area, drew up a plan. Under cover of darkness, protected by the mounted machine guns, the force would drive its armoured cars onto the bridge and remove any obstacles.

Lieutenant Michael Shannon led No. 6 Platoon in the first armoured car. The bridge had indeed been blocked. Obstacles included a bulldozer, iron girders and tree stumps but the platoon kept going until the armoured car's axle met the insurmountable force of a stone-filled barrel.

'It was a big, concrete road bridge,' according to Shannon.

And we'd been going full steam ahead. The defenders were on high ground to the other side and we took a tremendous exchange of fire.

When we couldn't go forward it was mutually agreed by me and the armoured car gunner to reverse but we were caught by the tar barrel, which was full of stones and cement. The corporal, Dan Kavanagh, was Irish; the gunner was Swedish. Kavanagh said, 'We'll move the obstacle,' and jumped down on his own side and with the help of the other gunner, Paul Murphy, removed the obstacle so that the Swedish gunner was able to reverse back from the bridge. [Kavanagh and Murphy were later awarded Distinguished Service Medals.]

Under heavy Katangan fire, all of the armoured cars then left the bridge and pulled back. Attempts to dislodge the obstacles by firing on them failed and at 19.45, Kane decided to withdraw and make a second attempt to cross the bridge at first light.

The troops were fed and retired for the night at 22.00 hours.

CHAPTER 5

We walked innocently into the jaws of a trap which slapped shut as soon as we arrived in Jadotville.

Captain (retired) Noel Carey

Jadotville. 13 September 1961

Before night finally fell, Katangan Gendarmerie in a house on the Jadotville road gave A Company what their commanding officer described as 'considerable trouble'.

Three snipers managed to completely pin down one of our sections until Sgt Monaghan, shortly before last light and using an 84mm anti-tank gun, exposed himself to great danger and silenced heavy fire from the house. The sniping ended.

Then it was night, and for a while almost silent. It was cold, too, in the inky black, and there was no knowing what the Katangans, who knew the terrain and its possibilities so much better than the Irish, were up to.

As the men of A Company waited, chilled by the drying sweat stiffening and stinking their clothes, Quinlan plotted tactics. Soon, under cover of the darkness and aware that their position would be 'untenable if the enemy attacked in strength or infiltrated at night', he 'thinned out' the forward platoon. Every man who could be spared from fighting was put to the digging of new trenches. Within an hour, the company was withdrawn and positioned in a new, carefully planned defensive position.

Meanwhile, Quinlan had far more than retrenching his troops to contend with. While the digging was going on, Jadotville's Mayor Amisi rang Madame Lamonfagne's number, asking for a ceasefire.

Sergeant Wally Hegarty accompanied Lars Fröberg to Mme Lamonfagne's home when the Swede went there to interpret the call for Quinlan.

'She insisted I take a cup of milk,' Hegarty wrote. 'It was like manna. She sent the company consignments of cakes and chips. When Comdt Quinlan offered to pay her for these, she roundly refused.'

Quinlan, through Fröberg, spoke on the phone with Mayor Amisi.

The mayor said he was trying to arrange talks. I agreed to this and all firing ceased. An enemy ambulance and two cars drove to the villa that had been hit by our 84mm anti-tank fire and evacuated the dead and wounded, including the three snipers.

With signalman Frank Williams, he radioed this news to Battalion HQ.

1830 HRS. JADOTVILLE: ARRANGING CEASEFIRE AND TALKS. ONLY ONE WOUNDED. ENEMY CASUALTIES EXPECTED HEAVY. IN TOUCH WITH REINFORCEMENTS BUT RECEPTION POOR.

1851 HRS. ELISABETHVILLE: REINFORCEMENTS HELD UP AT THE BRIDGE.

1851 HRS. ELISABETHVILLE: REINFORCEMENTS UNDER FIRE AT BRIDGE.

Then, at last, Quinlan managed to make brief contact with Force Kane at Lufira Bridge.

1858 HRS. JADOTVILLE: ARRANGING CEASEFIRE AND TALKS HERE. HOLD YOUR POSITION. DON'T ACCEPT RISKS.

He radioed HQ in Elisabethville again.

1940 HRS. JADOTVILLE: HAVE INSTRUCTED REINFORCEMENTS TO HOLD AT BRIDGE RATHER THAN RISK CASUALTIES UNTIL AFTER TALKS. THE FCA HAS LEARNED A LESSON. OUR MORALE VERY HIGH, HOPE YOU ARE ALL RIGHT. GOD BLESS YOU ALL.

Elisabethville radioed the relief patrol, passing on this last message.

The Gendarmerie continued to evacuate their dead and wounded while the ceasefire, pending talks, continued. But Quinlan was uneasy.

2115 HRS. JADOTVILLE: TALKS NOT STARTED. CEASEFIRE STILL OBSERVED. NOT SURE WHAT TO EXPECT. HOW IS OVERALL SITUATION? MAY REQUIRE HEAVY REINFORCEMENTS MORNING.

His caution was well founded. As soon as the Katangans had collected their dead and wounded,

…they broke the ceasefire, opening fire again without warning. Sporadic firing continued throughout the night at intervals and talks as promised did not take place. At approx 2130 hours a person the mayor called his 'White Adviser' rang. This man said he was a Red Cross official and could offer us good advice.

Madame Lamonfagne asked to speak to him. When she did so, she told us she didn't recognise his voice, that he was new to Jadotville and she suspected he was a mercenary. She said his accent was definitely French, not Swiss as he claimed he was. Her advice to us, not to believe anything this 'Adviser' told us, was very sound. Instead of arranging for a conference, this man demanded our capitulation and threatened again that a mob was coming to attack us.

He assumed the role of our saviour and friend, someone who would protect us from the wrath of the mob whom he said were almost out of control because of heavy casualties inflicted by us. I replied through my interpreter, Lieutenant Lars Fröberg, that if he could not stop the mob, then we would.

I thanked him for his concern for our safety and told him not to worry, that we were quite capable of protecting ourselves.

I suggested to him that he should protect the mob by preventing them from attacking us.

Fröberg, interpreting all of this for Quinlan, took a characteristically robust approach:

They waged psychological warfare against us: one minute full of pleasant promises, such as our safe passage to the Rhodesian border; the next ugly and threatening us with massacre. It was all meant to force us to give in, a way of making us surrender to them.

Wally Hegarty's perspective on events was, as always, succinct and sharply evocative:

Night fall, great activity rat-tat-tat on all sides then again silence. During the evening they rang looking for us to surrender. Quinlan wouldn't even discuss it. Battalion HQ assured us of help in the morning. During the night isolated firing on all sides.

And so the Katangan night took over, ever more chilly and black with distant dogs barking, toads croaking, the unknown everywhere and, sporadically, gun fire.

A Company was positioned in the new location by 2000 hours. Quinlan fully expected they would be closely surrounded under cover of the darkness; his preparations were intended to meet a full-scale attack at first light.

Tireless effort by Frank Williams and the company's radio operators failed to make contact with the reinforcements at Lufira Bridge. They did, however, receive a message from Battalion HQ.

2145 HRS. ELISABETHVILLE: ELISABETHVILLE STILL IN UN HANDS AND STRONG REINFORCEMENTS AT BRIDGE NEAR YOU. MAKE YOUR OWN ARRANGEMENTS WITH THEM.

Contact with Force Kane continuing impossible, there was only one feasible reply to this.

2200 HRS. JADOTVILLE: FCA WILL NOT HAVE TALKS UNLESS WE CAPITULATE. SUSPECT CLOSE SURROUNDING OF POSITION. GET HEAVY REINFORCEMENTS TO ME FIRST LIGHT.

CHAPTER 6

It's not the bullet with my name on it that bothers me; it's the one that says 'to whom it may concern'.

Anonymous, Belfast, 1991

Over the next five days, the men of A Company would become intimately acquainted with every sun-baked inch of dusty road and scrubby bush, every unfriendly building, grassy hill, valley and slope of their position. None of them, however, ever became quite so familiar as their commanding officer did.

Quinlan's tenets of tactics and a good defence were, he knew, their best, and maybe their only, hope. The tactician in him set about intensely detailing every inch and centimetre of A Company's new position, his soldier's eye graphically itemising the topography of the patch of African soil on which his troops would make their stand. Nothing, not a twisted root or dusty hollow, was left unaccounted for as he planned for their defence.

And a rout of the Katangan enemy.

Our new defensive position was almost circular, approx 250 yards by 180 yards astride the main Elisabethville–Jadotville road. The ground on the right of the road, facing Jadotville, was covered with close bush sloping gradually down for a distance of 400 yards and then rising again for a distance of approx 1700 yards to the skyline. Fields of fire and observation close in were limited to 20 or 30 yards in most of the area, but we had fairly good observation on the rising ground from 600–1600 yards and could bring effective mounted machine guns and mortar fire on this area. Along the road to Jadotville we had perfect observation and covered the road with fire up to 1000 yards.

On the left of the road a belt of approx 200 yards wide and extending all the way to Jadotville was tightly covered with small residential gardens, some villas and thick bush. Observation and fields of fire at ground level were limited to 15–20 yards.

Farther to our left, extending around to within 150 yards of the Elisabethville road on our rear, there was unlimited observation as the bush had been cleared.

The Union Minière works were situated on a hill approx 2500 yards distant.

At a distance of approx 1200 yds a native commune was situated on the side of the hill.

To our immediate rear there was another belt of very close bush, approx 400 yards wide and extending along both sides of the road for a distance of about 600 yards, where it dropped abruptly to form a large area of dead ground. Three small villas with out-offices were situated along the roadside in this area.

Approximately one mile to our rear a big hill rose steeply to over 300 feet. The road to Elisabethville wound around the base of this hill and over a culvert. The hill was strongly held and we observed the mast of a wireless on the top.

This hill commanded the whole area, was our most dangerous sector and was where I expected the main attack to come from. Large forces could assemble in the dead ground and approach very close to our position through the bush unobserved.

He gave serious thought to taking this ant, or termite, hill.

I considered attacking and taking this hill as it would afford us a very strong position where we could hold out indefinitely if we could be supplied with water, rations and ammo. But as we could take with us only the water we had in portable containers, and as this was very limited, I decided to hold out in our present position.

I had, however, plans prepared to spring the obvious trap there as soon as our reinforcements crossed the Lufira Bridge. We were not attacked from this position and, although we could bring mounted machine-gun fire on it, I decided to leave it alone, hoping to secure surprise by my attack when the reinforcements were coming through. Perhaps the enemy also expected to achieve a surprise ambush on the reinforcements and were hoping that we had not observed their position.

A Company's defence, once again and in principle, depended on trenches, on soldiers dug in on small ant hills on the perimeter of their position and on others in the strategically placed villa they'd named 'Red House' and in Purfina Garage. All of this was supported within the location by fortified villas.

Quinlan's painstaking detail illustrates this organisation of his company's defence:

- No. 1 Platoon on the right of the road with elements of Company HQ—the mounted machine gun Section in Number 1 Platoon location to cover the main road to Jadotville and the bush area, and another road leading around our position to Lufira. We had observation on this road at two points at 1250 yards and 1500 yards.
- No. 2 Platoon on the left of the road facing Jadotville.
- Two armoured cars as mobile-mounted machine-gun fire support to move quickly to any threatened area. Tracks were cut through bush and hedges to firing position for the armoured cars.
- Two high buildings (two storey), Purfina Garage (which was also my HQ) and Red House which gave good observation over the area were occupied with two light automatic teams in each. I assigned the area of Red House to Coy. Sgt Prendergast with a force of 15 men from Company HQ.

- Two 84mm anti-tank guns were situated covering the main road, one towards Jadotville and one towards Elisabethville. The third 84mm was in mobile reserve.

My plan was to break up all attacks at long range and prevent the enemy from coming into the close bush country near our position, where his superiority in numbers could force a break-in.

A concentrated attack, if vigorously executed, could have broken into our position in any sector. I planned to catch any break in force in cross fire from the fortified within the position.

But the limitations of their supplies, as well as their position, posed a continuing problem.

We had very few sandbags for these fortifications and we used beds resting on window sills with mattresses draped over them to give the men protection from grenades and some protection from mortar fire.

They weren't to know it then but none of the villas occupied by A Company would take a direct hit from either mortars or aerial bombs. Quinlan recalled:

This was so even though some mortar shell fell beside two villas and caused considerable damage and four aerial bombs fell beside the Purfina Garage. One unoccupied villa got a direct hit from heavy mortar shell and was almost totally destroyed.

A Company's mortars (3 x 60mm) were located in the centre of the Support Platoon position. Each one was laid on a specific SOS target (a target of special importance), though all three could and did fire on selected targets as well as SOS targets. Liam Donnelly prepared range cards to check the distance to predetermined targets during the battle. Quinlan worried about injuries and medical facilities:

The First Aid Post was situated in a garage in No. 1 Platoon location. Treatment of the seriously wounded caused me much anxiety as there was very little our Medical Officer could do in the case of serious internal wounds and there was no means of evacuation.

Dr Joe Clune was tireless and made the most of a much less than ideal situation.

Quinlan furiously bemoaned the inadequacy of their communications.

We had two 31 wireless sets and two 38 sets which had given out completely during this, our first day of battle. Even when they worked, they were most unsatisfactory and fire orders and corrections for our mortars were passed from trench to trench. The resourcefulness and efficiency of many of the private soldiers in passing on fire orders and corrections, and the cooperation of everyone, was both admirable and praiseworthy.

We had two C12 sets used as a rear link to HQ in Elisabethville. Reception was not possible during the night from 2359 hours to 0600 hours. At times it was possible to get through on voice and when this was not possible, morse was used.

Reception during daylight was very good despite continual interference by an enemy set which was tuned in on our wavelength and broadcast a chattering garble whenever we came on the air.

We still had only intermittent radio contact with the reinforcement group at Lufira Bridge. But could hear mortar fire....

The sound of that mortar fire, and echo of the explosions, caused 'hearts to soar', according to Noel Carey.

It meant our relief was at hand. It lasted for just over an hour and then there was silence. We waited, and waited, and waited. In the darkness, our cooks began to prepare a stew meal and to boil water on their petrol cookers. To our delight, we were able to have one good meal and hot tea that night, in relays, as we still had to man the trenches.

Leo Boland also remembers, 'how we could hear the reinforcements at Lufira Bridge, how we were hoping all the time that they'd get to us....'

CHAPTER 7

I went for adventure. As boy soldiers you didn't expect to go into battle. When you heard United Nations you immediately thought 'peace'.

John Gorman (17-year-old Private in Jadotville)

DAY TWO
Jadotville. Thursday, 14 September 1961

The morning of the second day arrived for A Company at 0400 hours. Each man got tea, and a ration of 'dog' biscuits.

At 0530, they came under sudden, intense and worryingly accurate mortar fire, with three or four shells landing together. Quinlan recalled:

> Many of the shells fell around Company HQ in the Purfina Garage and were accompanied by heavy machine-gun and rifle fire from all sides. This fire was vigorously returned.

What he would describe as 'a very long and tiring day, with the merciless sun beating down on top of the men sweltering in their trenches' had begun.

Cook Bobby Allan describes the heat on that, and other days, as 'unreal. If you put an arm on the bonnet of a car at two in the day, you'd burn the arm. It was 45–46 degrees....'

Quinlan wrote:

Fire went on for almost an hour before the enemy mortar positions were located by Sgt Prendergast and Private Michael McCormack, who were in the Red House. They discovered them situated in the bush on the left of the road near the bus depot at a range of 950 yards. Fire orders and corrections were passed back to Capt. Donnelly at our mortar position. He engaged, silenced and completely destroyed the enemy mortars. Some of the enemy crews were cut down with light automatic fire as they ran for safety.

Donnelly's mortar division was proving, for a second day, both zealous and ceaselessly accurate. Donnelly's own report on the day's activities is coolly professional, and to the point.

Firing started on this morning by enemy mortar fire which was exceptionally accurate and lucky for us was NOT continued for long. The enemy mortar position was located at the bus garage and with prompt and accurate fire Sgt Kelly silenced the enemy mortars.

Wally Hegarty, more laconic in style, describes the same event:

Dawn was shattered by machine-gun and mortar fire coming and going. It took us some time to locate them ... their bombardment stopped midway through ours.

Contact was made again with Battalion HQ.

0559 HRS. JADOTVILLE: ENEMY ATTACK HAS COMMENCED. PLEASE SEND STRONG REINFORCEMENTS IMMEDIATELY.

0620 HRS. ELISABETHVILLE: REINFORCEMENTS AT BRIDGE. CAN YOU CONTACT THEM?

But A Company's radio operators failed, despite countless and exhaustive attempts, to make contact with Force Kane.

0650 HRS. JADOTVILLE: VERY HEAVY ATTACK ON US. SEND VERY STRONG REINFORCEMENTS IMMEDIATELY. VERY URGENT.

An hour later, the situation hadn't changed.

0738 HRS. JADOTVILLE: NO CONTACT WITH REINFORCEMENTS. SEND VERY STRONG REINFORCEMENTS PLEASE.

The mortar attacks on A Company continued, from different positions, the accelerating whine of the explosions followed by the sound of shrapnel cutting through the air as the Gendarmerie adopted the tactic of firing three or four shells from one position before moving swiftly to another. Some of this fire was accurate; most was inaccurate.

The accuracy of A Company's mortar fire, on the other hand, was uncanny. Quinlan, impressed by this accuracy during battle, was awed afterwards to be told by a South African mercenary mortar officer with the Gendarmerie how a shell from one of the company's mortars had all but gone down the barrel of a Gendarmerie mortar. 'He didn't say,' Quinlan remarked, 'how many casualties he suffered from that shell.'

On that Thursday, the second day of battle, A Company's commander felt confident his men had 'destroyed all enemy mortars. The enemy did not use mortars against us on Friday. They did bring them in again on Saturday morning, however.'

As time and the battle went on, it became apparent that intelligent common sense had become a factor in A Company's defence. According to Quinlan:

Cooperation between men in trenches in forward positions and mortar crews was unstinting, with private soldiers passing back fire orders and corrections to the mortar position. Responsibilities like this had not been part of the men's training.

That second morning also saw a bloody encounter fiercely test A Company's defences—as well as Gendarmerie loyalty to their mercenary leadership.

This happened when Gendarmerie troops, marshalled by their mercenary officers and moving on A Company in an open formation of company strength, found themselves in the teeth of the Irish soldiers' invulnerable defences. Quinlan recalled:

> They were cut down at a long range of 800–1100 feet by concentrated fire from all weapons which could be brought to bear. These included a mounted machine gun dug into an ant hill covering the road in this area, light automatic fire from Company Sgt Prendergast and Pte McCormack in the Red House, two armoured cars firing from prepared positions and mortar fire. When the first wave was broken up, supporting Gendarmerie infantry located behind the brow of the high ground did not come forward.

But enemy numbers were growing, reinforcements pouring into Jadotville from surrounding villages.

At 0820, Quinlan managed to make voice contact with his Battalion OC Lieutenant Colonel McNamee in Elisabethville, and to tell him just how serious things were with A Company. McNamee assured him that reinforcements would arrive in Elisabethville that day, including heavy weapons.

Uncertain, in the absence of radio contact, how things were with the patrol at the Lufira Bridge, Quinlan again asked that a strong force with heavy weapons be sent to relieve A Company. The Battalion OC replied that he expected the reinforcements at the bridge to break through but that he would send further reinforcements if necessary.

Not long after this, around 0900 hours, the sound of mortar fire from the direction of the Lufira Bridge came, 'as pleasant music to our ears and was vastly reassuring to the company. We expected the reinforcements to capture the bridge, opening our line of road communications....'

But a message from Force Kane, intercepted by Frank Williams and his operators within minutes, diminished the likelihood of this positive scenario.

0922 HRS. FORCE KANE: ARRIVED AT THE BRIDGE LAST NIGHT. CAME UNDER FIRE. RETURNED FIRE. WITHDREW FOR NIGHT. SAME PROCEDURE THIS MORNING, WITHDREW AND NOW SHELLING BRIDGE WITH MORTARS ON BRIDGE.

0925 HRS. ELISABETHVILLE: REINFORCEMENTS FIGHTING AT BRIDGE. NO CASUALTIES SO FAR.

0943 HRS. JADOTVILLE: IS FÉIDIR LEIS AN FCA DUL TIMPEALL MO SUÍOMH GO DTÍ AN DROICHEAD [The FCA can go around my position to get to the bridge].

1018 HRS. FORCE KANE: PUTTING IN FINAL ATTACK. MUST RETURN TO ELISABETHVILLE IF NOT SUCCESSFUL.

Quinlan was not impressed by this last: 'We felt strongly that this message anticipated the result.'

> I realised that our fate depended entirely on holding the Lufira Bridge and sent a message immediately to Battalion HQ to contact Comdt Kane and to get him to hold on at the bridge in order to contain the enemy. Capt. Dermot Byrne, my Second in Command, got on by voice to Lieut Col. McNamee and explained the absolute importance of consolidating and holding near the bridge if it could not be taken. It was vital to A Company that the FCA be contained at the bridge.

Within 20 minutes of this, a message from Battalion HQ to Force Kane was intercepted.

1058 HRS. ELISABETHVILLE: INFLICT AS MANY CASUALTIES AND DO AS MUCH DAMAGE TO ENEMY AS POSSIBLE. STAY TRYING AS LONG AS POSSIBLE.

Twenty minutes later, Jadotville got a voice message through to Battalion HQ asking them to contact Force Kane and tell the men that when they arrived in Jadotville, they would be able to identify A Company's position by a UNO flag flying on the first villa. They were to be warned, too, to be careful as the company's armoured cars were camouflaged.

The soldiers of A Company carried on defending themselves, the sun becoming hotter hour by broiling hour, fatigue and thirst growing, the whining howl of mortars incessant and hopes high that reinforcements would get through, any minute.

CHAPTER 8

The troops had no body armour. A stray bullet in the lower chest and they were dead....

Col. (retired) M. Shannon

Lufira Bridge. Thursday, 14 September 1961

Transport problems delayed Force Kane's early-morning movement and it was 0830 hours before a second attempt was made on Lufira Bridge.

As Lieutenant Michael Shannon's platoon headed for the railway bridge and Lieutenant J. Farrell with No. 5 Platoon made for the Lufira Bridge, both came under heavy machine-gun and small arm fire. With the river bank offering absolutely no cover, they were horrendously exposed.

Within an hour, ill-equipped and with no way of getting past the obstacles, it had become clear that it would not be possible to cross the Lufira Bridge.

'We sent messages to Elisabethville that it was unpassable,' Shannon recalls. 'And were told to go back to Elisabethville.'

Before leaving, Force Kane subjected the Gendarmerie to sustained machine-gun and mortar fire.

Meanwhile, in Elisabethville, two Irish soldiers, Corporal M. Nolan and Trooper P. Mullins, were killed when they were ambushed by Gendarmerie using anti-tank weapons. Commandant Patrick Cahalane and Sergeant T. Carey were injured and taken prisoner with the rest of the patrol.

CHAPTER 9

*When the Fouga dropped its first bomb, it was the beginning of a
nightmare which got worse and worse.*

Lieut Lars Fröberg, Swedish Interpreter

Jadotville. Thursday, 14 September 1961

Comdt Pat Quinlan's ongoing account of the second day's battle
becomes one of military understatement:

> Extra mortars were brought into position at longer range
> and we were subjected to very heavy shelling all that day. I
> still thought this to be a ruse and that the main effort would
> come on my most vulnerable sector on the Elisabethville
> road, where we were under fire from the bush. But no major
> attack developed.

Nothing of the scalding heat and sizzling, unmoving air, the
fatiguing dehydration, the buzzing clouds of flies, the insects
sucking at the corners of eyes and mouths, the stinking clothes
and growing stench in the trenches. All realities which, along
with the certain knowledge that disease was inevitable as the
approaching night unless they got water and food and rest, would
be acknowledged later.

Everyone tried not to voice the increasing fear that the relief
patrol might not get through.

Quinlan was unashamedly appreciative of the men in his charge,
awed by their courage, adaptability, tenacity and by 'the resourcefulness
and efficiency of many of the private soldiers in passing on fire orders
and corrections':

The cooperation of everyone was both admirable and praiseworthy.

Ireland never reared better sons. The men never wavered and my slightest sign was obeyed without question. They seemed to think I could do no wrong. It was very heartening to have such unconditional loyalty. No man ever got the loyalty I got from those boys. When things were darkest, they were always smiling. 'How are we doing, sir?' was the usual query. Oh, God, they were great.

At midday, with Force Kane gone from the Lufira Bridge and A Company much embattled, the Fouga jet arrived overhead.

1206 HRS. JADOTVILLE: ENEMY FIGHTER JET HERE NOW.

1210 HRS. ELISABETHVILLE: ANY AIR ATTACK?

1210 HRS. JADOTVILLE: NO, IT IS OBSERVING. DO YOU KNOW WHERE IT HAS COME FROM?

1212 HRS. ELISABETHVILLE: NO.

The Fouga circled, and circled, then headed back to its Kolwezi base 100 miles away.

Some of the troops, unable to get a clear view of the aircraft against the sun, thought it might be a UN plane. Someone even stood in a trench and waved. Quinlan and others saw it for what it was.

We identified it immediately as one of the Katangan planes that had been at the airport at Elisabethville. It circled our position four times then headed away towards Kolwezi. We knew we could expect another visit, when it would strafe us. We arranged a reception with small arms.

In the meantime, they kept going, full of the will to live and to win, hoping against hope for reinforcements, believing against the evidence that they would get through, until, at 1300 hours, the word came:

A message from Battalion HQ told us that the attack on the bridge had failed. We knew this anyway as all sound of firing from that direction had ceased shortly after 1000 hours.

When Elisabethville advised that they were, 'endeavouring to send further reinforcements', Quinlan replied:

1307 HRS. JADOTVILLE: GOD BLESS YOU. SEND NEW REINFORCEMENTS SOON AS POSSIBLE.

1330 HRS. JADOTVILLE: WHAT IS POSITION IN ELISABETHVILLE?

1333 HRS. ELISABETHVILLE: POSITION SAME. HOLDING OUR OWN.

1410 HRS. JADOTVILLE: SUGGEST THAT JET IS RHODESIAN RECCE PLANE.

1430 HRS. JADOTVILLE: PLANE POSITIVELY IDENTIFIED. RED TIPPED WINGS. THIS MAY BE PLANE MISSING FROM AIRPORT WHEN A COMPANY TOOK OVER THERE [in August].

Then, and for more than an hour, A Company fought against heavy mortar fire. Coming up to 1600, Quinlan radioed again:

1540 HRS. JADOTVILLE: IS PATROL STILL AT BRIDGE? GIVE ESTIMATED TIME ARRIVAL NEW REINFORCEMENTS.

1545 HRS. ELISABETHVILLE: ETA [estimated time of arrival] NEW REINFORCEMENTS NOT KNOWN. WILL LET YOU KNOW SOON AS POSSIBLE.

Quinlan now knew definitively that Force Kane had left to return to Elisabethville. He would have to trust in Battalion HQ officers to get a second force of reinforcements together.

Mortar fire became ever heavier. And the Fouga returned. This time the roar of bombs followed its high, whining approach.

Corporal Williams went on messaging.

1550 HRS. JADOTVILLE: JET AIRCRAFT HERE AGAIN. POSITION BEING BOMBED BY AIRCRAFT.

1555 HRS. JADOTVILLE: JET NOW BOMBING AND MACHINE-GUNNING POSITIONS.

Quinlan wrote:

> ...after circling our position once it dived on Red House— or on our machine-gun position, both were on the same line. Instead of strafing, it dropped two bombs which gave us all quite a jolt. Each time it came, it arrived out of the sun.

And each time it left, the men of A Company 'prepared a further barrage of small arms should it come again'.

Quite a jolt, as described by Wally Hegarty, amounted to the jet 'dropping two bombs and giving us three strafing runs. That guy terrorised me....'

He terrorised and angered everyone. Hegarty recalls a soldier standing in his trench, furiously blowing raspberries at the Fouga. According to Sean Foley, 'people were so angry, they were firing their Gustavs at him; some were even firing pistols.'

But their efforts, Bobby Allan admitted, 'were like throwing pebbles at a crow.' Quinlan described how:

> The bombs dropped very near our machine-gun position and two men were wounded. One, Pte James Taheney, was thrown into the air and suffered from shell shock. Pte Edward Gormley was hit in the shoulder by a big boulder of a stone.

When the jet came in again on strafing runs, its targets were Red House and Purfina Garage. But Quinlan had anticipated this.

> I had ordered the evacuation of Purfina, a tall building, after the earlier recce by the Fouga as I expected that to be the target. Two men didn't get my order, however, and they had a very lucky escape when machine-gun fire from the Fouga

tore the windows and walls around them. They just had time to take shelter behind an angle of a wall.

As soon as the Fouga left the area, I dashed across the road to No. 1 Platoon position as there was intensive firing from that location. The entire area on the front-line trenches was covered with dense smoke and dust cloud from the bombing. I met Sgt John Monaghan and asked what all the firing was about.

'It's okay, sir,' he said. 'These men are sound. They're firing through the smoke in case some of the Gends may be coming into attack under its cover. They all started firing together without even an order given to them. They're okay, they'll never crack up,' he said.

Quinlan took comfort from his sergeant's reassurances.

I must confess that I was very elated to hear this as I was worried about the effects of the bombing and continuous attacks on the troops. Not one officer or man in the company had ever been under fire until the previous day. None of us knew what our reactions would be.

Hegarty had already given some thought to this very point:

I found that every man thought he himself would come through and that only the other guys were mortal. I suppose it's some kind of anaesthetic provided by nature.

What worried everyone in A Company, constantly and throughout, was how their families and loved ones were dealing with news and misinformation about their embattled state.

'We wondered what the hell people at home were thinking,' Dr Joe Clune remembers. 'This was the great worry people had. Bullets flying overhead didn't worry us half so much.'

But with all this, Quinlan marvelled, 'I never saw a man waver. The morale was excellent and every man gave of his very best, accepting orders without question. *Every man would have fought on until death if the situation had warranted it.*'

The 'Tigers of Jadotville', the UK's *Daily Mail* was already calling them, getting its animals and continents confused but echoing the general media view of things.

The outcast years when their bravery would be decried, and the battle they had fought denied, were inconceivable at that point.

CHAPTER 10

The first casualty when war comes is truth.

Hiram Johnson, US Senate, 1918

Across the world. Thursday, 13 September 1961

Reactions to UN action in Katanga, and A Company's plight in Jadotville, varied worldwide.

In Belgium, *La Libre Belgique* reported that 'the UN opened fire, killed and continue to kill Africans who lived in peace and hope.' Elsewhere in Belgium, the UN was accused of 'premeditated crime' and Dr Conor Cruise O'Brien compared to the Nazis.

Swedish opinion supported the UN action. London papers demanded an explanation of events. Portugal's press was critical, announcing that 'Mr Hammarskjöld must have been brainwashed by the Russians in the corridors of the UN building.'

Wire reports arriving in newspaper offices in Dublin asserted that:

Twenty of the encircled Irish company in Jadotville are said to have been captured and executed ...

The chief of 1,000 fierce Bayeke warriors has declared war without quarter on the Irish troops at Jadotville....

And, more accurately:'Outpost being bombed and strafed from the air and machine gunned from the ground....'

CHAPTER 11

No marksmanship can help you against hunger and thirst.
Lieut Lars Fröberg,
Swedish Interpreter with A Company, September 1961

Jadotville. Thursday, 14 September 1961

Shortly after the first air attack on A Company, the 'White Adviser' rang again. He wanted Quinlan's capitulation within ten minutes.

Fröberg brought his message to Quinlan who immediately returned with the Swede to Mme Lamonfagne's villa. On her phone to the 'Adviser', he operated a psychological game of his own.

> I decided to play for time and said I was awaiting instructions. I did this, as I knew that although reinforcements had left the Lufira Bridge for Elisabethville, I'd had a Battalion message to the effect that they were endeavouring to send further reinforcements. When the 'Adviser' came on the phone again, he was both aggressive and cajoling at the same time. He eventually said 'We have cannon too, you know, and we can use that'. I sent my reply through Lars Fröberg: 'What are you waiting for? You have sent everything else.' This finished that conversation.'

Quinlan then brought Elisabethville up to date on the situation.

> 1630 HRS. JADOTVILLE: ENEMY HAVE ASKED FOR OUR DECISION NOW. I HAVE REPLIED THAT I AM AWAITING INSTRUCTIONS. CUIR CÚNAMH AN-LÁIDIR GAN MOILL. TÁIMID AG FANACHT GO DTÍ AN FEAR DEIREANACH. [Send very strong reinforcements without delay. We are holding out to the last man.]

And so they were:

> Throughout Thursday, A Company mortars were continually in action against troop concentrations, machine-gun positions and counter bombardment of enemy mortar positions. We were running very short of mortar ammunition and thereafter we fired only when urgently required...
>
> During the late afternoon we detected convoys moving along the road to the right of No. 1 Platoon towards the Lufira Bridge. Lieutenant Leech, OC of that platoon, had two men continually observe this road with field glasses and on the codeword STABLE two mortars, two mounted machine guns and two armoured cars opened fire. Two vehicles were put out of action and blocked this road. The road was cleared during the night so we knew further convoys were moving. We fired on these but did not know what the effect was...
>
> The enemy also attempted to use a road on our left flank but this was very open and after the first jeep was overturned with mortar and light automatic [Bren gun] fire it was not used again.
>
> Corporal Timothy Quinn who was in charge of one 60mm mortar, went out onto an ant hill for better observation and shouted his fire orders back to the mortar position. A shell landed immediately in front of the jeep and overturned it. Lt Carey, with a light automatic team, cut down the enemy in the jeep.

Major Jose Denlin, piloting the Fouga, had not yet finished for the day and returned at 1745 hours to,

> ...drop more bombs and carry out three or four strafing runs. One bomb fell on the roadway beside Purfina and caused considerable damage especially to the buses which were located there. The other bombs fell on the lawn in front of Red House. Red House was also strafed and Company Sgt Prendergast had a very narrow escape as he was coming down the stairs and the staircase was cut beside him by a burst of fire coming through the window.

The indomitable Hegarty, wandering abroad as he tried to 'get some water for the lads and find out why help had not come', was about to discover that he was not invulnerable.

> I was going back to my hideout with the water when I heard the Gends opening up with mortar ... I was caught in the open but unworried as the bombs could be going anywhere. I hopped into a convenient fold in the ground and waited, but damned if the first one didn't land 20 yards away. While waiting for the second to land, I nearly died with fright. I'd say I learned what fear is right there. Indescribable but I remember trying to dig myself into the ground, and my legs extended stiffly behind me. The second landed 10 yards away and I knew I was hit but I moved away like a rocket....

Quinlan described what happened next:

> With several small pieces of shrapnel wounds from his ankle up along his right side, he got up and ran in a shocked and dazed condition towards the enemy lines, to where some of the enemy, led by mercenaries, had crept through the bush and small gardens very close to our positions. Some distance beyond our forward trenches, Hegarty collapsed and was rescued by Company Sgt Prendergast....

Sheltered behind the trees in his platoon area, Hegarty was patched up as well as possible by Private John Broderick who, Hegarty recalls, 'put patches on the two wounds on the left side of my rump and one in each calf.'

> I got our blankets together and wrapped myself up. About five minutes later, I was in shock.
>
> After this primary shock and with Broderick's help during a lull in fighting, I staggered off towards Company HQ lines, ambitions to reach the Medical Officer. After 100 yards, I went down with weakness and had to be stretchered fully conscious but very embarrassed. Of course the word went

out that I was wrecked. Several corporals began wondering how they'd look in two stripes [indicating a sergeant's rank]. After the doc came, he said there wasn't much danger, gave me a shot of morphine and packed me away in the house which was also company HQ and in the centre of things. The shot made me dopey and I believe I spent the night asking for my gun, which I had under the stretcher. That night I was so miserable I didn't care if they came and cut my throat....

Quinlan's account fills in what Hegarty's does not include:

After dark the next night (Friday), Hegarty left the First Aid Post and returned to his trench. His cool courage, self-sacrifice and devotion to duty throughout the battle and indeed throughout his whole service in the Congo was an inspiration to all.

As for the man who rescued him:

...Prendergast was christened 'The Tiger' by some of the men during the battle. This man was untiring; his personal bravery earned him the name. During normal 'peacetime', he was a strict disciplinarian but always very fair. He saw to it that every NCO and man did his duty but he also saw to it that they got their rights.

He was in command of Red House sector which, together with the right flank of Lieutenant Tom Quinlan's adjoining No. 2 Platoon, took the brunt of the major attacks on that Thursday, as well as close-range grenade attacks on that night and on Friday too. Sgt Prendergast was inspiring to us all.

Paddy Neville also marvelled at Prendergast: 'He was our sniper and a crack shot. Lying down, he could fire accurately at 500 yards. An almost impossible thing.'

And Hegarty remembers an incident after he had been injured and was recovering:

Jack Prendergast said to me—'Come here, Hegarty. look at that house.' It was a place at least 200 yards away, max 300 yards, and there were Gend. officers out on a balcony surveying our position. Beside them was the gable end and he blasted that gable end. You could see holes popping out of it. You could see those Gends go like jack rabbits! And this was in the midst of battle! He could have killed them as easily as turning off a light but he didn't.

If Prendergast was inspiring to all, so was Quinlan himself. As the fighting continued that hideously long Thursday, he was never less than fully attentive to the role played by each man, moving ceaselessly between sections, encouraging, cajoling, forever alert and forever fine-tuning tactics.

According to Hegarty, 'Comdt Quinlan grew to giant size in every man's eyes as the fighting continued.'

Quinlan also, and through it all, took note of the contribution of individual men at different times, as can be seen in his tribute to Lieutenant Tom Quinlan, commander of No. 2 Platoon adjoining Red House Sector.

Lieutenant Quinlan was a fine officer, solid as a rock. He organised his own platoon sector and included the Red House sector in his command also. Each night he placed himself in the most dangerous position where the enemy was always attempting to infiltrate. His presence and example gave courage and strength of purpose to the men in this dangerous sector.

Lieut Tom Quinlan, Company Sgt Prendergast and Sgt Hegarty were three right men in the right place at the right time.

CHAPTER 12

The main reason for the complete misunderstanding of UN action is a complete lack of knowledge of the Congo situation....

Dag Hammarskjöld, September 1961

Leopoldville, Congo. 14 September 1961

Confusion and dysfunction continued in the capital of Katanga. The UN Secretary General, in Leopoldville, was disturbed by reports from Dr Conor Cruise O'Brien that Moise Tshombe could not be found and that UN buildings were being attacked by the mercenary-led Gendarmerie forces.

In the hope that a ceasefire could be arranged, the UN released Vice-President Kibwe, the only Katangese minister to have been detained by its troops during Operation Morthor the day before. The expectation was that he would make contact with President Tshombe.

Reports of Tshombe's whereabouts did indeed filter through: He was later in the day reported to be sheltering in the British Consulate. When Cruise O'Brien made plans to capture the Katangan President, he was refused authorisation to do so by Dag Hammarskjöld.

Rhodesian troops, armoured cars and planes lined up along that country's frontier with the Congo because of what Rhodesia's Prime Minister, Sir Roy Welensky, called a 'serious threat' to his country's security. 'Nothing so disgraceful in the whole history of international organisations has ever before happened,' he said furiously of UN action in the Congo.

Concern and confusion continued about the fate of A Company, beleaguered and embattled in Jadotville, without reinforcements and now repeatedly being bombed and strafed by the Fouga jet. Katangan radio continued to broadcast demoralising reports of their massacre, torture and death.

CHAPTER 13

*I'm not very happy about our Battalion Plan. There is no coordination
at Battalion level so I'm just minding my own company....*

Comdt P. Quinlan, August 1961

Jadotville. Thursday, 14 September 1961

As the second night of battle fell in Jadotville, sharp and sudden as
always, Battalion HQ got in touch with A Company.

1800 HRS. ELISABETHVILLE: AIR DROP BEING PREPARED. GIVE
REQUIREMENTS IN ORDER OF PRIORITY RE WATER, RATIONS AND
AMMO. ULTIMATUM BEING BROADCAST AT 1800 HOURS TO FCA
BY MINISTER KIBWE TO SURRENDER BY 2000 HOURS OR BE SHOT
FOR TREASON.

Kibwe was the Katangan Vice-President. Hopes were raised.

Fifteen minutes later, Quinlan and Fröberg were once more
caught up in what Fröberg describes as 'a psychological war within a
war, waged by telephone'.

At 1815 hours, according to Quinlan,

...the 'White Adviser' phoned again and gave us an
ultimatum to capitulate by 1830 hrs or we would be
destroyed. He said the mob was now coming in and that
they would eat us. I told him (through Lieut Fröberg) to
be careful of his mob and that they might get indigestion
and I invited him to do his worst. I also told him to listen
to Kibwe's broadcast but he said nobody would pay any
attention to such a broadcast and that he did not believe
Kibwe would make it anyway.

Shortly after this, two mercenary officers were captured and brought to Quinlan. Believing A Company to be wiped out, its troops either killed or surrendered, they had driven a car into the company's position and been taken prisoner.

Quinlan spoke with them.

> They gave their names as Pierre van der Weger, an ex-soldier of the French Foreign Legion, and Michel Paucheu, a Frenchman, as far as I know, although they both said they were Belgians and employees of Union Minière. They were in civilian clothes but both carried pistols and grenades. The car in which they had been travelling contained more grenades, a submachine gun, an FN rifle and an ample supply of ammunition for these weapons.

Sean Foley describes seeing them drive through No. 2 Platoon's position,

> ...in a duck-egg blue coloured Volkswagen. They thought we were all finished and didn't take too kindly to being arrested. They became amenable however when they realised they weren't going to be shot. One of them looked British and wore a British Para beret with a badge. I negotiated the beret from him though he wouldn't give me the badge. I still have the beret. When we were taken prisoner, I put a slit in my tunic and stitched it into it.

Quinlan set about questioning the captives.

> In the course of questioning, they admitted they were members of Tshombe's mercenary army. They had left Elisabethville that day and had been informed by Tshombe before leaving that we had been overrun and captured in Jadotville and were being held as hostages. The Gends garrison at the Lufira Bridge told them the same story and so they drove right on to our position through other Gendarmerie roadblocks and were captured by our men.

Van der Weger told me that the garrison on the Lufira Bridge was only about 50 strong and that another force of the same size was at the crossroads about halfway between the bridge and our position. I did not know whether to believe him or not but sent the information to Battalion HQ in Elisabethville, in Irish.

He radioed other information, too, spelling out what had happened earlier.

1840 HRS. JADOTVILLE: ULTIMATUM WAS ISSUED TO A COMPANY BY FCA TO CAPITULATE BY 1830 HRS. A COMPANY REFUSED. JET PLANE ATTACKED OUR POSITION TWICE. INFO THAT TWO JETS ARE AT KOLWEZI—PILOTS ARRIVED THERE FROM RHODESIA YESTERDAY. OUR AIR DROP REQUIREMENTS LATER. FCA OFFENSIVE FIRE CONTINUES.

He sent word of their air-drop requirements and, nearly an hour later, another message coded in Irish.

1955 HRS. JADOTVILLE: FCA ANSEO. NÍL SIAD CUN AN N-ÁIRM DO CHUIR SÍOS NÁ ÉISTEACHT LE SOS TRODA. [FCA here. They are not going to lay down their arms or consider a truce.]

Quinlan, during his further questioning of the two men, had asked them why they had become mercenaries.

They just answered, 'The money is good, 25,000 Francs every fortnight.' At the rate of exchange, that amounted to Irish £180. An Irish lieutenant's salary at that time was about £20 per month.

They had also informed me, earlier, that a car left Elisabethville on the previous day, Wednesday, the day the battle began, to collect two fighter pilots. One of these was the pilot of the Fouga, a Belgian, Major Jose Denlin. This information too I immediately passed on to Elisabethville.

The prisoners were placed under guard—but not before angry members of A Company suggested they deserved to be executed as they were mercenaries and would have killed members of the company had they not been apprehended.

'Thankfully, good sense prevailed on this,' Noel Carey recalls. 'And, after taking their weapons, I put the prisoners in the loft of Purfina Garage.'

They were, according to Fröberg, 'well treated in this hastily prepared guardroom.'

Quinlan, combining the newly gathered information together with earlier data, formed a graphically realistic and even more frightening picture of the reality of the forces opposing A Company.

The bulk of the mercenaries in Katanga were recruited from ex-French Para Commandos who'd fled Algeria after the rebellion in 1960. After Operation Rumpunch on 28 August [a successful UN offensive during which A Company had captured the Gendarmerie HQ in Elisabethville], all mercenaries who were not captured (between 200 and 300 of them) went into hiding in Shinkolobwe, the old uranium mining village 10 miles west of Jadotville. There they lived in luxury with women from Jadotville to entertain them. Some ventured into the city in civilian attire. This strong force of mercenaries was available for the operations in Jadotville.

I was not aware at the time of the overwhelming strength of Gendarmerie and mercenaries opposing me but, as the volume of fire on our positions increased, it was obvious that reinforcements were being brought in. I estimated the opposing force at approx. 2000 men or two full-strength battalions plus mercenaries and other white paramilitary personnel. In actual fact, it was confirmed by intelligence sources that the force opposing us was much stronger.

In the area of Jadotville and Kolwezi alone, there were three Gendarmerie and one Para Commando Battalion (less one company on duty in Elisabethville) as well as an Engineer Company and other elements with a total strength of 3,300. These facts, in a UN intelligence report, did not include mercenaries or the white population of Jadotville who took up arms against us according to a statement made to Mr Cruise O'Brien by Lassimore, a French mercenary officer. Lassimore was second in command of the force opposing us (and said to be the man who shot Prime Minister Patrice Lumumba). I do not say that all this force was used against us but the greater part was and it should have been sufficient to overrun my position in a couple of hours. [Weeks later, when the soldiers of A Company were prisoners, Captain Tschipolo of the Gendarmerie in Jadotville would tell Quinlan that the battle had been expected to end in two hours.]

The propaganda on A Company given to Michel Paucheu and Pierre van der Weger by Moise Tshombe was by now being broadcast by Rhodesian radio. Picked up worldwide, the broadcast announced that the Irish had been massacred and defeated. The distress and confusion in Ireland were enormous.

Added to this was Rhodesian radio news, which, within hours and throughout the next day, told of how the two mercenaries had been captured by A Company. There was now no doubting how superior Katangan intelligence was to that of either the UN or the Irish Army—and how far-reaching its tentacles. According to Quinlan:

We heard it broadcast on Rhodesian radio that the mercenaries we had captured had given us vital information. This was when it became clear that someone who understood Irish was monitoring the messages between my HQ and Battalion HQ. Only later did I discover with disgust that Irishmen mining in Rhodesia were employed to monitor our Irish messages. The identity of these renegades was known and in fact one of them on a later visit to Ireland confirmed our suspicions....

However, for now and days to come, Quinlan had to concentrate on the battle.

Our left flank, which was occupied by elements of No. 3 Platoon and the cook staff of company HQ, was in the most exposed area and was where the enemy had excellent observation. But it also had the advantage of very good observation (by us) of enemy positions. This flank was under continuous fire, especially machine-gun fire, on Thursday and Friday.

Lieut Carey, who was well forward, located the enemy machine guns with the aid of field glasses. His orders to armoured cars and mortar brought concentrated and effective fire on the targets. One mortar shell from Corporal Timothy Quinn's mortar, with Pte Joe Mahoney as layer, scored a direct hit on an enemy M6 which was causing us considerable discomfort.

Lieut Carey's leadership was of very high quality and inspired confidence in his men.

Our pre-prepared trenches saved us from severe casualties. All our casualties were suffered when men were caught in the open.

One trench on our left flank suffered what was almost a direct hit when a mortar shell hit less than three feet from the edge of the trench. The men in the trench heard it coming and got down so that the worst that happened was that the side of the trench was thrown in on top of them.

The inky splendour of the African night failed to impress. Filled with shadows and the oppressive unknown, it stretched ahead of A Company.

Quinlan was feeling the strain. He wrote:

This had been a very long and tiring day, with the merciless sun beating down on top of the men where they sweltered in their trenches. The comparative cool of the night was a blessing and water bottles were refilled from our almost exhausted stock. The water in the containers and bottles got very hot under the sun although the men tried to keep it in the shade in the sides of the trenches, but the hot sun penetrated everywhere. The water in baths and open vessels was already putrid.

The last message received from Battalion HQ that night indicated that there was at least a partial observance of a ceasefire, which I took to refer to the ceasefire which Kibwe was to arrange.

The message was mostly, and uselessly as an intelligence ploy, in Irish:

2305 HRS. ELISABETHVILLE: FIRE IS MUCH LESS TONIGHT INDICATING PARTIAL OBSERVANCE OF CEASEFIRE. BEIDH SCÉAL AGAM AR BALL FAOIN IMEACHT FÓRSAÍ CHUN CABHRÚ LEAT. TÁ SÉ BEARTAITHE TREALAMH A CHUR SÍOS CHUGAT ÓN AER AR MAIDIN. NÍ MÓR AN ÁIT A MHARCÁIL ACH NÁ HÚSÁID BRAILLINÍ. [I will have news presently concerning troop movement to help you. It's arranged to drop equipment to you from the air in the morning. The (landing) place should be marked but don't use sheets.]

Quinlan took this last to mean that they were to receive an air drop of supplies the following morning. It was, he felt, 'good news'.

Except that the night of the second day was anything but over:

Heavy fire continued on us from all side. This was intended of course to keep us from sleep and so wear down our resistance and morale. Despite this, I managed an hour's sleep as I did every night. It was imperative that I get some sleep or I would not be able to conduct the battle. It was amazing how refreshing an hour's sleep was. Some of the men got a few winks of sleep now and again but, by and large, it was impossible to sleep with the din, and those in the perimeter trenches had to remain constantly on the alert.

Not easy, then, given their lack of sleep, their increasing thirst and hunger, to keep their eyes fixed on the dark, moving corners of the African night, blacker and more unknowable the more they looked into it.

They were learning, too quickly, the reality of how shrapnel and shell tore flesh from the body. They also now knew that if they did not get out of the trenches soon—if the enemy bombardment continued to hinder movement—they would be seriously at risk of infection and gangrene.

But they knew, above all, how a direct mortar hit could end everything. For one soldier, as the third day of battle approached, that dread became a near-fatal reality. Quinlan recalled:

> During the night, groups of enemy penetrated to within 20 yards or less of our perimeter in Red House area. The field of fire was very poor, with small gardens and scrub. This was our most dangerous sector and was where Pte John Manning was shot through the shoulder from very close range by a group that got into a shed in front of his trench. Company Sgt Prendergast came to the rescue when, under cover of fire of two other men, he destroyed the enemy group in the shed with hand grenades.

Hegarty's account of events after Manning's wounding leaves less to the imagination:

> [Prendergast] asked Manning where the sniper's shot had come from…
>
> 'There, I think,' says Manning, pointing to a native house.
>
> 'Stand back,' Coy. Sgt ordered, goes up and throws 36 mills grenade in the window then blasts the door in case yer man tried to come out. He has many notches on his Bren gun.

Manning was evacuated to the First Aid Post.

Quinlan recalled that another soldier marked the night with an act of extraordinary courage:

> Pte Noel Stanley showed very great bravery in going alone to patrol a dangerous route where enemy could infiltrate between our trenches.
>
> It was on this night too that the supper which was our only meal each day got its name. When Corporal Bobby Allan, our cook corporal, arrived at one trench with the food, a soldier asked, 'What's on the menu, Corporal?'
>
> 'Stew, boy, stew,' Allan replied.

'Oh, yeah?' the soldier responded. 'Jadotville Stew, is it, Corporal?'

And so it was named. The stew consisted of bits and scraps of everything that was edible. There was not enough tinned meat left to go around and as the biscuits were very hard and tasteless by themselves, the cooks minced some with the tinned meat. While it was not very appetising, it was palatable.

Some of the men were feeling sick and had no mind for food but there was always an NCO or some comrade to see to it that these men ate whether they liked it or not. The continued perspiration under the broiling sun was dehydrating to the body and some sustenance had to be taken or collapse would occur very quickly. Salt tablets which the Medical Officer had were also distributed.

Allan says of the stew, that he, 'even ate it myself. Hunger is great sauce. The stew in Jadotville was easy done. The dog biscuits, corned beef from cans, and beans—anything I could get hold of bar toenails!'

The resourceful and intrepid Quartermaster staff were led by the Company Administration Officer, Captain Tom McGuinn, Quartermaster Sergeant Paddy Neville and the much-regarded and fearless Allan. Quinlan recalled:

The Cookhouse was in an open shed, and was located on our exposed left flank and it was absolutely impossible to work there by day. We considered moving it to No. 1 Platoon location but as Company Quartermaster Sergeant Neville said, it wasn't worthwhile moving it for the amount of food we had left to cook.

The cook staff fought in their trenches all day long and at last light set to immediately to prepare food and distribute it to every trench. As soon as that was over, it was time to prepare the morning cup of tea and a biscuit which was again distributed. All had to be finished, including cleaning of utensils, before 0500 hrs, at which time all of the men had to be at their posts. On the rounds with the food, McGuinn and Neville replenished ammunition.

Tension continued through that night, A Company constantly on the alert to the screams and sudden silences that heralded more firing.

When the 'White Adviser' rang three times that night on Mme Lamonfagne's phone, Fröberg, according to Quinlan, 'took him on at his own game':

When this 'Adviser' wanted an immediate decision, Fröberg informed that he would have to wait until morning as the commander (myself) was in bed and could not be disturbed. I was far from in bed at that time.

To the threat of being eaten by the mob, Fröberg replied, 'Why? I can't understand that. Are your people hungry or what?'

'Remember you are not in Europe now,' the 'Adviser' said. 'This is Africa and things are different here. This is not a civilised country.'

'I thought you always claimed that the Belgians had civilised the Congo?' Fröberg replied.

'By the way,' Fröberg then asked the 'Adviser', 'you are Belgian, I take it?'

'Yes, of course I am Belgian.'

'Then tell me,' said Fröberg, 'have you turned cannibal too?'

Fröberg turned to me after this conversation and, despite the heavy and continuous machine-gun fire, could not contain himself with laughter. He was a fine character and typical of the Swedes I met in the Congo. He refused to be browbeaten and he was both humane and courageous.

This was all very amusing but it had a sinister side too as we realised only too well that our fate depended entirely on strong reinforcements getting through to us.

As to being eaten, I don't think it worried any of us unduly what happened to us after we were killed. In any case, the propaganda did not get down to the men. Three or four men who were in positions at the windows of that villa knew of it all right and they seemed to enjoy the joke.

My estimate of the situation on this night was that we could possibly hold out until Saturday morning unless a fully coordinated attack on a large scale was made. I was apprehensive of a strong build-up very close to our position during the night with a mass attack at or before first light.

This would result in terrible slaughter (of the enemy) but there was a grave danger too that we would be overrun by force of numbers.

I did not then contemplate a break-out towards the bridge at Lufira as I considered that my main task now was to pin down as large a force as possible in Jadotville and hold a bridgehead for the promised new reinforcements which I felt would cross the Lufira Bridge in the morning.

There would be no reinforcements in the morning, nor at any time on Friday.

CHAPTER 14

We are not permitted to choose the frame of our destiny. But what we put into it is ours.

Dag Hammarskjöld, Diaries

Leopoldville. Friday, 15 September 1961

In Leopoldville, with nothing resolved, the UN Secretary General decided to prolong his stay in the Congo.

In Elisabethville, the Katangan Fouga jet strafed and bombed UN troops, and attacked Dr Conor Cruise O'Brien's HQ in that town and the airfield at Kamina.

It returned continuously to bomb and strafe A Company's position in Jadotville.

Dag Hammarskjöld sent urgent requests to Ethiopia, Sweden and India for a small number of fighter aircraft to aid the UN cause. Ethiopia immediately agreed to supply such aircraft.

The aircraft failed to materialise, however, when Britain prevaricated and would not give the clearance needed to allow the aircraft to overfly Kenya and refuel in Uganda.

Hammarskjöld ordered the UN Military Commander-in-Chief, General Sean McKeown, to go to Elisabethville and report on the situation there.

A breakthrough seemed imminent when Conor Cruise O'Brien, through intermediaries, arranged to meet Moise Tshombe at the British Consulate in Elisabethville in the late afternoon. He was fully intent on discussing an immediate and unconditional 48-hour ceasefire.

Mr Tshombe failed to turn up.

During a dinner in his honour that evening, the Secretary General was told about a Radio Katanga broadcast claiming that 57 members of A Company in Jadotville had been killed and 90 taken prisoner.

With a ceasefire more than ever an absolute necessity, Hammarskjöld drafted a letter to Tshombe, setting out the UN position and proposing a meeting between them, somewhere outside the Congo if necessary.

CHAPTER 15

*Men should be properly equipped to do their duty—otherwise it is
the improper use of valuable lives.*

Lieut Joe Leech, September 1961

DAY THREE
Friday, 15 September 1961

The third day of the Battle of Jadotville began too early, neither
sleep nor quiet dividing it from the exhausting day which had gone
before.

Most of the 156 men defending their lives because of what the
UN's Military Adviser to the Secretary General, Indar Jit Rikhye,
called 'a delicate mission and a weak mandate' had by now passed into
that state of exhaustion which makes sleep impossible.

With a young man's diffidence, Noel Carey tells how it was:
'Lack of sleep was a great strain on the men and made it very
difficult indeed to concentrate during the heat of the day.'

In the dark just before light, Paddy Neville ingeniously built
a shelter in a narrow passage. The wounded Hegarty watched
as he 'stood bed springs on end diagonally across the length of
the passage and then packed the top with mattresses. Ostensibly
this was for the wounded but the company "O" group [the HQ
group which assisted the CO] used it too.' In the pre-dawn, all
was silent, briefly, Hegarty says, with 'a light meal distributed' in
the minutes before it became light.

Earlier, at 0040 hours, Williams had tried several times to get
messages from Quinlan through to Elisabethville. Interference had
been strong and his attempts unreadable at Battalion HQ.

He went on trying.

0622 HRS. JADOTVILLE: POSITION DESPERATE SEND REINFORCEMENTS IMMEDIATELY.

0710 HRS. JADOTVILLE: IN AINM DÉ [In the name of God] SEND REINFORCEMENTS NOW. PROMISES OF SUCH ARE NOT SUFFICIENT.

0750 HRS. JADOTVILLE: HEAVY AIR BOMBARDMENT.

The Fouga returned, dropping two bombs and making strafing runs. A Company fired on all fronts and from all platoon locations. Liam Donnelly's Support Platoon used mortar and mounted machine guns.

'We laid a trap for him on the second day,' Bobby Allan recalls. 'We gave him everything we had. He spun and we saw smoke....'

'It came out of the sun,' Hegarty says.

...and dropped two bombs. The house shook, armoured cars got into position fast and when the pilot came in on a strafing run, their mounted machine guns gave him hell. After that, he gave us a wide berth, stayed high. Too busy elsewhere, probably.

Busy, but impaired now and wary too. The jet returned to Kolwezi airport with bullet holes. From then on, it would fire on the company positions from a higher altitude and be less accurate. It busied itself elsewhere by dropping bombs on Elisabethville airport later in the day.

Carey recalls:

Dawn on the third day brought sudden and colourful streaks in the sky, flicking towards us. I all at once realised they were tracer bullets. They clattered off the walls of the outhouse behind us and off the villa walls. We stared, fascinated, at this colourful display until the thud of bullets [was] felt on the front of our trench. Lieut Kevin Knightly and one of his armoured cars darted out from the side of a villa near us and sprayed a full belt of 250 rounds towards the Katangan fire. We all in turn commenced firing.

After some time the attacking forces discontinued their firing.

Enemy groups who tried to organise into assault positions were 'deterred' by very heavy and accurate long-range light artillery fire.

At 0800 hours, Quinlan finally made voice contact with Elisabethville and spoke with McNamee.

The Battalion OC assured him that further reinforcements were being organised—'a real heavy force,' he said, but was unable to give a time for its arrival in Jadotville. The air drop of supplies was also discussed. Quinlan emphasised his company's water requirements. He recalled:

> The proposed force was to have Indian heavy mortars. We calculated the ranges to three important targets which were well outside the range of my weapons and I proposed to get the reinforcements to fire one or two shells at one of them and telephone the 'Adviser' and let him swallow some of his own medicine by asking for his decision. I was quite certain that the reinforcements would get through before Saturday. I did not like to contemplate what would happen if help did not arrive by Saturday morning as it appeared to be beyond our physical endurance to hold out any longer.
>
> My greatest worry at this stage was the shortage of water. Because of the perspiration, combined with the heat and excitement, the lack of food and lack of sleep, the body craved water until it almost became an obsession.
>
> The water which we had left was very stale and tasted badly because of the purification tablets. [By Saturday, it would be almost putrid and by Sunday would make the men sick.] There was a grave danger of disease due to burst sewers from bombing and shelling. There was a vile smell and flies were swarming everywhere.

A half pail of water was later 'sucked' from a tap for the wounded. This was tried, without success, at other water points.

Radio communications with Battalion HQ were ever more difficult and intermittent on the C12 sets—'fighting conditions' had degraded batteries and there were HF transmission difficulties. The indefatigable Williams kept going, as Quinlan remembered:

> I saw Cpl Williams sending messages when the hut he was in was being raked with machine-gun fire from the Fouga. Though his two operators were very competent, he insisted on manning the set continuously himself. With his wireless, he was our only link with the outside world and, despite the tension and the fire, as well as the exasperation of wireless blackouts and hostile jamming, he recorded meticulously all incoming and outgoing messages.

At 1030 hours, a message got through to Elisabethville, advising that an aircraft had appeared over A Company's position. The reply, as far as Quinlan was concerned, gave a very real indication of Battalion HQ's understanding of the situation in which A Company found itself.

1030 HRS. ELISABETHVILLE: ARE THEY ENEMY?

1030 HRS. JADOTVILLE: SUSPECTED TO BE ENEMY.

1035 HRS. ELISABETHVILLE: YOU MAY CLOSE DOWN AND SWITCH OFF, TRY AND GET SOME REST FOR YOURSELF.

Rest not being an option, the men of A Company carried on defending their lives and position.

The anti-tank weapon in No. 1 Platoon position was now used 'once again and very effectively', according to Donnelly, this time against a villa containing snipers. It was also used in No. 3 Platoon position against Gendarmerie who tried to infiltrate from an ant hill.

The dust, heat, noise and stench got worse as the sun rose higher.

So did thirst, exhaustion, the need for reinforcements and the sense, impossible to accept but forever growing, that they had been abandoned. They carried on fighting.

Quinlan and his signal corps went back on air.

1050 HRS. JADOTVILLE: 30 FCA MARCHING OUT FROM LOCAL TOWN.

1051 HRS. JADOTVILLE: FIGHTING IN PROGRESS.

The strong Katangan group moved on A Company through the area of the bus station and the scrubby, grassy spaces leading to No. 2 Platoon position. The Katangans did not get far. Taken on by the Support Platoon, armoured cars and No. 1 Platoon, they were driven back.

And all the while, infuriatingly out of their weapons' range, A Company could see Gendarmerie troops moving towards Lufira Bridge.

A radio message, just before midday, gave word of ceasefire talks with President Tshombe and wished A Company good luck. The men took heart.

Hegarty, confined with his wounds to the medical centre at the HQ building, was an uneasy patient after the Fouga's early-morning attack:

> As the day wore on, I was suffering in that house, expecting the 'B' in the jet to come back. After midday the Gends opened up with mortars and we put the run on them again. I tried out my legs but was weak and the meds tied me up again.

Carey, recalling that day, echoed Hegarty's sense of a day wearing on:

> As the day wore on, the mortar fire was concentrated on our positions. The fire was intense, initially going over our heads but then falling just short of our trench. As a Mortar Officer, I knew that with proper bracketing the next salvo would certainly fall on our trench so I ordered four members of my platoon to withdraw to the rear while I stayed in the trench.
>
> Those were some of the worst moments I experienced during the whole action, all alone with mortar shells

falling around me. I thought of my loved ones at home—
but don't recall being over religious even though I was
facing a critical situation....

Carey states, wryly, 'the fact that I had actually volunteered for this
mission was also uppermost in my mind...', before continuing:

> With the mortar bombs exploding ever nearer I put a
> sandbag on my plastic helmet in the hope that I might be
> able to protect my head from splinters.

At 1430, Hegarty's worst fears, and everyone else's too, were realised
when the Fouga returned to bomb and strafe the company's
positions again. But this time, made wary by the damage caused
by the morning's fusillade of fire, it stayed higher and was far less
accurate.

Gendarmerie fire on the ground intensified each time the
jet appeared, but then so too did fire from A Company. The air, as
described by Allan, 'was grey with lead'.

After the Fouga's departure, the afternoon, according to Quinlan,

> ...was comparatively quiet. The enemy made four or five
> separate attack attempts, each time firing on us from all
> sides while, at the same time, a group of about 60 came
> forward. These groups came from an assembly area out
> of A Company's 60mm mortar range; they were on high
> ground too so we couldn't bring machine-gun fire to bear
> on them.

Clever as this tactic was on the part of the Katangans, it was as
nothing against the ruthless determination of A Company.

> Once the Gendarmerie groups came within range, we broke
> up every attack with devastating fire from our armoured
> cars, mounted machine guns and mortars. These groups may
> have been the first wave of an attack or they may have been
> uncoordinated efforts.

Quinlan, like the rest of A Company, was lavish in his praise of the Bren gun's value to the company:

> It was an excellent weapon, its fire devastating at a range of up to 1000 yards. The accuracy too of our 60mm mortar crews and the handling of these weapons was of an extraordinarily high standard. The credit for our safety, were it to be attributed to human endeavours, must be given to a very large extent to our mortar crews.

Carey, recalling that third afternoon, says,

> ... at one point, I saw what appeared to be a wounded Katangan soldier sitting in the open some 500 yards from us and told the Bren gunner in the adjacent trench to discontinue firing as he appeared to be wounded. Many Katangans must have been injured in the area of Numbers 2 and 3 Platoons during the initial attack, when caught in the open and again in No. 1 Platoon and Support Platoon area.

At 1455 hours, Quinlan made voice contact by radio with John Kane, soon to be in charge of a second reinforcement patrol.

COMDT KANE: 'CAN YOU BREAK OUT?' [of Jadotville]

COMDT QUINLAN: 'NO. WE HAVE NO TRANSPORT.'

COMDT KANE: 'CAN YOU BREAK OUT ON FOOT? WE WILL MEET YOU AT THE BRIDGE.'

COMDT QUINLAN: 'BRIDGE ABOUT 20 MILES, FIR TRAOCHTA [men exhausted]. WE DO NOT KNOW THE KATANGAN FORCE BETWEEN HERE AND BRIDGE, UNABLE TO TAKE ALL AMMO AND SUPPLIES, THIS WOULD BE SUICIDE. ONLY HOPE REMAIN HERE, YOU REACH US.

The two men then discussed getting strong reinforcements to the bridge by first light on Saturday.

COMDT QUINLAN: THIS FORCE MUST GET THROUGH.

Quinlan knew well the inadequacy of their transport. He was just as certain that his dehydrated, exhausted men would not be able to make the 18–20 miles to Lufira on foot and under a blazing sun. Fire would be opened on them from all sides once they moved from cover of their defensive positions.

A breakout would have resulted in the slaughter of most, if not all, of the men of A Company.

Messages received from Elisabethville by Williams throughout the afternoon advised that the ceasefire conference 'was continuing', asked for a casualty report and assured that the 'air drop' was being prepared. Quinlan replied:

> 1555 HRS. JADOTVILLE: BETTER AWAIT OUTCOME OF CONFERENCE ROIMH TUIRLINGT AER [before air landing] CÚIGEAR GORTAITHE [five wounded] SGT HEGARTY, PTE READY, PTE MANNING, PTE GORMLEY, PTE TAHENY. DÉIN SOCRÚ IAD A THÓGAINT AMACH [make arrangements to have them evacuated].

Within the hour, the nature of the air drop was revealed, and was a shock.

CHAPTER 16

GRIM NEWS FROM KATANGA. Irish at Jadotville said to have surrendered. Katanga Radio claims 57 killed.
Evening Herald, Dublin, Friday, 15 September 1961

Dublin and Athlone. Friday, 15 September 1961

The distortions and inaccuracy of reports carried in Irish newspapers and on radio about events in Jadotville were a measure of the devastating success of Katangan propaganda.

Reports in Dublin newspapers variously claimed that: 'The chief of 1,000 fierce Bayeke warriors has declared war without quarter on the Irish troops at Jadotville' and that: 'Twenty of the encircled Irish company at Jadotville are said to have been captured and executed.' It was variously reported too that 'five of the men in Jadotville' had been killed, and, the story most strongly going the rounds, that 57 members of the company had been killed.

The Irish Times reported heavy losses in Jadotville and said the UN was unable to confirm reports that the garrison had surrendered. It went on to tell how Dr Conor Cruise O'Brien had told journalists in Elisabethville that A Company had 'suffered heavy losses in desperate fighting against greatly superior Katangan forces.'

The country was deeply shocked. Church bells tolled and Masses were said across the land. Newspapers were devoured in the street and discussed in pubs and on buses. The non-paper-buying public huddled together reading poster headlines. People spoke of little else for days.

All of this gave rise to the second biggest story of the day, the one telling of 'the great wave of sympathy across the nation'. With people speaking of little else, this was a great deal more accurate than the stories coming out of Africa. By the time the army issued a statement discounting agency/Katangan radio reports, everyone was ready to believe the worst.

Through it all, the families and loved ones of the men in Jadotville prayed and agonised and tried *not* to believe the worst.

According to the wife of Lieutenant Joe Leech, Mrs Lola Leech, who was 26 years old at the time, the news reports brought 'sheer terror' to the families of A Company in Athlone:

> They were absolutely devastated, really in an awful state. All the information they had was this terrible stuff coming over the radio and in the papers all the time. The insensitivity of the army authorities was inexcusable.
>
> They should have contacted the next of kin and assured them—us—that all relevant information would be passed on. But they didn't. All they said was that they had no information—they should have made contact and said 'we're here and aware of you' but it was as if we had nothing to do with any of it.
>
> In the absence of any contact with army authorities, some members of the families descended on Custume Barracks main gate, looking for information.

But the gates remained closed and information stayed behind them. Lola Leech continues:

> Carmel Quinlan [Comdt Quinlan's wife] and I were lucky to have friends who could interpret the propaganda for us. When we heard that some of the families thought we'd had information passed on to us by the army HQ, I went and called on them. We were all in the same boat and shared our fears, just sitting and talking. I told them too that if Carmel and I heard anything, we would make contact immediately.
>
> Of course communications in 1961 were unreliable, and this type of situation was new to Army HQ—who themselves were victims of a clever propaganda operation on the part of Belgium and Katanga.

But after five days' battle, peace terms were negotiated and A Company were prisoners for a further five weeks. During this time, apart from media reports and visits from army comrades, and friends, and some reports from sources in the Congo, our first real contact was letters taken out by the Red Cross.

The first official communication from army authorities I received was a notification of the handover of prisoners, which we already knew about. The sheer insensitivity of the army authorities was inexcusable.

The families of A Company went through more than their share of suffering, which did not end entirely with the return of their men folk but has been with us all for these 45 years. A certain distress continued because of the slur on their courage through all those years.

Radio Free Katanga continued to add to the distress and confusion of the time. Monitored in Rhodesia on Friday, 15 September, its broadcasts told of threats to shoot Irish Jadotville troops held as hostages if Katangan prisoners were executed.

'We want the people who have 11 Irish prisoners who surrendered yesterday (Thursday) to keep them as hostages,' its broadcast said, 'because if the UN detain Katangan prisoners we want them to know that for every prisoner shot we will shoot ten of their mercenaries [*sic*].'

There were no Irish prisoners.

Taoiseach Seán Lemass issued a statement outlining the government's policy on the Congo. He also announced that he was sending External Affairs Minister Frank Aiken to the Congo for discussions with UN officials there, so as to get 'reliable information'.

In the confusion, all people felt able to do was pray, which they did in their thousands, in churches everywhere. Children prayed too, in schools everywhere, for 'the soldiers in Jadotville'.

CHAPTER 17

Truth is rarely pure, and never simple.

Oscar Wilde

Sector B. Swedish Brigade. Katanga. Friday, 15 September 1961

On Friday, too, Colonel Jonas Waern, OC Sector B and the Swedish Brigade as well as acting UN Intelligence Officer, sent the following message to Brigadier Raja, Senior UN Military Officer in Katanga, requesting permission to carry out a mission in connection with relief of A Company.

REQUEST PERMISSION TO CARRY OUT THE FOLLOWING OPERATION IN CONNECTION WITH RELIEF OF IRISH COY AT JADOTVILLE. TASK [tasks]. ALPHA [a] SENDING OF HELICOPTERS AND/OR AC C47. BRAVO [b] DESTROY ENEMY COY AT BRIDGE BY FLANKING MOVE CMA [comma] REMOVE BARRIER FROM BRIDGE. CHARLIE.[c] ADVANCE TO JADOTVILLE AND ASSIST BREAK-OUT OF JADOT COY. DELTA. [d] TROOPS REQUIRED CMA ONE IRISH COY NOW IN FARM [in Elisabethville] CMA SP [support] ARMS IRISH NOW IN FARM CMA ONE GURKHA COY TO BE DECIDED [one Gurkha Company was needed but which one was not specified]. FOUR IRISH ARMD CAR [armoured cars]. ENGINEER PERSONNEL AND EQUIPMENT. ALMOST ALL TRUCKS IN SECTOR B.
    SHORT APPRECIATION AS FOLLOWS. GENDARMERIE ARE CAPABLE OF PITTING

MORE TROOPS AGAINST COY IN JADOTVILLE THAN AGAINST ALL THE FORCES IN EVILLE. RESUPPLY OF COY BY MEANS AVAILABLE IS NOT GUARANTEED. IF THEY ARE NOT RESUPPLIED OR RELIEVED THEY MAY BE WIPED OUT. THIS RISK MUST BE CONSIDERED AGAINST POSSIBLE LOSSES IN EVILLE WITH REDUCED STRENGTH. POSSIBLE REINFORCEMENTS TO EVILLE COULD OFFSET DEPLETION IN STRENGTH. <u>SUCCESS OF THIS OPERATION WOULD BE A GREAT BOOST TO UN OPS. FAILURE TO RETRIEVE THIS COY WOULD BE A CRIPPLING BLOW TO UN</u>. REINFORCEMENTS MORE AMMN [ammunition] SUPPLIES [food] TPT ARMD CS [transport and armoured cars] FROM OUTSIDE SECTOR B ARE A MUST IF WE ARE TO SUCCEED.

The document was signed by Col. Waern and a second officer, S. Rosen.

The underlined areas of emphasis are Waern's.

CHAPTER 18

It was only because I was an Irishman that I could understand fully, I
think, the whole scheme of wrongdoing at work in the Congo.

Roger Casement, 1906

Jadotville. Friday, 15 September 1961

The first indication that a helicopter would be used to airdrop supplies
came in a late afternoon radio message.

> 1617 HRS. ELISABETHVILLE: KEEP EYES OPEN FOR HELICOPTER
> ARRIVING FROM ELISABETHVILLE. GIVE PROTECTION WITH FIRE,
> SMOKE ETC. FOR LANDING.

Quinlan was not well pleased. Their position was totally unsuitable for
a landing and he conveyed this.

> 1635 HRS. JADOTVILLE: HELICOPTER CANNOT LAND HERE.

The Fouga arrived overhead at 1710 hours. While Jose Denlin was
dropping his bombs and making a couple of strafing runs, another
message arrived.

> 1710 HRS. ELISABETHVILLE: O'BRIEN, BRITISH CONSUL AND
> MR. KIBWE HAVE HAD DISCUSSIONS. MAIN ITEM JADO. KIBWE IS
> TO TRY CALLING OFF JADO AGGRESSION. HAS GONE TO TSHOMBE
> 1530 HRS. SHEASAMAR AN FÓD OBAIR SHÁR MHAITH. BEIDH
> BRÓD IRLANDE AS COMPANY A. HOLD YOUR GROUND. [Superb
> work. Ireland will be proud of A Company.]

> 1710 HRS. JADOTVILLE: WE ARE BEING BOMBED. HE IS HERE NOW.

Then it was dark again, and the company was battling the heaviest night firing so far. This, Quinlan said, 'was more than adequately replied to by all company weapons and armoured cars.'

Attacks on all fronts were stepped up; the psychological warfare waged by the Red Cross 'Adviser' on the Burgermeister's phone from Jadotville took on an urgent malignancy. Quinlan, on Mme Lamonfagne's phone,

> …got word that the 'Adviser' had an urgent message for me to do with ceasefire talks. When I arrived in the villa, it was to find it had been badly damaged by two mortar shells which had exploded on the pathway and yard just beside it. The glass in all the windows had been blown in. We put a telephone call through and while I was waiting for the connection, I heard a shell screaming in and knew it would land close.
>
> I shouted to everyone to get down. Madame Lamonfagne did not understand English and stood frozen in front of a broken window. As I pulled her to the floor beside the wall, a heavy shell (4.2' I think) exploded just outside the window, about two feet away, where it made a crater. Another shell came screaming in and exploded close to the other wall of the room. Mme Lamanfagne got her legs pretty badly cut on broken glass, which was lying around after an earlier bombardment had broken all the windows. She never complained.
>
> These last shells made a shambles of her home; doors were shattered as was furniture, a part of the ceiling and plaster off the walls. A chandelier was smashed and the room was choked with the smell of explosives and with smoke, dust and debris.
>
> That lady risked her life, first of all, in staying, which meant she was subjected to the enemy fire directed at us. As well as that, she ran a grave risk of being shot if our position was overrun and she was captured. She was a very courageous lady. She well knew the penalty for aiding the UN.
>
> She also risked, and, I dare say, suffered, the scorn, of her own people. Her actions were motivated by the highest ideals

of humanitarianism and as she will probably never get any reward in this life except the undying gratitude of a group of Irish soldiers, I have no doubt that she will get her reward hereafter.

The telephone call was probably a ruse to catch me with the mortar fire.

When the 'Adviser' asked that an ambulance be allowed approach their position to pick up Katangan dead and wounded, Quinlan refused. The Katangans were known to mount machine guns inside ambulances, opening fire once they had infiltrated. He was not going to have his men blown to pieces from an ambulance.

His caution, it later transpired, was well founded. The proposed ambulance had contained mercenaries with mounted machine guns.

The simultaneous psychological warfare being waged *outside* Mme Lamanfagne's shattered walls was less subtle. Hegarty, who by now had earned himself the moniker 'lead-ass', saw it all:

The Gends were roaring at us 'Kill! Kill! Kill! Choppy-chop (we will eat ye)'. Our lads replied with everything they'd got and when they stopped, there were howls of agony and pain on the Gends' lines. For the remainder of the night, there was wholesale firing on both sides. They tried to infiltrate that night. In fact, Pte Michael Tighe's trench reported a guy screaming in pain about 30–40 yards away; though, come morning, there was nothing there.

Firing which came from the bush in front of Joe Leech's platoon position was dealt with by small arms fire. But the Verey lights (one worked out of the entire platoon allotment) failed to function and, Leech drily reported, 'once more did not endear themselves to us'.

Leech reported, too, that, as it had during the day, light machine-gun fire came at them from the 'native village. This was searched by our light automatic and small gun fire and quietened considerably.'

Carey, 'as dusk was approaching' finally left his trench and made his way to his platoon sergeant, Kevin McLaughlin and radio man Private Donal Manley who were behind him.

> I reorganised my platoon and rotated the personnel giving the front trench men a well deserved rest. That night, I visited Pte John Manning and a few others who were in a villa used as a medical centre and being cared for by Doctor Comdt Joe Clune.

All the men of A Company were by now very critically dehydrated. Sewage pipes were damaged, rats were gathering and there were insects everywhere. Food was all but gone and hunger gnawed viciously. The heat had cracked open dried skin and parasites were breeding underneath. Inside and outside the trenches, the fetid, humid air carried disease.

Hegarty listed a harsh litany:

> By Friday evening, in spite of high morale, a tired company had much to contend with within their lines with water running out, biscuits and tea as their sole grub, and the rising certainty that the UN could not help us. As well, the danger of disease was imminent, as the flies were rampant (the C/O's word …) The batteries of the C.12s [radios] were running low and communications were bad. The disease represented our great internal danger; our latrines and refuse dumps were swarming and stinking, and worse still we're under fire….

As another night settled dark, chattering and noisy around them, all hope of survival was vested in the hope that reinforcements would arrive in the morning and, with them, food, water and ammunition.

Acutely aware of this possibility, convoys of Gendarmerie were seen moving in the direction of the Lufira Bridge. While his troops fired on them, Quinlan sent a forceful priority message, in Irish, about the plight of his men.

2014 HRS. JADOTVILLE: EOLAS ANOIS NÍL ACH 50 NAMHAD AG AN DROICHEAD. DREAM BEAG EILE AG CROSBÓTHAR LEATH SLÍ ANSEO.

TÁ SIAD AR BUILE ANSEO TOISC TUBAISTÍ TROMA, NÍ STOPFAIDH SIAD SCAOILEADH. TÁIM AG BRATH ORT ANOIS AN DROICEAD A THÓGAINT AG CÉAD SOLAIS. BEIDH TÚ ANSEO IN UAR A CHLOIG TAR ÉIS SIN. DEIN É IN AINM DÉ. TÓG UISCE AGUS LÓN LEAT. FREAGRA GAN MHOILL. SUÍOMH I GCOMHAIR HELI ULLAMH, BRAT BÁN AIR. DEATACH RÉIDH, ABAIR NUAIR ATÁ SÉ AG TEACHT. [Information now is that there are only 50 of the enemy at the bridge. Another small group at a crossroads halfway here. They are furious owing to serious casualties, they won't stop firing. I'm depending on you now to take the bridge AT FIRST LIGHT. You'll be here in an hour after that. Do it in the name of God. Take water and supplies with you. Answer without delay. Location for heli ready, white cover on it. Smoke ready, say when it is coming.]

Despite having asked for an immediate answer, he got none at all. He radioed again, and again.

2023 HRS. JADOTVILLE: SEND WATER URGENTLY.

2030 HRS. JADOTVILLE: ANY REPLY TO MY 151940?

2031 HRS. JADOTVILLE: WE ARE CLOSING DOWN BECAUSE OF BATTERY SITUATION. WE WILL MAKE CONTACT EVERY HOUR.

2219 HRS. JADOTVILLE: CAN YOU GIVE ME ANY INFO. ON GENERAL SITUATION?

2359 HRS. JADOTVILLE: PRIORITY MESSAGE AGAIN.

It would be hours before he got a reply.

In the meantime, he called a meeting of his officers to tell them that a second relief column would set out the following morning. The officers reported spirits high in the company and left to give news of the reinforcements to their platoons.

In the dark, they could see more vehicle lights crossing the valley, heading for Lufira Bridge to reinforce the Gendarmerie already there. A Company's armoured cars fired on them again, but they were too far away.

Hegarty wrote:

Friday night saw more threats and requests to give in. Through the night, I stayed near a window and by first light I got my cuppa and biscuits, and watched. Much blasting through the long night.

For Carey, Friday night brought sleep, short and of a kind:

It was the first night in three days that I slept, and it was the sleep of the damned. I was completely exhausted, mentally and physically, and slept in the trench with my platoon sergeant and radio man protecting me. However, it was hard to dispel the fear I had felt all alone in the forward trench, with mortar shells falling all round, and at the same time ensuring my men were not aware of this fear, as I had responsibility towards them and for ensuring that morale remained high.

He was 24 years old.

And so, every man giving his all, they fought through another long night, fearless and hopeful, ignoring telephone calls to surrender or die, all too aware of the difficulties facing the patrol making for and hoping to cross the Lufira Bridge the following day.

CHAPTER 19

We were so few against so many that they thought all they had to do was come and take us....

Comdt P. Quinlan, September 1961

DAY FOUR
Jadotville. Saturday, 16 September 1961

The next word about reinforcements came, in Irish, as Friday became Saturday and the fourth day of battle at 0033 hours. It was brief, and it was encouraging.

'Ag tósnú ón áit seo [Setting out from here],' it said.

Quinlan sent messages to Elisabethville at 0205 hours, and again at 0320 hours. Neither was replied to.

At 0645 hours, he got a message from General Sean McKeown, overall UN Force Commander in the Congo. McKeown was based in Leopoldville; the message was relayed via Battalion HQ in Elisabethville and it read:

> We all here admire you and commend you and your men on your gallant stand. The whole UNO force and our own people and in fact the world are watching the outcome of your brave efforts. Inform all men of your command go bhfuil cabhair ag teacht go luath [help arriving soon], and that you have already earned yourselves the name of heroes.

Elisabethville HQ added its own, separate, assurances: '*Cabhair láidir imighte as seo 0630 hrs* [Strong reinforcements left here at 0630 hours].'

Quinlan replied to McKeown unequivocally, and immediately.

0645HRS. JADOTVILLE: MANY THANKS TO FORCE COMMANDER FOR MESSAGE. SEASAMIAD GO DTÍ AN FEAR DEIREANNACH ACH CUR AN CABHAIR ANOIS AGUS GO LÁIDIR. CUIR UISCE. [We will fight/stand to the last man but send help/reinforcements now, and strong. Send water.]

The reinforcements on the way consisted of two companies, one of Irish and one of Indian (Gurkha) troops, along with sections of Swedish and Irish armoured patrol cars.

At 0900 hours, Quinlan got through to Battalion HQ and had a conversation with Commandant J.J. Barrett there. He was given 1100 hours as an estimated time for the arrival of the reinforcements at Lufira and was told that the helicopter would be in Jadotville 'soon'.

The helicopter arrived at 0928 hours.

CHAPTER 20

Katanga's one Fouga jet trainer, modified as a fighter, gave it complete air superiority....

Indar Jit Rikhye,
Military Adviser to the UN Secretary General

Elisabethville. Saturday, 16 September 1961

The second, much larger Force Kane included Indian Gurkha troops and transport which, this time round, was augmented by 16 locally acquired single-decker buses. These were reinforced and protected by knocking out the windows and piling ration packs against the sides.

Setting out from Elisabethville, the force planned to arrive at Lufira Bridge at 0530 hours, or at first light.

But by 0745, the troops had got only as far as Jadotville Junction, 6 km outside Elisabethville.

Michael Shannon explains how things went:

We had 81mm medium mortars plus Vicker machine guns and from the time we left Elisabethville to go to Lufira Bridge, we were visited every hour-and-a-half by the Fouga jet; the time related to how long it took him to get back to Kolwezi and reload. So, when it was coming up to the one-and-a-half-hour time, we'd disperse and go into the jungle, then regroup when he'd gone. Our only defence was to fire light machine guns.

The jet dropped bombs and strafed each time it attacked. Sergeant J. Gallagher of the medical section was wounded in the legs by shrapnel.

The second Force Kane finally arrived to assemble south of Lufira Bridge at 1000 hours.

CHAPTER 21

Our brave helicopter crew ... landed in an inferno with all hell let loose....

Comdt P. Quinlan, September 1961

Jadotville. Saturday, 16 September 1961

The helicopter was first spotted, Hegarty recalls, 'high in the sky—and a small, innocent, harmless thing it looked.'

It circled their position several times, staying high, then came in along the valley, UN white and markings very clear. In the sky above it, the Fouga jet, still cautious of A Company's fire, also circled, also staying high.

As he came in to land, the pilot of the helicopter, 39-year-old Norwegian Bjerne Hovden, heard ground instructions from the Gendarmerie at the Lufira Bridge telling the Fouga's pilot to shoot him down. Meanwhile, Gendarmerie everywhere on the ground opened frenzied fire on the UN helicopter, using all of their weapons, including .5 mounted machine guns.

This was not a wise move. Their barrage of fire revealed their positions to A Company who, immediately seizing the moment, took them on with devastatingly accurate fire.

The air, according to Lars Fröberg, 'literally glowed with bullets.' The helicopter continued slowly down through it all until Hovden and co-pilot Eric Thors, a 25-year-old Swede, quite suddenly found that they had more than flying bullets to contend with.

Because Elisabethville had omitted to tell the helicopter pilots that the Irish troops had had to pull back from the earlier designated landing area, they had been heading for the wrong spot. They would have continued, too, with fatal results, if they had not been diverted by the quick thinking and actions of a couple of members of A Company

Everyone remembers it well; accounts graphically describe the debacle of the helicopter's mission and the heroism of their comrades. According to Hegarty:

> Paddy Neville and Bobby Allan ran out, braving the leaded elements to lay down marker sheets. The Gends had gone frantic; every man of them must have been firing at that poor helicopter. We of course opened up with our Vickers and Brens against every known Gend position. The din was frightful and, strangely enough, oddly exciting. Over the slopes of the mines a .5 machine gun opened up on Neville and Allan—standing jump records were broken but the sheets were laid out.
>
> Allan was narrowly missed by .5 mounted machine-gun fire....

Allan's own retelling is modest:

> Paddy and myself went out and put down the markers. As we did, the lead began to fly. I felt it at my heels and by God it made me jump! We laid the sheets ... there was a wall and I ran for it; I could see bullets bouncing off it as I did. I caught a bar and somersaulted over that wall. A fellow from Mullinahone caught me and pulled me over and down and said 'you f...ing Cat, get down'—I'm a Kilkenny man, you see. He saved my life. I would have broken my back but for him. He said I ran faster than Roger Bannister ever did. I broke special track records covering that bit of ground!

Sean Foley describes the scene as, 'grey with the mortar and other fire all round while the jet was trying to land'.

> We couldn't even see the other fella, the enemy, to take aim at, just caught fleeting targets as a fella might flit between the termite mounds....

Wally Hegarty continues his account:

Having taken note of the new landing place, the helicopter went out over the town then came in very fast and dangerously low, spun like a top and landed dead on the spot where the sheets had been laid. This was only a matter of feet from Sgt Kevin McLoughlin's hideout. Himself and Pte James Myler (both short men) had in the course of the four days improved their trench with all mod cons, including a sunshade. Lieutenant Carey was visiting them when the 'copter came. Every bit of cover over that trench was lifted by the swirling air from the 'copter. Carey said 'get out' and fast they were, expecting mortars as well as machine guns to open up on the 'copter.

The mortars did indeed come, but later.

'By the grace of God,' according to Foley, 'the pilot landed safely.' With a groan, he continues his story:

Ah, but the jerry cans and our lovely water … and the 81mm 14lb mortar ammo sent us when we only had 60mm mortar guns that took 3lb weight. They were useful for doorstops.

Hegarty tells how things went on:

Bjerne Hovden and his co-pilot Eric Thors were volunteers who, on volunteering, were informed that it would be a suicide mission. Knowing this, they were very brave to come but to cap it all they were flying a drill purpose (i.e., useless) grounded helicopter. During the journey to Jadotville, the Red Panel light, the utmost sign of danger, came on twice.

So they risked their lives to bring us supplies which consisted of four jerry cans of contaminated water, 260 84 rounds plus a half sack of letters. The jerry cans held 22½ gallons of water which was undrinkable because it had been filled into new, uncleaned mineral jellied cans. So they could have stayed at home. They didn't know what was on board. However, the fact that a 'copter landed provided the UN with a valuable face saver.

Comdt Pat Quinlan (seated) observes and checks on the digging of defensive trenches at Jadotville.

embers of A Company,
the days before
ey were attacked in
dotville, take a break
om digging defensive
nches.

Comdt Patrick Quinlan, commanding officer of A Company, Congo, 1961.

Digging in at Jadotville before the attack, September 1961, l to r, Sgt Walter Hegarty, Lieut Noel Carey, Sgt Kevin McLaughlin and Lieut Tom Quinlan.

Tented area at Jadotville, 14 September 1961.

Identification tag from the tail of the Fuoga plane that bombed A Company in Jadotville. It was appropriated by Private Billy Ready in Elisabethville after being shot down there in December 1961. The date of manufacture, clearly shown as 4.10.60, belies the information given to A Company that the Fuoga was a much older plane.

After the battle Katangan Gendarmerie, refusing to believe there were not fatalities, search A Company trenches for the bodies of Irish soldiers. Capt Liam Donnelly is in the centre wearing a UN beret. Lieut Lars Fröberg, Swedish interpreter, is behind him.

Saturday, 16 September. Evening of ceasefire in Jadotville. Lieut Noel Carey, on extreme left, with members of A Company's Support Platoon.

Lieut Noel Carey and Lieut Joe Leech outside A Company HQ/
Purfina Garage after the end of the battle, September 1961.

Cpl Bobby Allan (left) Private
Charlie Tomkins (right) and
Quartermaster Sergeant
Paddy Neville in the cockpit
of the UN helicopter flown
to Jadotville by the valiant
Scandinavian crew.

Saturday evening, 16 September. Lieut Eric Thors, the red-bearded co-pilot of the UN helicopter that made a brave, but futile, trip to Jadotville, after he and Norwegian pilot Bjern Hovden were taken captive along with A Company. A Company members queue for food in the background.

Lieut Noel Carey and members of his No. 3 Platoon pose with the UN helicopter flown to their aid in Jadotville by a Scandinavian two-man crew. Carey is in the front row, wearing a beret.

Lieut Joe Leech in Jadotville after the end of battle.

Capt Liam Donnelly, centre, wearing a UN beret, and a group of A Company soldiers outside Company HQ/Purfina Garage after the fighting ended.

Capt Liam Donnelly in Jadotville after the end of the battle, September 1961.

Sunday, 17 September 1961. With fighting over, Cpl Sean Foley poses in the gun position of an armoured car. Sgt Kevin McLaughlin and Private Anthony Roper pose with him.

Carey, in that festooned trench, had a much closer view than he wanted of the helicopter:

> The noise grew louder and suddenly all our overhead cover was whipped from our trench. I looked up to see the rotor blades spinning literally above our heads. It was at this point that my radio man, Private Myler, asked, 'In real war, would it be anything like this?' and I answered, 'This is as real as you get it.'
>
> Realising that we were prime targets in the event of mortaring, I ordered Sgt McLoughlin and Pte Myler out of the trench and was able to help the two helicopter pilots from the aircraft to the safety of a trench nearer the villa.
>
> The co-pilot, Eric Thors, congratulated us on our stand. He said it was 'just like Dien Bien Phu (which happened during the French fighting in Indo China). The pilot was a very courageous Norwegian called Lt Bjerne Hovden who knew that the helicopter would not be able to return as it was showing the emergency light from Elisabethville but bravely flew himself and the co-pilot into our positions.

Thors and Hovden had flown the only helicopter available to the UN. Now, having thrown in their lot, they would fight alongside A Company for the rest of the battle—and share their imprisonment after it ended.

Carey, debating whether or not their 'almost suicidal effort was worth it', concluded that it was not:

> Apart from a large boost to our morale, initially, and a huge worry for the surrounding Katangans, the only supplies we received were a number of jerry cans of polluted water (the cans had not been cleaned out), a few boxes of ammo and a sack of post. Indeed, as firing went on from all directions near our new trench, one of the NCOs called out my name and handed me a letter which was a bill for three pounds from The Book Club. I felt like replying that I was otherwise engaged just now, but would write to them later.

Hegarty tells of the aftermath:

> After the excitement of the landing, the Gends went off for
> their siesta. So we thought, at any rate, but in fact they went
> to sack their white officers. If we'd only known then, could
> we have moved out and taken over the town, I wonder?
> Kearney [Charlie Kearney from Wexford, helpful to A
> Company and who had been in Jadotville as a civilian] said
> we were outnumbered 30–1 at all times. He estimated that
> there were 600 Belge under arms against us. If that was so, I
> imagine they were only waving the flag.

But by revealing their positions when they fired on the helicopter,
the Gendarmerie had played right into Quinlan's strategic hands. He
explained:

> We retaliated with every weapon which could be brought to
> bear and proceeded to hit with accurate and devastating fire.
> Some enemy positions were very close, between 50 and 100
> yards. Our men unloaded the 'copter under fire but were
> covered by fire from our own weapons. Over 20 gallons of
> water, our most urgent requirement, was undrinkable. Also,
> it would have been scarcely enough to supply 20 men with
> water for one day under our conditions.

Neville echoes all of this:

> After I got the bundle of bed sheets and spread them with
> Bobby Allan, a Kilkenny man and a brave man, the pilot
> landed, cursing and blinding. A cool man, he'd volunteered
> and stayed there with us. There was no way out. His Swedish
> co-pilot timed the shooting coming at us and in five minutes
> he reckoned there were 4,000 in opposition to us.
>
> After the helicopter landed, I rushed into an old house. I
> was fit as a fiddle. A fellow advanced toward me and I hit him
> a belt of the Gustav and opened down the side of his face. I
> felt terrible. Poor divil.

Fighting went on without cease for two hours, after which there was a lull of about an hour. Then A Company was back in action, returning concentrated fire for another hour.

While the battle went on, the wounded Billy Ready, still mattress-buttressed under the stairs, had a visit:

> After the helicopter landed, Pat Quinlan and Paddy Neville came for me where I was confined and said they were getting me out of there. They carried me between them, under fire, to the helicopter. When we got there, the pilot said he wasn't taking off and they had to carry me back. On the way back, one of them tripped—I don't know which one—and the three of us went down in a heap, them on top of me! But they got me back in under the stairs. They should have got a medal at least for that....

The Katangans, it was clear to Quinlan and his men, were completely demoralised by A Company's intense fire. Large numbers of them were seen fleeing into the bush where many died of their wounds. Others died or were wounded when their white officers opened fire in an attempt to stem this retreat, or to get the men back into the battle again.

The whine of the Fouga was regular as ever as it flew overhead from its base at Kolwezi, where it was constantly refitted with bombs. But its prime target now was the reinforcements intent on crossing Lufira Bridge.

A Company still did not have radio contact with these reinforcements, nor any way of knowing whether they had in fact arrived at the bridge. Then, with the thunder and reverberations of a long, rumbling explosion, came the fear in A Company that the Lufira Bridge had been blown.

Quinlan radioed Battalion HQ in Elisabethville.

1120 HRS. JADOTVILLE: ZETO [code for the Fouga] SEEMS TO BE BOMBING BRIDGE AND ELISABETHVILLE. EACH TIME IT PASSES HERE WE WILL SIGNAL ZETO. SHOULD BE OVER BRIDGE IN THREE MINUTES, ELISABETHVILLE TEN MINUTES.

CHAPTER 22

*No one visualised we'd get into military conflict with another force.
We were soldiers of peace—men of Ireland inspired by religion and
peacekeeping!*

Col. (retired) M. Shannon

Lufira Bridge, Katanga. Saturday, 16 September 1961

As the second Force Kane arrived at Lufira Bridge, local men
appeared to tell them that, because of the heavy casualties inflicted by
the earlier Force Kane, the Gendarmerie had been strongly reinforced
by troops from Kolwesi. Proof of this came when a group from the
reinforcements moved out to recce the situation and came under
sustained attack. The men were forced to withdraw under cover from
the armed cars.

The Fouga jet continued to bomb and to strafe. Three Gurkha
soldiers were killed. Five were injured.

Michael Shannon recalls:

> We began to mortar the bridge and the high ground behind
> it. Capt. Cyril McQuillan was in command of mortar and
> machine guns. When firing mortars, you need observers to
> go forward. I was an observer and the thing remains in my
> mind … we hit their transport car and there was immediately
> explosions and smoke and debris. That must have been
> immensely frightening to them.
>
> Our machine guns came into action then. We engaged
> the whole area with fire. Meanwhile, the plan was hatched
> that Gurkhas would move out through the bush and attack
> the railway bridge to the left. But the enemy must have seen

the Gurkhas moving through the bush because they blew up the railway bridge.

We were reporting all the time to Elisabethville and the Gendarmerie were monitoring all of our calls. But the Gendarmerie still couldn't be sure where the Gurkhas might come from....

Nevertheless, it was becoming increasingly obvious that a daylight attack so as to force a crossing without air support was not going to be possible.

Or at least not without very serious losses.

CHAPTER 23

Never, for the sake of peace and quiet, deny your own experience and convictions.

Dag Hammarskjöld, Diaries

Katanga, Congo. Saturday, 16 September 1961

Fighting throughout Katanga worsened. The Fouga upped the ante, more than ever strafing the reinforcements as they attempted to get to the troops in Jadotville, bombing the airfield at Kamina, Elisabethville, shooting at a UN DC-3 transport plane in the air.

General McKeown left Leopoldville for Elisabethville. His plane, a DC-6B called *Albertina,* was to return at once to Leopoldville in case it was needed by UN Secretary General Dag Hammarskjöld.

A message from Katangan President Moise Tshombe, delivered by Sir Roy Welensky of Rhodesia, made any ceasefire conditional on all UN troops leaving Katanga. Tshombe threatened 'total war' if this did not happen.

Transport planes, requested by Hammarskjöld the day before from the United States so as to fly reinforcements to Elisabethville from Stanleyville, were recalled 'by higher authority' while *en route* to the Congo.

At a meeting with Lord Lansdowne, the British Parliamentary Undersecretary of State at the Foreign Office, Hammarskjöld asked if the British government would arrange a meeting with Tshombe in Ndola in Northern Rhodesia. The Swedish Secretary General was convinced that, once away from the influence of Munongo and his white advisers, Tshombe would be agreeable to a meeting with Prime Minister Adoula of the Congo's central government.

President Tshombe replied, through the British Consul in Elisabethville, that he would meet with Dr Conor Cruise O'Brien in Bancroft, Northern Rhodesia the following day. But O'Brien was reluctant to agree to this and Hammarskjöld, who believed that his detachment from the violence, rumour and intrigue devouring Elisabethville was imperative if the talks were to be successful, said that he would go ahead with his own plan to meet Mr Tshombe in Ndola.

CHAPTER 24

The Irish troops have done a wonderful job and have got little support from a lot of people who should have supported them.

Minister Frank Aiken, en route to Congo

Dublin and Athlone. Saturday, 16 September 1961

Reports throughout a tense day repeatedly suggested that, 'in spite of a gallant stand', the garrison at Jadotville had been overrun and its troops either killed or taken prisoner. A variation on this reported that, in spite of strafing from the Katangan jet, the company was 'putting up an excellent fight' and that helicopters [*sic*] had dropped food and ammunition. Quinlan was commended for bravery by Brigadier Raja, UN Commander in Katanga.

The *Evening Herald* headlined another piece of Katangan propaganda when it carried a threat from Moise Tshombe which had been broadcast by Katangan radio. 'New Threat to Irish troops: Tshombe claims 130 prisoners, warns of "ten lives for one"' read the paper's front page.

Athlone, where the families of almost 50 members of A Company lived and waited for news, was, according to an *Irish Times* reporter, 'a town of grim expectancy tempered by hope.' The reporter, keeping a waiting vigil in Athlone, described a town where, 'mothers await news of their sons, wives of their husbands and children of their fathers', continuing:

> Over all the steadily falling rain keeps the streets unusually quiet.
>
> In Custume Barracks, from where A Company departed just three months ago, the mess is full of officers awaiting word

of their comrades. They express confidence in the ability and quality of the Irish troops to hold their own. The Irish had time to dig in and consolidate their positions and it would, they say, 'take a lot to drive them out'. They are angered by British reports that the Irish soldiers are participating in a war in which 'all rules had gone by the board.'

The news that the chief of the Bayeke tribe had ordered 1,000 tribesmen to march on Jadotville and 'show no quarter to the Irishmen' strikes a strangely pathetic note of incredulity in the quiet homes of a townspeople who know that their menfolk went out not as conquerors but to help a young country in its first and difficult days of independence.

CHAPTER 25

We are all angry and bitter at the blundering fools who left us isolated here.

Comdt P. Quinlan, September 1961

Jadotville. Saturday, 16 September 1961

Noon came and went in Jadotville. The fighting had intensified but there was still no word of reinforcements. Quinlan radioed again, in Irish.

> 1255 HRS. JADOTVILLE: AON SCÉAL FAOIN CHABHAIR? NÍ CLOISIM AON TORANN FÓS. TÁIMID AG SCAOLEADH AR FCA A BHÍ AG IARRAIDH DUL AR CHÚLBOTHAR I DTREO DROICHID. CUIR SCÉAL CHUGAM. [Any news about help? I don't hear any noise yet. We are firing on FCA who were attempting to take a back road in the direction of the bridge. Send word to me.]

A reply sent at 1259 hours did not get through to Jadotville until more than an hour later.

> 1403 HRS. ELISABETHVILLE: BHÍ AN CHABHAIR BUAILTE ÓN AER. TÁ SIAD AG LEANUINT ID' THREO ANOIS. NÍL SIAD TRASNA AN DROICHID FÓS. CAD IAD AINMNEACHA NA BEIRTE PHRÍOSÚNACH ATÁ AGAT? [The reinforcements were hit from the air. They are heading in your direction now. They are not across the bridge yet. What are the names of the two prisoners you have?]

While this was going on, at around 1400 hours, Mayor Amisi's 'White Adviser' rang on Mme Lamonfagne's phone to say that Amisi wanted

114

a ceasefire. Quinlan refused to discuss this, or anything else, on the telephone. If the Mayor was genuinely interested in a ceasefire, he told the 'Adviser', he should come under a flag of truce into No Man's Land.

The 'Adviser' said that he would phone again at 1500 hours with a response to this.

Quinlan, after this call, again radioed Elisabethville for an update on the reinforcement situation.

1410 HRS. JADOTVILLE: AN BHFUIL AN CABHAIR ÁBALTA A BRISEADH TRÍD? CAD É AN SUÍOMH? NÍ RAIBH DO SCÉAL SOILÉIR. SÓRT SOS COGAIDH ANSEO. MERCENARY PRISONERS MICHEL PAUCHEU AGUS PIERRE VAN DEN WEGER. AN BHFUIL AN DROICHEAD SÉIDTE? [Has help managed to break through? What's the situation? Your message wasn't clear. A ceasefire of sorts here. Has the bridge been blown up?]

Quinlan was given scant details of events around ceasefire talks but heard enough to help him decide how he would deal with requests for a ceasefire when, and if, they came from the Gendarmerie in Jadotville.

The information I had was that high-level ceasefire negotiations were going on and that, in fact, apart from some sniping, a ceasefire was to all intents and purposes being observed in Elisabethville. Given this as the situation, I decided to negotiate agreement of a local ceasefire pending the outcome of these high-level talks. The enemy were also aware that high-level ceasefire talks were going on. They too were agreeable to a local ceasefire pending the outcome.

The 'Adviser', as agreed, rang at 1500 hours on the still-functioning phone in Mme Lamonfagne's shattered home. He asked for a ceasefire and promised Quinlan that the Gendarmerie would withdraw from around A Company's position. Quinlan warned him that 'any man seen moving forward or backward' would be shot, on sight.

The 'Adviser' asked for permission to send officers to forward positions so as to order the Gendarmerie in those positions to stop firing. Quinlan told him to get the officers to walk upright and to carry a white flag.

After a lot of discussion, the 'Adviser' agreed, eventually, to come himself, along with Mayor Amisi and the officer commanding the Gendarmerie, to an appointed place in No Man's Land. They would be there at 1600 hours and would discuss ceasefire terms.

As the conversation ended, a burst of fire resulted in a white Gendarmerie officer's leg being shot off. This provoked huge anger and disruption among the Katangan forces. Quinlan was unmoved:

> The man was both senior and useful and they claimed that he was going forward to get his men to stop firing. I doubt it very much. He didn't carry a white flag and there had not been enough time to make such arrangements anyway. The Katangans didn't press the point too far.

The man lived but had his leg amputated.

Twenty minutes late, at 1620 hours, the Burgermeister, the Gendarmerie OC and the white 'Adviser' arrived at the designated No Man's Land. Quinlan met them with Lars Fröberg and Fr. Joe Fagan. The mood, in the dully simmering afternoon heat, was swollen with anger, frustration and a crucial lack of information on both sides.

What both sides *did* know was that, without doubt and with very little provocation, a bloodbath unlike anything that had happened up to now was inevitable unless an agreement, of some sort, could be reached. Quinlan, distrustful of his enemy, negotiated hard.

> I knew that the Lufira Bridge was very strongly held now by the Gendarmerie and I wanted to avoid casualties to our men who were, in any case, completely exhausted. So I agreed to a ceasefire under certain conditions.
>
> I told them, at the outset, that discussion was useless unless they agreed to ground the Fouga jet and ensure that their troops at Lufira Bridge cease firing. At first, they didn't want to discuss the action at Lufira as they said they were

fighting Indians there. I refused to consider a ceasefire in Jadotville alone and said emphatically that the jet must be grounded and that I would fire on any troops moving around my position towards the bridge.

After some time, they stated that the troops fighting at the bridge were not under their command as they had come from North Katanga. After some more time, however, they agreed to get the troops on the bridge to cease fire if I could get UN troops there to cease fire also.

I undertook to convey this to HQ in Elisabethville.

Crucially, neither side was yet aware that the reinforcements had already been beaten back at Lufira Bridge. Liam Donnelly's view of things at this stage is unequivocal:

Radio signals from Elisabethville were telling us they were negotiating a ceasefire there and what Pat thought was if they're negotiating a ceasefire in Elisabethville, why wouldn't I negotiate one here?' But they were doing it from a position of strength, we from one of great weakness.

At 1700 hours, Quinlan radioed Elisabethville to say that ceasefire talks were being arranged and to advise Battalion HQ to await their outcome. Almost certain now, too, that the bridge was mined (following the earlier sounds of an explosion), he warned about this and said that the reinforcements should consolidate.

1737 HRS. ELISABETHVILLE: I HAVE INSTRUCTED KANE TO CONSOLIDATE PRESENT POSITION. GOOD LUCK WITH TALKS.

CHAPTER 26

There was a dearth of awareness of the real situation on the ground
in the Congo, and of the political intrigue abounding.

Col. (retired) M. Shannon

Lufira Bridge, Saturday, 16 September 1961

Force Kane, still on the Elisabethville side of Lufira Bridge, had
reached an impasse. Some time around 1700 hours, the final position
was reported to Battalion HQ and the force ordered to return to
Elisabethville once again.

Michael Shannon's account tells how things then unfolded.

There is no doubt in my mind that the defenders of the bridge
were under severe pressure. Which is why their masters contacted
UN HQ or whomever to suggest negotiating a ceasefire. This
suited the Irish because of A Company's position in Jadotville.

We got a message that the whole force was to disengage and return to Elisabethville because negotiations for a
ceasefire and relief of the company in Jadotville had reached
an advanced and sensitive stage.

The UN, whose job it was to keep peace, said to call off
the action at Lufira Bridge and it was called off.

But there were still 156 hostages to fortune in Jadotville.
The Belgians, who once again had total control over A
Company, went on to withdraw from negotiations and to
bring in reinforcements from Shinkolobwe. Water had run
out in Jadotville and the water sent to them was contaminated
so there was stalemate and a huge increase in pressure on the
Jadotville company.

In Shannon's view, 'one of the defects in the second critical assault on Lufira Bridge was the air attack. Ethiopian jets left Addis Ababa to go to Entebbe in Uganda (these were war planes badly needed to support us on the ground) and the Brits wouldn't allow them to take off. It's quite reasonable to say that the Brits said "No, don't take off" so as the *status quo* would be maintained, so that the Rhodesian and Katangan mines would be kept working.'

On its return journey to Elisabethville, Force Kane was ambushed and five Irish soldiers injured. On the continuing journey, five Gurkhas were injured. Closer still to Elisabethville, an accident involving two vehicles and exploding shells resulted in the deaths of two Gurkhas and injuries to another ten.

CHAPTER 27

...with treachery, under cover of the ceasefire and when Kane had left the bridge ... they brought up more paratroopers and others to close in on us.

Comdt P. Quinlan, September 1961

Jadotville. Saturday, 16 September 1961

Quinlan's reply to the misleading message on consolidation at the Lufira Bridge was in Irish and impassioned. With no idea that the reinforcements had been recalled, he was already planning tactically.

1800 HRS. JADOTVILLE: SÉ AN FÁTH IS MÓ LE SEO, NÁ STOP A CHUR LE TROID. TÁ AN DROICHEAD AN-LÁIDIR ANOIS, SÍLIM. IS FÉIDIR LIBH BHEITH RÉIDH LE FÓRSAÍ NÍOS LÁIDRE I GCEANN CÚPLA LÁ MÁ TÁ SÉ RIACHTANACH. BEIDH DROICHEAD EILE AG TEASTÁIL, SÍLIM, AGUS PRÉACHÁN NÓ DHÓ CHUN MO DHUINE A CHUR AS GNÍOMH. NÍL ANSEO ACH SOS TRODA. IS FÉIDIR LEIS NA POLAITEORÍ AN CHEIST A PHLÉ ANOIS. TÁIM I SUÍOMH LÁIDIR ACH BEIDH MÉ NÍOS LÁIDRE TAR ÉIS CUPLA LÁ SOSA. BAIL Ó DHIA ORAIBH GO LÉIR. [The most important thing about this is to put a stop to the fighting. The bridge is very strong now, I believe. You (HQ) can be ready with stronger forces within a few days if it is necessary. Another bridge will be needed, I believe, and a crow (préacháin/helicopter) or two to put my man (enemy) out of action. Here it is only a ceasefire. The politicians can debate the matter now. I am in a strong situation but I will be stronger after a few days' rest. God bless you all.]

This message was not cleared until 1844 hours. Meanwhile, A Company got word from Elisabethville that President Tshombe had broadcast a message to the Gendarmerie telling them that a ceasefire was in the offing. The Katangan President was worried, however, that outlying Gendarmerie units might not get the word in time.

As a consequence, Quinlan was asked to inform Gendarmerie in Jadotville of how things stood. He did this, passing on their President's message about a ceasefire to the Gendarmerie in Jadotville. Then he continued to try to make contact with the reinforcements, sending messages to Elisabethville to be relayed to Kane.

> 1813 HRS. JADOTVILLE: CONSOLIDATE PRESENT POSITION. DO
> NOT ATTACK AGAIN. AWAIT FURTHER INSTRUCTIONS.

More than an hour, and several messages, later, he still had not received a reply and nor, apparently, had contact been made with Kane's force. There were no replies from the Lufira Bridge. But the ceasefire talks, in Jadotville at any rate, reached conclusion, and, by 1930 hours, a deal had been struck.

> 1930 HRS. JADOTVILLE: MAYOR ASKED FOR CEASEFIRE. AGREED
> ON CONDITION THAT BRIDGE GARRISON OF FCA WOULD ALSO
> CEASEFIRE AND THAT JET WOULD BE GROUNDED. THIS WAS AGREED
> TO. WE ARE GETTING WATER AND FOOD. WE HAVE NOT, REPEAT
> NOT SURRENDERED. PRESENT ARRANGEMENTS WILL AVOID HEAVY
> CASUALTIES ON ALL SIDES. HIGH LEVEL TALKS CAN FIX THE REST.
> TÁIMID AR FAIRE AGUS ULLAMH [We are ready and waiting]. MAYOR
> AND PEOPLE HERE DO NOT BELIEVE TSHOMBE BROADCAST.

However, the agreement was struck in continuing ignorance, on both sides, of the fact that the reinforcements had been beaten back at the bridge. According to Quinlan, he:

> …agreed to a ceasefire under certain conditions, then radioed
> the reinforcements to dig in and consolidate at the bridge. I
> knew that the ceasefire would be broken if they thought they
> had the bridge secured.

Unfortunately, the reinforcements were returning to Elisabethville in disorder at the time.

Quinlan called an A Company meeting, outlined the situation and got individual reports from the Platoon and Armoured Car Commanders. Morale was high, he was assured, and everyone was well, apart from the small number of casualties, general fatigue and lack of water. He then gave them details of the deal, and conditions, agreed upon.

a) Gendarmerie to withdraw from around A Company's position to their barracks.

b) A joint patrol of ten Irish and ten Gendarmerie to patrol the road area which had until then not been designated No Man's Land.

c) A cordon of unarmed police, accompanied by some Irish troops, was to form a cordon between A Company's position and Jadotville to keep back 'sightseers and other undesirables'.

d) The water was to be turned on to service A Company's position immediately. [When the negotiators claimed this would not be possible for some time because the pipes had burst, Quinlan demanded they get a tanker of water to A Company's position that night. The water was not turned on and the tanker did not arrive. But they did, Quinlan said, 'send me 30 doz. minerals to tide us over the night until water could be arranged in the morning.']

e) The Police Chief and Assistant Police Chief (the latter English speaking) were to tour the town and native compound with Comdt Quinlan at 1000 hours on Sunday to assure everyone that all was well.

All of these terms, Noel Carey affirmed, 'were acceptable to us.'

We had defended ourselves honourably and our role in the Congo was peacekeeping so we had no difficulty accepting the terms of the ceasefire. Comdt Quinlan praised our efforts, and was obviously relieved at the outcome of events, having directed his company with great bravery, visiting every area and certainly putting himself at serious risk in a tireless display of outstanding leadership.

Sean Foley had no doubt that:

Everyone there would have died for Pat Quinlan. The effort he had us put into the training saved us from another Niemba and many deaths. He used go round all the trenches at night, at two and three in the morning, calling out that he was coming, reassuring us, making sure we stayed on the ball and were alert. He would tell us we were going to be victorious no matter what happened. He would always stop and exchange the cúpla focal in Irish with the men from Renmore.

The men of A Company left their trenches and headed for their various and original billets and sleeping quarters. The officers found their Purfina Garage HQ riddled with bullets, most of the windows smashed and broken. And the entire company found, very quickly, that the ceasefire would be anything but peacefully agreeable.

The word from Elisabethville was initially reassuring. Frank Aiken, Ireland's Minister for External (Foreign) Affairs, was on his way to Congo.

1945 HRS. ELISABETHVILLE: COGAIRDEACHAS PAT. TÁ DÓCHAS MÓR AGAINN AS AIKEN. TÁ SÉ AR A BEALACH. TÁ JOHNNY TÚGAITHE SLÁN. [Congratulations Pat. We place great trust in Aiken. He is on his way. Johnny (Kane) is safe.]

Fifteen minutes later, in Jadotville, a group of white Gendarmerie arrived to form a patrol with A Company. Quinlan was irate and 'refused to recognise them and the Mayor ordered them away. Later, African Gendarmerie arrived and the joint patrol was set up....'

Carey recalls that the mood was good, verging on euphoric.

The Katangans even engaged with our lads in playing football in the forecourt of Purfina Garage. The atmosphere was excellent, and to all intents and purposes victory was ours and we had acquitted ourselves well.

However, for the mercenary soldiers, a ceasefire was not an option, and Katanga, anyway, was not their country. Football and civilities were not what they had come to the Congo for and, soon, what Quinlan described as a 'lorry-load' of white, mercenary Gendarmerie, arrived at A Company's cordon:

They were very loud and demanded to be allowed through to Elisabethville as the fighting had stopped in Jadotville. They wanted further action in Elisabethville. I sent instructions to these people that anyone coming within our area would be arrested. The Chief of Police approached me and asked for an escort to come with him to disarm these mercenaries. I agreed immediately.

Sgt Prendergast was to take charge of this escort and, in briefing his men, was very businesslike. He appeared to frighten the Chief of Police who now asked me to allow him to endeavour to get the mercenaries to go away. He stated that he was afraid of the consequences if further fighting started. He said that these people (the mercenaries) would be disarmed by the Gendarmerie in Jadotville as they had been thrown out earlier anyway when the Gendarmerie had mutinied against them during the fighting.

The Chief of Police approached the mercenaries and, after a long discussion and when our escort eventually moved up, they left.

2100 HRS. JADOTVILLE: TÁ AN-ÁTHAS AR GACH ÉINNE ANSEO AS AN SOS TRODA. GO MÓR MÓR AN FCA. NÍL AON FONN TRODA ORTHU ANOIS. AN RAIBH AON DUINE GORTHAITHE AG JOHNNY? SÉ AN SÍOCHÁIN AN CHUID IS FEARR DEN TROID. BA CHÓIR DO JOHNNY FANACHT AG AN DROICHEAD. [Everyone here is very pleased with the ceasefire. Especially the FCA. They have no desire to fight now. Did Johnny sustain any casualties? The best part of this war is the peace. Johnny should remain at the bridge.]

It was then that he got word back that the reinforcements had left the bridge and were returning to Elisabethville.

'B'éigean do Johnny rith ón Jet [Johnny had to run from the jet]', he was told, 'tá formhór an fhorsa ar ais [the greater part of the force is back].'

Quinlan's reply was bilingual, with the English part of the message upbeat and positive for public consumption and the ears of the listening Gendarmerie, while he gave the sober truth of the situation, for ostensibly army consumption only, in Irish.

2230 HRS. JADOTVILLE: WONDERFUL NEWS HERE. MERCENARIES THROWN OUT. POLICE VERY FRIENDLY, GOING ON TOUR OF TOWN AND NATIVE VILLAGE TOMORROW WITH CHIEF OF POLICE TO SHOW PEOPLE ALL IS WELL. JOINT IRISH/FCA GUARD ON ROAD TONIGHT. TROID FÍOCHMHAR INNIU. DEIRTEAR 150 AR FAD MARBH. THEITH FORMHÓR EILE. DEIRTEAR SUAS LE 2000 AR FAD. NÍL SÉ DEIMHNEACH (FEROCIOUS FIGHTING TODAY. 150 IN TOTAL REPORTED DEAD. THE MAJORITY OF THE REST FLED. SAID TO BE ESTIMATED AT 2000 IN TOTAL. THIS IS NOT CONFIRMED.) THIS IS A MIRACLE. MY SINCERE THANKS TO YOU AND JOHNNY AND ALL WHO HELPED. NOTIFY IRISH RADIO ALL WELL AND NO SERIOUS CASUALTIES.

This message was passed on by Battalion HQ to Dr Conor Cruise O'Brien and General McKeown

Quinlan then called a meeting, at Purfina Garage HQ, where he told officers Donnelly, Leech, Knightly, Tom Quinlan, Byrne, Carey and others of the company that the reinforcements had again returned to Elisabethville.

'This was a shock,' Carey admitted. 'Later that night we discussed the situation among ourselves. The outlook did not look good.'

They knew by now, too, that the water was not going to be turned on, that there was no tanker on its way. Not having a choice in the matter, they had to settle for the 30 dozen bottles of fizzy minerals and further promises of water the following morning.

Donnelly's Platoon remained in defensive position, 'awaiting further orders'.

Leech was even more cautious. 'Firing stopped due to mooted ceasefire. The Platoon remained in defensive positions and with a 50% alert.'

Pat Quinlan himself was soberly realistic: 'On this Saturday night, we still manned our trenches. The difference was that, apart from one sentry in each trench, the men actually slept in their trenches.'

Their wary vigilance would prove both wise and justified.

CHAPTER 28

*When the climb seems endless and suddenly nothing will go quite as
you wish it, that is when you must not hesitate.*

Dag Hammarskjöld, *Diaries*

Leopoldville. Sunday, 16 September 1961

At 5 a.m., Secretary General Hammarskjöld got word that
Gendarmerie troops in Jadotville had thrown out their white officers
and were fraternising with Irish troops. 'At last,' he wrote, 'they seem
to have got our point.'

He was more than ever convinced that a positive meeting with
Tshombe in Ndola would work things out.

Hammarskjöld's plane, the same *Albertina* which had taken
General McKeown to Elisabethville, was hit by a bullet while taking
off to return to Leopoldville for the Secretary General's journey to
Ndola. The bullet penetrated the cowling and struck the exhaust pipe.
The exhaust pipe was replaced and the *Albertina* arrived at Ndjili,
Leopoldville, at 8 a.m. The crew, with the exception of the chief pilot,
was the same as that which had flown McKeown to Elisabethville the
previous day.

At 10 a.m., the British Consul gave Dr Conor Cruise O'Brien a
reply from Mr Tshombe; the Katangan President agreed in principle
to an immediate ceasefire, but he also demanded that UN troops
be confined to their camps and that all troop movements and
reinforcements by ground and air should cease. He agreed to go to
Ndola but wanted three of his ministers to go with him.

Hammarskjöld replied that these terms were totally unacceptable
but, timing and events proving unmanageable as ever, the British
Consul got this reply too late to give it to Mr Tshombe. The Katangan

President was aboard a chartered plane ready for takeoff for Ndola. With no option left to him, the Secretary General decided to go to Ndola anyway. He sent Lord Lansdowne ahead of him to see to arrangements.

A further request from Hammarskjöld to Britain to allow the Ethiopian jets to fly over Kenya and refuel in Uganda got a further negative response.

By midday, a 'sudden change' was reported from Jadotville: A Company was being held hostage and all communications had been cut off.

Plans for the Tshombe/Hammarskjöld meeting and talks went ahead and, just after 4.30 p.m., the UN Secretary General and his party arrived in Ndjili Airport to fly to Ndola. The cabin was given a final, searching check and the *Albertina* took off at 4.51 p.m.

CHAPTER 29

With no hope of more help, my only concern was for the lives of my men. Before God and their Irish mothers and wives and fathers I am satisfied that I have done my duty. Further fighting would have achieved nothing except useless slaughter.

Comdt P. Quinlan, September 1961

DAY FIVE
Jadotville. Sunday, 17 September 1961

Noel Carey found it strange, on Sunday morning, 'not to have the Katangans firing at us. All was very quiet. We had only a skeleton presence in the trenches but it was noticeable that Katangan forces had moved closer into our area during the night....'

Carey, along with everyone billeted in Purfina Garage HQ, was having breakfast—'something to eat'—when the strange became the Jadotville everyday.

> Suddenly the Fouga jet appeared, dived on the garage. We all crouched, desperately seeking cover. To our relief he flew past without bombing us. So much for grounding the Fouga. The quiet was ominous.

As it was in the beginning, so it was now, near the end. About one-third of the men were at Mass, again in the open air, and at 0725 hours, when the jet flew over. Quinlan 'immediately suspected a break in the ceasefire.'

> Later we observed large groups of Gendarmerie still around our position. These included many paratroopers.

Mayor Amisi and the white Red Cross Adviser arrived at around 0800 and I protested very strongly about the jet, and about the encroaching Gendarmerie. The 'Adviser' said that it was a mistake about the jet and said the Gendarmerie would be withdrawn. We discussed the accommodation to be occupied by us. Some of our villas had been badly damaged and the Burgermeister was to requisition other villas in the same area for us. All seemed well at this stage.

What would be a series of radio and voice messages relaying mis-information, or at best confusion, began soon after this when Quinlan, speaking with Barrett at Battalion HQ, passed on word of the jet's threatening reappearance and A Company's continuing lack of water. In the course of this conversation, he was promised that two helicopters would be sent with water that day.

Quinlan replied that these would have to make about four round trips to bring enough water and that this would be impossible to do with the jet overhead. He said that he was worried, also because of the jet, about sending the injured out in a helicopter.

In any event, Quinlan was perplexed at the promise of not one, but two, helicopters. Thors and Hovden, the crew of their own, now disabled, helicopter, had been, and continued, adamant that there were no other helicopters available to the UN.

The situation on the ground at Jadotville was no less confusing.

Some time later, Major Makito arrived. I suspected his attitude. He demanded that we store our heavy weapons in one villa. I asked for water to be turned on in accordance with the original agreement. He insisted we store weapons first and then he would turn on the water.

I now knew this was a trick and they had no intention of keeping the ceasefire agreement. I refused to move from our position and continued negotiations and arguments hoping to get relief as soon as possible.

The mood in Jadotville changed rapidly. Hope was replaced by disbelief. The relative calm in A Company's position returned to battle-alert.

130

The foul and fetid stench from villas, latrines and the trenches was all but unbearable. Rats were making their rampant way into things; Liam Donnelly had already killed two in Sergeant Tom Kelly's dugout and Kelly himself had just killed another. Disease was without doubt imminent and inescapable.

No one had enjoyed anything as basic as a change of clothing for six days, nor proper nourishment, nor sleep. It was the lack of sleep particularly, as the day grew once again relentlessly hot, which made it hard for the men to concentrate.

And it was still only 0900 hours.

At ten minutes past the hour, Quinlan, in a voice message from Captain P.J. Stewart at Battalion HQ in Elisabethville, was advised that three UN jets would be arriving in Elisabethville that day. He was told to tell Mayor Amisi and the Gendarmerie in Jadotville that the Fouga would be shot down if it left the ground.

Quinlan gladly brought this news to the Mayor, telling him that 'three UN jets would be over Jadotville if they tried anything'. The news had the desired effect. 'They wilted visibly,' Quinlan recalled.

But there were no jets. Nor even the possibility of jets for at least three days.

Tension grew. The water was not turned on. Heat and thirst became more and more unbearable and, according to Quinlan:

> The enemy had a full company of paratroopers on my very vulnerable rear. They had withdrawn them from the bridge. They had rallied the Gendarmerie during the night and they were ready to attack us again. I begged HQ for instructions and asked when I could expect help....

It was almost noon when he sent one such message, in Irish.

> 1155 HRS. JADOTVILLE: TÁ ATHRÚ MÓR AR AN SCÉAL ANSEO. AN BHFUIL NA TRÍ PRÉACHÁIN AGAIBH? AN FÉIDIR BIA AGUS UISCE A CHUR CHUGAINN? CÉN T-AM GUR FÉIDIR TOSÚ AG CUR TRODA MÁ GÁ? CAD É AN SUÍOMH POLAITIÚIL? TÁIMID BEAGNACH MAR HOSTAGES. TABHAIR TREORACHA LÁITHREACH. [Situation here has changed greatly. Do you have the three

crows? Is it possible to send us food and water? What time is it possible to commence fighting, if necessary? What's the political situation? We are almost hostages. Give instructions immediately.]

Quinlan 'sent about six messages and did not even get a reply. McKeown was in HQ and he got my messages. I asked for a decision from Aiken and McKeown. Aiken was in Leopoldville. Still no reply.'

Meanwhile, the Katangans, getting over their fear of the threatened jets,

> …became more harsh in their demands, insisting that we move to a hotel in town. There was still no question of surrender on my part. They claimed the reason we should move to town had to do with there being no suitable accommodation available elsewhere. They said they could not turn on the water because it was Sunday and no plumber was available to re-air the pipes.
>
> I was very suspicious at this stage that the Gendarmerie were planning another attack on my men, some of whom were now out of the trenches. I knew also that a large group, at least a company of paratroopers, were on my very vulnerable rear. These paratroopers had been withdrawn from Lufira Bridge and I am satisfied that the Mayor was responsible for preventing the Gendarmerie from attacking us again at this time. [Later that night, and again on Monday, 18 September, the Mayor had to hide from Gendarmerie keen to shoot him dead because of his perceived sympathy for the UN.]

Quinlan's message shortly after 1 o'clock was adamant:

> 1306 HRS. JADOTVILLE: I REQUIRE DECISION ON OUR LAST MESSAGE FROM AIKEN. REPLY BEFORE 1400 HOURS. SUÍOMH ANSEO AS MO CUMAS. [Situation here beyond my control.] WE ARE BEING OFFERED ACCOMMODATION IN HOTEL WITH PERSONAL WEAPONS AT 1600 HOURS. THIS IS OF COURSE BEING

HOSTAGES. Níl bia nó uisce san suíomh atá againn faoi láthair. (In our present situation, we have neither food nor water). Decision Aiken and McKeown now.

1328 hrs. Elisabethville: An t-Árd Ceannasaí anseo. Tá do theachtaireacht aige. [Commander-in-Chief here. He has your message.]

Quinlan continued to negotiate and argue with Amisi and the Jadotville Gendarmerie chiefs, insisting on a written ceasefire agreement.

I was still hoping for some information on reinforcements to come to my assistance. The men at this stage were very fatigued—all had lost considerable weight and suffered from lack of sleep.

Our only food now was some biscuits. We had absolutely no water whatsoever. At approx. 1400 hours, I insisted on going into Jadotville town on the pretext of buying some beer, and if possible to get water, for the men. My real reason was to get the feel and the attitude of the people.

I asked two policemen to accompany me and also took Eric Thors, the Swedish co-pilot of the helicopter, with me as interpreter.

I drove through the town. It was an armed camp with several hundred Gendarmerie and armed civilians on the streets. One group of civilians jeered us.

The police with us showed me a bar where I could get beer. There were approximately 100 Gendarmerie in the street outside. I pulled up in the car and when I got out, a murmur went through the crowd.

Then someone shouted 'le majeur Irlandais' and they all rushed forward and began to shake my hand and to cheer me. They appeared to be friendly …

I went into the bar. There appeared to be about 80 people inside. Someone called them to attention. I was cheered again and offered drink. Some Gendarmerie showed me their wounds, of which they appeared to be very proud.

Quinlan bought a case of beer, then took the worried advice of his police escort and left.

Battalion HQ had been in touch in his absence.

1415 HRS. ELISABETHVILLE: AN PRÍOSÚNAIGH SIBH? TÁ PRÉACHÁN EILE AG TEACHT CHUGAT LE LINN TRÁTHNÓNA INNIU. AODHA. [Are you prisoners? There is another crow (helicopter) coming to you during this afternoon. Aodha/Hugh.]

Quinlan, unimpressed by this, continued to insist on a written ceasefire agreement and to demand the presence of the Mayor to sign it, Amisi being the one who had initiated the negotiations. Mayor Amisi, however, had not been seen or available since about 11.30 that morning.

Quinlan was still hopeful at this stage that the promised jets would, 'come over in a show of force. We estimated that there was little or no hope of ground assistance for at least some days and even without fighting we could not hold out another day without water. If we were attacked at this stage, it would develop into a massacre.'

At 3 o'clock, he fired off another radio message, unequivocal as those that had gone before it. It was entirely in Irish.

1500 HRS. JADOTVILLE: NÍL AON UN AG AN DROICHEAD AGUS TÁ CÚPLA MÍLE FCA TIMPEALL ORAINN ANOIS. NÍ MÓR BRIOGÁID A CHUR ISTEACH. BRISEADH AR AN NGEALLÚINT SOS TRODA NUAIR NACH RAIBH AON UN AG AN DROICHEAD. MÁ THAGANN PRÉACHÁIN EILE ANSEO INNIU CUIRFEAR DEIREADH LINN. TÁ SIAD MÓRTHIMPEALL ORAINN GACH TAOBH. FAIGH GEALLÚINT Ó TSHOMBE FAOIN ÁR GCÚRAM. NÍ ORAINN AN LOCHT. NÍ MÓR DO DHUINE ÉIGIN ARD–SOCRÚ A DHÉANAMH ANOIS. [There are no UN at the bridge and we are surrounded by a few thousand FCA now. A brigade needs to be sent in. The ceasefire pledge was broken when there was no UN at the bridge. If another crow (helicopter) comes here today, we'll be finished. They are surrounding us on all sides. Get a promise/guarantee from Tshombe about our safety. We are not to blame. Someone must make an important settlement now.]

Within the hour, he had sent another message:

1555 HRS. JADOTVILLE: BÍODH SÉ SOILÉIR DON DOMHAIN
NÁR THUGAMAR ISTEACH TAR ÉIS CEITHRE LÁ TRODA AGUS
THREATS DE GACH SORT. D'IARRADAR SOS TRODA AR NA
COINNÍOLLACHA A THÚGAS CHUGAT ARÉIR. NÍ RAIBH AON
TRÚPAÍ LE GLUAISEACHT. BHRIS SIAD NA GEALLÚINTÍ. TÁ SUAS
LE DHÁ MHÍLE FCA AGUS PARATRÚPAÍ TIMPEALL ORAINN
ANOIS. NÍ FÉIDIR LIOM NÍOS MÓ A DHÉANAMH GAN BIA AGUS
UISCE AGUS NA FIR TRAOCHTA. TÁ SPIORAD NA BHFEAR GO
HIONTACH. IS TOIL DÉ É SEO. [Let it be clear to the world
that we didn't give in after four days of fighting and threats
of all kinds. They requested a ceasefire on the conditions
I sent you last night. There was to be no troop movement.
They broke the pledges. There are up to 2,000 FCA
and paratroopers surrounding us now. I cannot do more
without food and water given that the men are exhausted.
The spirit of the men is wonderful. This is God's will.]

He got a reply within the half hour.

1618 HRS. ELISABETHVILLE: TÁ TÚ TAR ÉIS AN FÓD A SHEASAMH
AR FEADH SEACHTAINE. TÁ FAITÍOS MÓR ORTHU ROMHAT.
SCAOILFIDH SIAD ORT, B'FHÉIDIR ACH NÍ DÓIGH LIOM GO
BHFUIL AN MISNEACH ACU RUATHAR A DHÉANAMH. TÁ CUNAMH
MÓR AG TEACHT GO DTÍ AN DROICHEAD GO LUATH. BEIDH NA
PRÉACHÁIN AG OBAIR AGAINN AMÁRACH AG CÉAD SOLAIS. CUIR
AN PRÉACHAN EILE THAR N-AIS. [You have stood your ground
for a week. They are greatly in fear of you. They will fire on
you, perhaps, but I don't expect them to have the courage
to attack. Considerable assistance is on its way to the bridge
soon. We will have the crows (helicopters) working tomorrow
at first light. Send back the other crow.]

But there *were* no helicopters, as Quinlan knew. And no word now of
the promised jets either (they were still being denied permission to
fly over Uganda).

'When I begged them [HQ in Elisabethville] to send the jets, all I got was silence, silence,' Quinlan recalled. The suggestion that the existing, malfunctioning helicopter be flown through the Fouga-besieged skies back to Elisabethville seemed to him bizarre, at the very least. He was finding it very hard, too, to have faith in the arrival of new reinforcements at Lufira Bridge, and impossible to have faith in their ability to cross it.

His reply to the 1618 hours message, transmitted immediately but not received until 1715 hours in Elisabethville, was superseded by events in Jadotville.

1715 HRS. JADOTVILLE: Ní THUIGEANN TÚ AN CHEIST. Ní FÉIDIR LEIS AN BPRÉACHÁIN DUL THAR N-AIS. TÁ CAHBAIR RÓ-DHÉANACH ANOIS. TÁIM AG IARRAIDH CAINT A CHOIMÉAD SUAS. NÍLIMID I SUÍOMH COSANTA ANOIS. TÁIM AG IARRAIDH MO CHUID SAIGHDÚIRÍ A SHÁBHÁIL. NÍL BIA, NÍL UISCE. [You don't understand the problem. The crow (helicopter) can't go back. Help is too late now. I am trying to keep talks going. We are not in a defensible position now. I am trying to save my men. There is no food, no water.] McKEOWN'S DECISION NOW.

He summoned and held a meeting with his officers.

There was no doubt now but that our surrender would be demanded any time. We were all agreed that if we could get acceptable guarantees of our safety, we would have no choice but to accept, as there was absolutely no hope of help arriving in time.

We decided we now had to do the best to safeguard our own lives. If we could get surrender terms which would be acceptable from some person in authority, we agreed that we would have only the choice to accept or fight to the finish. It would finish quickly for us then as we were completely exhausted and had not a drop of water. We also knew of the high-level ceasefire talks in progress and, in view of that, further fighting, with the resultant heavy loss of life, would be unjustified.

But we determined not to surrender to Makito as we were not prepared to trust him. If we could not get acceptable guarantees from the Mayor or some other responsible person, we decided to fight to the last.

According to Carey:

Each officer was asked for his views. I was not in favour of a surrender; I could not accept that it had come to this. Nor could Lieutenant Tom Quinlan. But we were single and the decision easier. The consensus was that:

Our position was hopeless. We were surrounded by vastly superior forces and weaponry and jet aircraft. Our relief column had failed to get through at Lufira Bridge and in order to save themselves from being cut off fifty miles from base had returned to Elisabethville. There was no sign of air support. We had no water. Rations were almost gone. Ammunition was running out. Casualties were still light but serious fatigue was setting in.

A clincher was that, even as we contemplated a break-out towards the bridge (suicidal without suitable transport and heavy weapons), Lieut Kevin Knightly informed us his locks for Vickers machine guns were gone, that he had no replacements and our main source of fire power was virtually out of action.

The die was cast. The decision was now Comdt Pat Quinlan's.

He said we had come as a peacekeeping force to Jadotville. We had been attacked without provocation, had fought only in self-defence and had done so courageously. There was no hope of relief in the foreseeable future; our troops were out on their feet; supplies and water were an acute problem.

Pat Quinlan knew, quite simply, that in order to avoid further casualties, Irish and Katangan, he would have to agree to terms. He recalled:

> There was no other option. There was a choice of saving my brave men by that; there was only certain death in any future action and, even though we would have taken maybe 20 or 30 to one with us, it could not be justified by any standards: moral, military or political.

CHAPTER 30

Irish Crush Katangans in Jadotville!!
Sunday Review headline

Dublin. Sunday, 16 September 1961

The Sunday Review, in common with other national newspapers, gave extensive coverage to events in Jadotville. Its front page carried the news that: 'The 150-strong garrison at Jadotville, after four days, were this morning reported to have won the battle of the mining town.'

A government statement released an official UN communication from Elisabethville: 'News from Jadotville indicates collapse of Gendarmes attack. Gendarmes are said to have thrown out their mercenary officers. Comdt Quinlan is having talks with chiefs of police. Will send you confirmation.'

Swedish airmen, interviewed by reporters in Elisabethville, admitted that they had earlier in the week refused to fly a helicopter to Jadotville to supply A Company. The mission was, they said, too dangerous. A Swedish officer, at this point, told the airmen not to talk any further and asked the reporters to leave.

And, on a strangely prescient note, the *Sunday Review* ended its editorial with the view:

> The politicians who try to use the heroism of Jadotville without waiting for the facts will be poor men indeed. There may be much to debate; let us not do it in ignorance.

CHAPTER 31

I was not prepared to let my brave men die for nothing.
                            Comdt Pat Quinlan, September 1961

DAY FIVE
Jadotville. Sunday, 17 September 1961

Godefroid Munongo, tall, eyes hidden behind habitual sunglasses, and popularly said to be 'an African with a European brain', arrived to meet Quinlan at 1700 hours.

> He asked me to come to his hotel in the town for discussions. I felt that if he intended Katanga to be recognised as a state, he would have to see to it that our lives were protected. I took Fr Joe Fagan, Capt. Liam Donnelly and Lieutenant Lars Fröberg with me to meet him.
>
> After paying tribute to us for doing our duty as soldiers, Munongo and his people demanded our immediate surrender. I protested that there was a ceasefire and that this demand was outrageous. Munongo made it clear that there was no alternative. He made a long speech, mainly criticising the Indian (Gurkha) UN troops and praising the actions of the Irish and Swedes.
>
> He guaranteed our safety on pain of death to any person who attempted to injure one of us. I insisted that we keep our weapons stored with us in the hotel we were to go to. He agreed that we keep our arms stored with us in the hotel.
>
> This was written into the terms of the agreement.

We must be ready, he said, to move out of our position on Monday morning. If not, we would be attacked by the forces in Jadotville at his disposal.

But this and other promises were broken immediately we laid down our arms.

We decided that the only road open to us was to accept this surrender. Further action would have resulted in the complete annihilation of our men.

The ceasefire agreement between Comdt Patrick Quinlan and Minister Godefroid Munongo, signed in Jadotville on 17 September 1961, read as follows:

I, Comdt Patrick Quinlan, Officer commanding United Nations troops in Jadotville, do hereby agree to the terms of surrender of Minister Munongo because the Irish Force is here in a peaceful police role and any further action would result in the loss of African and Irish lives.

I also wish to state that my troops fought only in self-defence, having been fired upon while attending Mass on the morning of 13th September 1961 at 0725 hours.

It is also agreed that the Irish troops will have their arms stored at the location of the Irish troops' accommodation.

In the absence of orders from higher authority, I take the responsibility for this decision.

The agreement was produced in both French and English. Godefroid Munongo's document, handwritten in French, was translated as follows:

The Minister of the Interior of the State of Katanga hereby demands the Irish soldiers to surrender and to hand over their arms into the hands of the Katanga forces. In return, the Minister representing the State of Katanga is anxious to assure the Irish soldiers that their lives will be protected and misfortune will strike none of them. The *sine qua non* condition is to hand over the arms into the arms of our forces.

PS the arms in question will be guarded in a safe place.

Both men then signed both documents.

Surrender, for any soldier, is against the military instinct. For the soldiers of A Company, it was an especially bleak and terrible option: They had fought tenaciously and with courage against great odds. They had, to all intents and purposes, won the battle—only to be seen to lose the war. It went not only against their military instincts but against their moral instincts, too.

Surrender, in the culture of the time, also meant that every man in A Company would be letting down himself, his country, the army and his family. Quinlan was certain, however, that he had done the right thing:

> They had upwards of 4,000 with several hundred white mercenaries and civilian ex-soldiers attacking us but we fought them to a standstill until they asked for a ceasefire in the middle of the battle. Then with treachery under cover of the ceasefire, and when Force Kane had left the bridge (against all appeals from me to stay there and consolidate), they brought up more paratroopers and others to close in on us. We were on our last legs and further fighting would have been criminal on my part. We would have taken 30:1 but it would not be justified as we would not be furthering the cause of the UN in any way.
>
> I was not prepared to let my brave men die for nothing.
>
> We have no doubts and don't think I regret my decision. I have all my men alive and that is the greatest victory I could ever hope for.
>
> Of course, again with treachery, they broke all the surrender agreements except the sparing of our lives—and if anything went wrong, they would not have respected that either.

Private Leo Boland, with his 19-year-old's viewpoint, saw things simply and clearly:

> We had no ammo and we got no reinforcements and had to surrender. The whole thing was, there was a ceasefire all right, both sides agreed, but the other side broke it. They broke the ceasefire. I think it was right to surrender.

Dr Joe Clune was equally clear:

> It wasn't a surrender as such. It was an agreement which was
> broken. The Katangese started moving closer, our water was cut
> off and not turned on. The question was one of weighing up
> loss of life and, on the basis that it wasn't our problem, why suffer
> loss of life? We were peacekeepers.

Quinlan was incandescent with rage at the role played by the Belgian
mercenary officers.

> The Belgians claimed afterwards that they saved us but the
> dirty bastards—they wanted to kill us. They also claimed that
> they had only a few soldiers killed and wounded. But we killed
> at least 150 including whites. We could have killed many more
> but I stopped the slaughter twice. If only I had 81mm mortars
> (these had had to be left behind in Elisabethville…) and water,
> my 156 men against over 4,000 who were heavily armed
> would have taught them a lesson.

He radioed Battalion HQ.

> 1718 HRS. JADOTVILLE: BEIDH ORAINN DUL GO TGEACH ÓSTA. ÁR
> N-ARM PEARSANTA AGAINN. [We will have to go to a hotel. We
> have our personal weapons.]

> (OUT 1740 HRS) NÍL SUÍOMH COSANTA ANN. NÍL AON SLÍ AS ANOIS
> ACH ARDCHAINT. AIKEN, MCKEOWN DECISION NOW. [It is not a
> defensible position. There is no way out now except high-level
> talks. Aiken, McKeown decision now.]

Then came a message which Quinlan, his officers, men and Fröberg
found devastating, and incomprehensible:

> 1800 HRS. ELISABETHVILLE: TÁ CAINTEANNA SOCRAITHE IDIR
> CHEANNASAÍ NA BHFORSAÍ AGUS AN (RECEIVED 1905 HRS)
> TÚACHTARÁIN. *BHFUIL TÚ AG TREIGINT NA BHFEAR?* [Talks

have been arranged between the force's commander and the President. Are you deserting the men?]

To be asked if he was deserting his men was, to Quinlan, an insult on a scale unimaginable. Together with the message on the morning of the initial attack, telling him too late of Operation Morthor, it constituted a betrayal by the army to which he and A Company had given all of their considerable loyalty. To be asked if he was deserting his men was more than devastating to Quinlan at a time when he had been left hanging without assistance, had been (and was still being) stalled by Battalion HQ, had been left without the bargaining power of a UN presence at Lufira Bridge, and was desperately trying to do all he could for a company of men suffering fatigue, lack of food and dehydration—a company of men experiencing their own sense of betrayal at the lack of help forthcoming.

Carey was unequivocal:

This was a dreadful slur on the integrity of an outstanding commander, courageous and brave. It was like a slap in the face and the final indignity to an outstanding leader.

To have to make such a dreadful decision to surrender, for a soldier like Pat Quinlan, must have torn him apart. But he made it and so saved the lives of some 156 soldiers.

Fröberg saw it as 'a shockingly insolent question. Quinlan was a good officer with a strong fighting spirit who had certainly done whatever he could for the good of his troops in a terrible situation. We all felt so bad, so sorry for him at that moment.'

Hegarty too was present as the radio messages came in that afternoon and evening.

Comdt Quinlan didn't get one word to guide him, no statement of what was required. They left him on the cross … no matter what he did now, someone would say he was wrong.

Through a miracle, his company still lived. If he elected to fight without water or food, he could hold out for another few days, perhaps. If we surrendered, he was a coward. I for one think he took the proper course and, speaking from hindsight, events proved him right. However, he had many worried moments before he got back on form.

Quinlan himself was incensed and saddened, and said so:

> The final thing which broke my heart and set every man mad was a message from the Battalion Commander when it was over—'Are you deserting the men?' This message was known throughout the company long before I got it and Dermot and Liam kept it from me for over two hours. I did not discuss it with the men, naturally, but they were not fools and they knew....

He did not reply to McNamee's message until another arrived, at 1930 hours, asking if the situation was unchanged in Jadotville.

> 1935 HRS. JADOTVILLE: NÍOR DHEAS AN ABAIRT DHEIREANACH DEN TEACHTAIREACHT UAIT. BHÍOMAR TIMPEALLAITHE AR FEADH OCHT LÁ AGUS TROID FÍOCHMHAR AR FEADH CEITHRE LÁ. NÍ RAIBH BIA LE DHÁ LÁ, NÁ CODLADH LE CEITHRE LÁ. NÍ RAIBH UISCE. AN FUÍ LEAT NA FIR THRÉIN A MHARÚ GAN CHÚIS? D'IARR MÉ TREORACHA GO MINIC INNIU ACH NÍ BHFUAIR ME IAD. [The last sentence of your message was not nice of you. We were surrounded for eight days with fierce fighting for four days. There was no food for two days, nor sleep for four days. There was no water. Is it worth your while to kill the men without cause? I frequently requested instructions today but I did not get them.] I HAVE SURRENDERED HONOURABLY TO MUNUNGO. WE KEEP OUR ARMS IN HOTEL. REGRET THIS WAS NECESSARY.

A reply sent at 2015 hours arrived in Jadotville at 2040 hours.

> 2040 HRS. ELISABETHVILLE: RINNE SIBH GO MAITH. TÁ GACH ONÓIR CHOGAIDH TUILLTE AGAIBH. GACH BEANNACHT ORAIBH

GO LÉIR. [You did well. You have earned every military honour. Every blessing on you all.]

2055 HRS. JADOTVILLE: TÁIMID AG FANACHT FÚINN ANOCHT SAN ÁIT CHÉANNA. GARDA AONTAITHE SINN FÉIN AGUS FCA. GEALLAIM DUIT GUR CÚIS CHROÍBHRÚ DOM É, ACH NÍ RAIBH AON SLÍ EILE AS, ACH AMHÁIN BÁS LE TROID NÓ GALAR. CAD É AN SUÍOMH POLAITIÚIL AGUS MÍLEATA ANOIS? BEIDH MÉ AG FANACHT LE H-EOLAS ANOCHT. FREAGRA LE D'THOIL. [We are staying put tonight in the same place. United guard, ourselves and FCA. I assure you that it was a cause of heartbreak for me but there was no other way out, except death by fighting or disease. What is the political and military situation now? Answer, please.]

A message of encouragement arrived at 2200 hours. Relayed from Ireland, it was from the Officer Commanding the Western Command in Athlone. 'Proud of your gallant stand,' it read. 'You are constantly in our prayers and thoughts.'

A reply from Battalion HQ in Elisabethville, sent at 2226 hours, arrived in Jadotville an hour later.

2325 HRS. ELISABETHVILLE: CHUIREAMAR EOLAS I DTAOBH AN GHÉILLTE AGUS AN SHEASAIMH GHLÓRMHAR A DÉINEADH DO TSHOMBE. HAMMARSKJÖLD ETC. AG CAINT I NDOLA. IS COSÚIL GO BFHUIL SOS COGAIDH SOCRAITHE. NÍL AN SUÍOMH SOLÉAR ACH TÁIMID SLÁN LÁIDIR. [We sent to Tshombe information concerning the surrender and the glorious stand made. Hammarskjöld etc. talking in Ndola. It appears that a ceasefire has been arranged. The situation is not clear but we are safe and strong.]

However, in another of the bizarre twists and tragic consequences that so marked the war in Katanga, this message could not have been more wrong.

UN Secretary General Dag Hammarskjöld was dead, killed just minutes before as his plane was coming into Ndola. The

DC-6B *Albertina* had skimmed the treetops, then cut through the forest until a wing touched the ground. It had turned over and exploded in a mass of flame. Dag Hammarskjöld's body was the only one thrown clear, the only one of the victims to escape without burns.

The crash happened at approximately 10.11 p.m. GMT. With local time in the Congo one hour ahead, Dag Hammarskjöld died at approximately 2311 hours, Jadotville time.

Quinlan, knowing nothing of this, recorded a message for home consumption on Radio Éireann. Broadcast on the national airwaves, it was intended to give heart and reassurance most especially to the anxious and waiting families of the men of A Company.

2347 HRS. JADOTVILLE: PLEASE ASSURE OUR DEAR ONES AT HOME THAT ALL MEMBERS OF A COMPANY AND ARMOURED CAR GROUP IN JADOTVILLE ARE WELL AND IN HIGH SPIRITS. THE FIVE SLIGHTLY WOUNDED MEN ARE IN ABSOLUTELY NO DANGER. THE MEN FOUGHT A GALLANT FIGHT IN SELF-DEFENCE AGAINST OVERWHELMING ODDS. CEASEFIRE AGREED TO PREVENT FURTHER LOSS OF LIFE. FAMILIES ARE NOT TO WORRY, SAFETY OF ALL IS ASSURED. OUR THOUGHTS AND PRAYERS ARE WITH YOU AT HOME. WE KNOW YOUR PRAYERS SAVED ALL OF US. YOU WILL HAVE LETTERS HOME SOON. GOD BLESS YOU.

But things were far from well with A Company. Officers Liam Donnelly and Joe Leech, in their reports on the surrender, pointed out that the ceasefire had quickly deteriorated. Weapons were not permanently destroyed, 'as conditions of surrender include the storing of weapons in new company location—therefore they again, presumably, would be used by us.'

The men of A Company found it difficult, too, to come to terms with their new situation.

Carey was 'numb with shock and disappointment … a dreadful feeling of nausea in my stomach. For any soldier to have to surrender must be the worst feeling of all….'

Everyone thought of families and loved ones, worried what they would feel and think of A Company when they heard the news.

Sunday night, according to Carey,

> …was absolutely dreadful. Some of us discussed the possibility of a break-out, but without armoured car support and proper transport to travel the distance to Lufira Bridge, fight our way through, then travel the 80 miles or so to Elisabethville, it would not have been feasible. It would also be disloyal to the rest of the company … It was a sleepless night not knowing what the morrow would bring.

'We were always intended to be cut off in Jadotville,' Donnelly believed then, and believes now. 'The Belgians wanted us as bargaining power with the UN.'

On Monday morning, their arms were stacked in the garden of Purfina Garage and the troops of A Company became captives.

PART TWO

CHAPTER 32

Life was dull in the army of the 50s and 60s in Ireland. Then the Congo came up.

Comdt (retired) L. Donnelly

Ireland. May–June 1961. A Company comes together.

The men of A Company were no different from other soldiers who went with the Irish Army as peacekeepers to the Congo. They were decent, God-fearing, hard-up and bored.

They were of the Western command and many spoke Irish. The soldiers in the ranks were young—younger than they said they were, in a lot of cases. Some of the officers were not a lot older. The Irish economy was in the doldrums, poverty endemic, jobs and opportunities scarce. Life in the army was no exception to the national rule and was, for most, chronically unexciting. The men who formed A Company believed in the UN which, founded in 1945, was even younger than their youngest members.

Michael Shannon, remembering how it was, neatly encapsulated the mood and culture of the time.

> I was young and impressionable. I'd been through the exacting regime of the Military College for two years which was all about obeying orders and doing as you were told. I was 26 years old.
>
> The military function then was to look to the front and swing up your arms. In other words, to do as you were told. There were no political implications for us in the Congo situation; we were going purely and simply to restore order. No more. No less.

You didn't have to produce birth certs to join the army at the time. You came to army recruitment armed with a letter from your PP or Garda. If a young man was physically big, everyone assumed he was of age. Nothing was codified; there were no health or safety numbers. This was authoritarian Ireland; people need to appreciate how different the culture was at the time.

The autocracy in the country was enormous and went on in the army until army wives bucked the traces and demanded their husbands be properly paid. The men themselves couldn't do it; they'd have been accused of being disloyal.

Noel Carey felt, in Custume Barracks, Athlone, that 'the Chaplains had undue influence':

Religion could sometimes be great for peacekeeping but not so great for peace enforcing. They had no military training but wore uniforms. It was hypocrisy—too big a dichotomy between church and military training and thinking. Also, being over-religious makes it difficult to be a good military man.

Shannon saw this as part of the 'autocratic culture of the time':

If a Chaplain said Mass at 6 a.m., you went. As an Orderly Officer at 26 years of age, I would march the whole garrison, those not on military duties, to Mass on Sunday mornings and holy days. But that was no different to a merchant up town whose employees had to go to Mass or be sacked.

Shannon saw the culture of the time in the decision of those who went to the Congo, too:

No one visualised we'd get into military conflict with another force. We were soldiers of peace, men of Ireland inspired by religion and peacekeeping. There was a dearth of awareness of the real situation on the ground in the Congo, and of the political intrigue abounding.

We were delighted to be going from a humanitarian point of view, imbued with great spirit and also feeling, in the early days, that we were emerging from the Celtic Twilight and going to Africa to help the underdog. All this without any real idea of Africa.

Nevertheless, there's a thread of independent-mindedness running through the enlistment stories of the men of A Company. To a boy and man, they wanted to be in the army; to a boy and man, they persisted and got there.

Private Billy Ready, from Cavan, joined the army as an apprentice fitter at 16.

When I was being christened, given the names William Anthony Ready, my grand-aunt said I'd be in a war before I was 21. I was 20 in Jadotville. I wasn't with A Company in Elisabethville but a good few of the lads I knew from home were going to Jadotville so I volunteered and was sent on attachment as a fitter. That was how I happened to be with them.

We weren't expecting to see action. I was the first injured. When you went out on a peace mission, you didn't expect battle. We didn't really know the politics of what was going on. We were kept in the dark about the seriousness of the situation—or maybe they didn't know either.

Then there was Corporal Bobby Allan, the company's dynamic cook, destined to be inventive with recipes and brave beyond the call of duty in battle. From Kilmagarry, Co. Kilkenny, he describes himself as 'always a madly enthusiastic young lad for the army'.

I tried to get in when I was 14, went down to the barracks to join. They gave me soup and sent me home. I waited a while and tried again. I was 15 when I finally joined, a good, strong 15, as big as I am now but no meat on me. I was sent to Portlaoise and billeted in an old hospital near the jail. I was sent to Kildare barracks during the war and in January 1946, I was sent to Mullingar.

I wanted to go to the Congo—it was the thing to do at the time. A notice went up on the board and you volunteered. I've no regrets at all.

Sean Foley was a corporal with A Company in Jadotville who *did* have an idea of Africa:

I joined the army in Limerick in 1960. They were looking for Irish speakers for No. 1 Battalion [An Céad Cath] and I'd always had an interest in the Irish language and in music. I grew up six miles north of Nenagh, in Pucane, and went to Gaelic League classes and all that. I had a Leaving Cert with history and geography as my main subjects, and French too. [This would later come in useful.] I'd read about Africa and wanted to go overseas and was afraid of being left behind so I volunteered. I was 20 years old.

Foley, like many of his generation, came from a soldiering background:

My father had been a soldier. He'd served with the Gordon Highlanders in Sudan and India as a young man and in the old LDF too. When I was growing up, he used regale us with tales of the Khyber Pass and all that. I'd always had a yen to be a military man. My father came back in 1951 from his last camp and had the Glengarry cap with two green tails hanging down....

The officers, NCOs and ranking men of A Company came together to undergo training in Custume Barracks, Athlone, on 30 May 1961, as well as for 'medical and documentary processing in preparation for service in the Congo'.

The NCOs and ranks, according to Commandant Pat Quinlan,

...had been carefully screened and selected for good discipline and military competence. This careful selection paid dividends later in the difficult situations in which A Company found itself during the six-months tour of duty in the Congo.

From the beginning, the morale and discipline was of a very high standard—higher than I had previously experienced. I have no doubt that this *esprit de corps* was the chief factor in enabling A Company to survive and overcome many difficult situations and one situation at least which appeared to be hopeless ...

A wonderful team spirit of cooperation and comradeship existed throughout the company and, as conditions became more difficult, this spirit became more closely welded. Men had full confidence in their comrades to support them in any situation.

This spirit was built up from the formation of the unit in Athlone.

Quinlan frequently referred to his conviction that 'a good soldier will be a better soldier if he knows the reason why' and said that he, himself, 'at all times treated the men, who were expected to do a man's work, as men. Any instruction or detail that showed any taint of "Bull" was avoided. The men were always kept in the picture of political and military situations as far as possible.'

Training was rigorously intensive. Everyone was in agreement about that, unanimous that Quinlan was tough from the word go. Sergeant Wally Hegarty explained:

In Custume Barracks, Pat Quinlan found himself with the task of trying to mould together a mixum-gatherum of men into a fighting force. I'd been a gym sergeant in Galway and did a special line in unarmed combat, so, when Quinlan put unarmed combat to the fore, I was elected to do it. We were quietly killing ourselves one day when he came into view and, when we'd finished, said to me, 'By God, Hegarty, I'd hate to meet you on a dark night!' This had repercussions later, when we were POW's....

Quinlan himself described the training as 'intensive', saying that it had to be and that the allotted two weeks 'was not long enough to bring the company to a state of competence in all aspects of training.' It was, he said, 'compensated by the keenness of the men to learn and a very fine spirit which existed from the start. It was remarkable the amount of instruction that was absorbed in the short time.'

The men were given experience on all small-arm weapons and, towards the end of the training period, were issued with ten FN rifles with which to train. They did not get a full complement of FN rifles until three days before their departure for the Congo.

Weapon training apart, A Company was trained by Quinlan 'as far as possible on the type of operations which were anticipated'. This included such areas as mounted and foot patrol work, the setting up of roadblocks, searching areas, vehicles and prisoners, anti-ambush drill, imposing curfews and 'training on all aspects of aid to Civil Power'.

Time was put into conventional tactical training, too, with the company, platoons and Special Section working on defence and attack strategies, on night movement across country, and on street fighting. The need for security was constantly emphasised.

The company's fit and able gym instructor, Wally Hegarty, was born in 1932; he was 29 when he went to the Congo. He retired from the army as a company sergeant in 1963, after which he worked with Galway County Council and then Galway Fire Brigade. He and his wife, Sheila, had three children. His feelings about A Company are unequivocal:

> That company, A Company, was terrific. Jado was my second trip to the Congo. I was a sergeant both times. Niemba happened while I was on the first trip but I wasn't worried about trouble. I was my own boss at the time, no ties, so go I did.

Liam Donnelly was 33 in the Congo, and married. He retired as a commandant, after 26 years in the army, and was Personal Staff Officer to the army Chief of Staff by the time he did so. The army was in his blood:

> My father, Lieut Col. Bill Donnelly, joined in 1922. I joined in my turn, and so did my son. We were the first family to have three generations in the army.

Life was dull in the army in the 50s and 60s in Ireland. Then the Congo came up. There was something exciting about foreign military service. I was lucky to get back, I suppose. Cyprus, when I went there later on, was more inhuman, in a way. We went off in our Bull's wool to the Congo.

The Bull's wool of the army uniform comes up in the stories and memories of everyone. Paddy Neville, Quartermaster Sergeant with the company, says that the overcoat 'was great but awkward and if it got wet, it weighed about three stone.'

Neville's story parallels that of an emergent state and army, straddling the events and turmoil of a twentieth century familiar to every man in A Company. Now in his late eighties, he is robust and life-enforcing still.

I was born early in 1918. I did 44 years in the army and enjoyed every second of it. Including the Congo. I retired from the army in 1979 and joined in 1935. I joined in Limerick. I'm a Clareman. I joined as a recruit, a private. I'd a tendency always for the army types. My grandfather was in the Boer War with the British Army.

No one had anything at that time, in the 30s. I don't know how people survived. Every town in Ireland was the same. A few people had money—the chemist, the doctor.

My father was a carpenter and died aged 39. No dole, nothing in those days. I'd two brothers, one born in 1916 and little Gussie, born in 1921; he was a lovely young fella and he died.

The army itself was only 13 years old when I joined. There were a lot of British Army fellas in it then. Pat Quinlan was a very good man. A sound man. After joining the army in Limerick, I went to the Curragh and found myself in a unit of very smallish men. They were the crews of the armoured cars and I was a small man. We were the Armoured Car Division. After a few months, I was put into a horse squadron. There were no horses, only bicycles. We used be the laugh of the army! We'd stables and all for the bikes.

Anyway, I enlisted in Sarsfield Barracks and went to the Curragh and did all my training there. Every day's training anticipated the next day's. I lived every single hour of it. The Emergency started in 1939, when the war started, and I was put into a unit called the Fourth Cyclist Division and we were moved everywhere. Everyone was moved, whether they liked it or not. I was in every town in Ireland during the Emergency.

The Infantry cursed us for having bikes, but it was good-humoured stuff. For God's sake, humour was invented in the army!

In the Curragh, in the Internment camp, there was one camp for Germans and another for Brits and Americans. There were 200 Germans marched into the camp one night. They all came from Munich and they went into the German camp. The Germans were the most disciplined men I ever saw. One German swam three miles ashore after his plane came down and swam three miles a day when he was in the Curragh.

The Brits were useless people altogether. They wore beards; the Germans never did. The Germans sowed spuds, onions, garlic, and they got on to the Quartermaster General and said they'd provide the army with free vegetables. The man in charge of them, his word was taken as he meant it.

I married in 1941, a Donegal woman. She stayed in Donegal when I went to the Congo. She got £2.4s.0d. a week marriage allowance from the army and she was the richest woman up there. I had four children; three of them went to England.

When I came to Custume Barracks, Athlone, in 1951, to join the 6th Battalion, I was a sergeant for three days and a quartermaster sergeant for the rest of my days.

I stayed all my life after in Athlone, except for summer holidays in Finner Camp. In the early days of the 6th Battalion, we'd a trip to Ballinasloe!

The Congo started in 1960. In 1961, our block of service was picked to go—we'd been reading about foreign lands and wanted to see things: blacks and all the bloody things under the sun! We saw enough of them, God knows.

I joined A Company 35th Battalion. Mary, my wife, was delighted. It meant I'd get loads of money and we'd the four children then. The money and the excitement; it completed our love of soldiering. Nearly completed us altogether.

The 'loads of money' which delighted Mary Neville and her four children was hardly a fortune. Michael Shannon says it amounted to a UN allowance of about £2.12.6d. per day for officers, 'paid into an account at home. Other ranks got about a pound less, again to do with the old structures, and it was put into their payroll at home. We were also paid about a half dollar per day, which was called mingi money. The Swedes and others called it razor-blade allowance.'

Noel Carey, almost 20 years younger than Paddy Neville in Jadotville, has a different story to tell. Reared as part of a family of nine children, five boys and four girls, in Fairgreen, Ballysimon Road, Limerick, he was, and takes pleasure in the memory:

...a very big sportsman in my day. I knew nothing of the Congo before we went. I'd have heard of 'black Africa' and of Belgians, to an extent, nothing more. When we were going, the army couldn't find a map of the Congo anywhere so someone went to a school and got a roller wall map. Probably Pat Quinlan. We had a briefing and were told we'd encounter lions and elephants and whatnot. [He pauses, a thought striking him.] Even the helicopter pilot who arrived in Jadotville had no map! There simply were no maps!

We were told it would be peaceful, but that there could be rioting. We were expecting adventure, wanting adventure. The boredom in the army in those days was terrible. Morale soared as soon as Congo overseas duty became an option; there was no shortage of volunteers. When our brave soldiers died at Niemba, their funerals took on a national dimension as the funeral cortège was paraded through O'Connell Street in Dublin. The Congo took on a new perspective for civilians and the army alike. Training was stepped up.

I didn't know Pat Quinlan very well and didn't take to him at first. I found him abrasive, prickly, aggressive. God, but he made us train hard. He drew up a good riot drill in Custume Baracks before going. He crucified me! But the proof afterwards was that we were the best-trained troops out there. He was unmerciful then too. Gradually his professionalism, especially in Jadotville, the checking to see each man for himself, then the continual checking during battle, all made you see he was simply a great soldier, a very brave man.

And then there was John Gorman who, at 17, was one of the youngest of the private soldiers. From Wicklow, he joined the army in June 1959. He was at home, on leave in Finglas, Dublin—to where the family had moved—when he heard that volunteers were needed for the Congo.

I got onto the 35th Battalion. My mother didn't know because I didn't tell her. She wouldn't have let me go. The first she heard was when she got word I was a prisoner. I went for adventure. The very thought of going to Africa! You were going to a place where all the people were black. I was always an adventurous young fellow, a bit of a loner. I'd run away from home when I was 15 but I'd never been out of Ireland before.

Leo Boland was another A Company private and, at 19, not a lot older than Gorman. Originally from Donegal, he was stationed in Custume Barracks, Athlone, in 1961 along with his good friend, Private John Manning, from Leitrim, who was the same age. Both volunteered for duty in the Congo. Both were accepted and both fought in Jadotville.

For the young Manning, the Jadotville experience would have tragic consequences but Boland remembers with clarity:

My time with A Company in the Congo was my second time out. I was out with the 32nd Battalion in Goma in 1960. It was the first battalion to go abroad. Very shortly afterwards, the 33rd went and were caught in the Niemba ambush. With the 32nd, on my first trip, it was quiet. Just doing duties and installations. With the 35th I was based in Elisabethville. And in Jadotville.

A Company was 'activated' and moved out of Custume Barracks on 16 June 1961. Neville remembers how, '… on the day A Company left Custume Barracks with Pat Quinlan, thousands lined the streets of the town as we marched up them. We marched to Bunavalley Bridge and went from there to the Curragh and after to McKee Barracks in Dublin where the whole 35th Battalion was reviewed by An Taoiseach, Seán Lemass.'

Weather conditions delayed things but A Company finally left Collinstown Airport (Dublin) in four American Globemasters on Thursday, 22 June. Two of the planes were diverted to Malta because of bad weather conditions at Wheelus Air Base. Two planes landed at Wheelus, which was the American Air Force base in Tripoli, north Africa.

'We thought we were great fellas until we met the Yanks at Dublin Airport and then the crew of the plane,' Paddy Neville says, humour mixed with pride at the memory. 'We'd brown studded boots and butty leggings and we'd be heard coming a mile away. We wore grey woolly shirts, no collar and the army number across it like a convict.'

Sean Foley has a particular memory of the Malta stopover:

We were each given $20 advance pay, to tide us over for the delay in Malta. A soldier from the Aran islands saw a small, stuffed crocodile for sale in a souvenir shop, a taxidermy job. He bought it with his $20 and carried it under his arm. He put it in his kit bag when we flew on to Wheelus in Tripoli. We teased him no end. We wore tricolour braces over the grey shirts. One of the officers decided to lighten up things by allowing us wear pyjamas tops.

For Paddy Neville, the Globemasters provided wonder:

> They were World War II American Troop Carriers and they
> used rev up on the runway for half an hour to get power.
> Your teeth would be rattling! They were double deckers, all
> equipment included on the flight, including armoured cars
> and jeeps and trucks which went into the belly of it. We sat
> above that on two levels.
>
> Our Chalk, which was what we called each plane, landed
> in Malta on the way out. There were about 60 of us. They
> thought we were Koreans when we got to Wheelus, with our
> uniforms. As Quartermaster Sergeant with A Company, 35th
> Battalion, I looked after everything: food, clothing, arms.

Noel Carey remembers:

> …flying over England and France, passing close to Paris and
> eventually arriving at Malta where we stayed overnight at an
> RAF base. It was scorching hot and we slept in a billet to be
> awakened at 5 a.m. with a mug of tea. We had a big breakfast
> before we headed for the airport and the next part of our
> journey to Africa.
>
> As we flew over Libya, it was obvious we were in
> another continent as we looked down on mud-walled houses
> with date and palm trees in abundance and the azure blue
> Mediterranean in the background.

They landed at Wheelus and Carey recalls how, 'in a massive self-service dining area' many of his companions 'filled their trays with tubs of the sort of ice-creams they'd never tasted before.'

Carey himself went to the PX store and purchased a portable radio. It would later prove invaluable. He remembers too how their identity was mistaken: 'The Yanks actually thought we were from Korea as they'd never seen Irish troops before.'

As the temperature reached 90 degrees in the shade, the troops were allowed, 'as a concession', to take off their tunics. Carey recalls:

This revealed them wearing their collarless grey shirts with their army number stencilled in front and red canvas belts. All were wearing the heavy peaked cap of the period. Off the lads strolled to see the beautiful blue sea and bathe their feet in the cool water.

And so A Company made its way to the Congo.

CHAPTER 33

I am tired and sick of war. Its glory is all moonshine … war is hell.
                                        General Sherman, June 1879

Athlone. June 1961

A Company left Ireland for the Congo with fanfare, good wishes ringing, hearts high and eyes on adventure. But then so too did everyone else in the 652-strong 35th Infantry Battalion: the 56 officers, 200 NCOs and 396 privates who made up companies A,B and C, as well as Battalion HQ and Company HQ staff.

The Irish Independent, on Friday, 16 June, described A Company's leaving of Custume Barracks in a report full of the goodwill everyone sent with the troops. Under the heading 'Hearty Send off in Athlone' the report read:

> Headed by the 6th. Battalion Pipe, A Company of 35th. Battalion, comprising eight officers and 150 other ranks, marched out of Custume Barracks, Athlone, and paraded through the streets of the town before boarding their trucks to the Curragh and the first leg of their journey to the Congo.
>
> Col. J.P. Emphy, OC Western Command, took the salute as the company played out the barrack gate. The departing troops were cheered and clapped by members of the garrison lining the route.
>
> Cheering crowds lining footpaths of the town also gave the troops a hearty send off.
>
> At a ceremony in the barrack square a pennant was blessed and presented to Comdt P.J. Quinlan, a gift to A Company by officers of the Western Command.

CHAPTER 34

Much impressed with my company. The men are very good and I am proud of them, the officers are really terrific. We have a perfect understanding all round.

Comdt P. Quinlan, June 1961

Leopoldville and Elisabethville, June 1961

Pat Quinlan arrived in Leopoldville, capital city of the Congo and where the UN had its HQ, on 23 June. He wrote home immediately:

Leopoldville, 24th June 1961

My dear Carmel and children:
　　Arrived at 2am this morning after 14 hours flight over vast expanse of desert. Stopped for two hours at Kano in Nigeria. Tomorrow we go to Kamina (airport) and then on to Elisabethville. I was at UN HQ today and met General Sean McKeown and all the staff. The company will arrive on a number of chalks over a few days. Fond love and God bless you all.

Initial impressions varied among members of A Company but everyone, whatever their expectations, felt a shared excitement and sense of adventure. Noel Carey recorded his young man's perspective on it all:

The city (Leopoldville) was approximately ten miles from the airport and for the first time I felt apprehensive knowing, as we passed hundreds of natives walking along the roads or in the bush, that we were now a minority in a new world. We were billeted in a villa on the outskirts of the city and issued with green tropical uniforms. I received my UN beret too, a very special moment.

Leopoldville he describes as:

> …a magnificent city with sweeping highways, high-rise city architecture and posh restaurants and cafés. The local whites seemed to be living it up. The native women were absolutely beautiful and the Belgians seemed to have many of them in tow. This was certainly not what we had expected to find in darkest Africa and indeed we were surprised with the affluence we saw everywhere as well as the native deprivation.

He had every reason to be impressed. Boulevard Albert, the main thoroughfare, was a six-mile-long dual carriageway lined with fine hotels, star-rated world-class inns like The Stanley, The Regina and The Memling, where the foyer had a fountain and aviary. Every reason too to be shocked by the native quarter where homes were squalid mud huts and children played in filth.

The youthful John Gorman was also gobsmacked by it all. He remembers the heat when they arrived:

> It was very, very hot, of course, and we were wearing Bulls' Wool. I thought the weather fabulous and didn't know what was ahead of us. Nor did anyone else. All of the women worked in the fields. You'd see a patrol of them going off at five in the morning with tar barrels on their heads. The men did the house work.
>
> In Elisabethville, when we got there, the Irish camp was the one where the children were most welcome. And oh! to see the poverty, the poor children eating out of swill barrels was pitiful. Their cuts were always covered in swarms of flies. Awful poverty! Belgians took the wealth and Congolese slept in shacks at the bottom of their gardens. The country was fierce wealthy and still is. Is it any wonder they rose up?

On 25–26 June, A Company was airlifted from Leopoldville to Elisabethville, the capital of Katanga and a city of fine, residential avenues lined with Jacaranda trees. They came together at Factory Camp in that city on the afternoon of 26 June. This, their accommodation until 1 August, was not at all pleasing to Pat Quinlan who recorded as much in a journal entry:

> Elisabethville, 28th June: We're billeted in a disused sock factory. It's a shambles. Our accommodation consists of the bays of a disused factory and what were once the offices. We must also use the open bays for storing necessities. After a few days' hard cleaning and disinfecting it is now livable in, however.
>
> I feel strongly that such inferior accommodation and facilities are very bad for the morale of Irish troops and lowers their prestige in the eyes of the population and other UN contingents. It is so bad as to be degrading to any Irish soldier to ask him to sleep there.
>
> It is very bad for the UN effort as a whole to accept such inferior accommodation for its troops. It degrades them in the eyes of Europeans and Africans alike, with the resultant loss of prestige and respect which UN troops should command. The Swedish battalion, by comparison, has excellent accommodation and a highly organised welfare and PX system.

He later complained bitterly about the fundamental question of bedding:

> The bedding was in a terrible condition when we arrived; scarcely a sound bed or mattress available to us. Proper bedding for the troops was non-existent. The iron beds were of such inferior quality that they fell apart. This was NOT due to abuse. The mattresses were of the poorest quality I have ever seen and literally fell to pieces in a few weeks. (We never had sufficient mattresses at any time. Some men were always sleeping on bare springs, or on the floor.)

We have four house boys here, three Rhodesians and one Baluba. We are of course in a bit of a heap as we have no transport and are short of everything. Only three or four jeeps/trucks are working; our men are getting the others repaired.

Liam Donnelly too was unimpressed with the accommodation rented for the company by the UN's procurement officers. Neither the sock factory, he says, nor their subsequent accommodation in Sabena Villas at Elisabethville Airport,

> ...had any military deployment significance. We were, after all, in the Congo on a UN peacekeeping mission; a peacekeeping force with a delicate mission and a weak mandate. The Factory was an unclean, unhygienic place. We had to 'put up' with this location for many weeks, our job to safeguard a battalion store of Irish rations, spare parts and ammo which could have been more secure in any other location. Cleaning, scrubbing, disinfecting, started and continued all during our occupation of this location.

According to Sean Foley, their accommodation in the Factory Camp was 'worse than a disgrace':

> The shell of a factory building is what it was, with the toilet facilities in a building with a row of holes in the floor. You had to be able to aim well. A fellow was employed to come around with disinfectant, DDT, spraying the mosquitoes and flies and insects. He kept grinning and whistling away and wore a mask. We had no masks.

Donnelly, earlier, had been less than impressed too with the Transit Camp outside Leopoldville which he did *not* regard as, 'a good introduction to Congo duty for Irish troops':

> Looking back on the whole period in the Congo, this Transit Camp was the start of a long series of situations where the

168

Irish seemed to have adopted a 'putting up with it' outlook, an outlook I might add which was not shared by the majority of other nationalities.

But wherever or whatever their billeting situation, Quinlan continued to push the training boundaries, 'along the same lines as at home,' according to Donnelly.

Now, however, we were able to adapt our training to the terrain. Special attention was paid to anti-riot training and A Company evolved an anti-riot drill. [This anti-riot drill was adopted by the 35th Battalion and by subsequent Irish ONUC contingents].

Carey remembers Quinlan as being

...relentless, putting us through our paces persistently, making the training as realistic as possible. I fell foul of his tongue on many occasions. He never seemed to be happy with my platoon drills and this caused much frustration both to myself and to my platoon who were working very hard. But we soon settled down and even managed to pass Pat Quinlan's tests! I was in charge of soccer activities and we played soccer against other contingents: Indians, Italians, Swedes and Nigerians as well as local teams.

Becoming acclimatised was vital, Carey says, 'as it was winter in Africa with cold nights and warm to very hot days with the temperature getting up to 90 degrees by noon, which was very energy sapping. But we acclimatised quickly and found the climate quite good as Elisabethville was 5,000 feet above sea level and not as oppressive as the rest of Katanga province. We took salt tablets daily and quinine tablets to keep the dreaded malaria infection at bay.'

And then there was the issue, and non-issue, of suitable clothing and uniforms for the troops. Quinlan was irate, and vocal, about the embarrassment, lack of dignity and discomfort this caused the soldiers of A Company:

The green cotton uniforms were of all shape and sizes except the shape and size to fit the man. They were entirely unsuitable for wearing on off-duty hours in the town. Result tended to give men an inferiority complex, especially when compared with the Swedes and other nationalities.

In time, and with the hindsight wisdom of 20/20 vision, the army itself accepted that 'the non-issue of a national tropical uniform was a disadvantage' and acknowledged that 'Irish troops were alone (among ONUC troops)' in not having one such.

The official Battalion report of the 35th acknowledges too that 'the type and quality of Irish issue boots were unsuitable', a problem overcome by a number of ad hoc arrangements which managed to get the troops shod in supplies of canvas jungle boots, UN boots and even the black boots issued to Katangan forces.

When it came to the uniform proper, Quinlan's criticism is more than borne out by the report:

> ...the sizes available were not sufficient to allow for correct fitting and our troops could be seen wearing the trousers with large waists and several turn-ups to compensate for the length of the trousers. [The army issued suitable uniforms later that year.]

Quinlan's insistence on treating his troops fairly, as adult men and with due regard to their intelligence, put him at odds with the autocratic ethos in the army. He railed in particular about curfew and other restrictions placed on Irish soldiers, bitterly complaining that:

> Battalion instructions re local leave during 'peace time' are too severe in my opinion. Local leave was granted up to 2230 hours during our first two weeks (in the Congo), thereafter the time was brought forward to 2100 hours and later still to 1800 hours. On the other hand, the Swedes were out at all hours of the night. The restrictions on the Irish may be explained because of a few who got drunk and misbehaved. Punishment of all for the sins of the few is fundamentally wrong. The men felt that the

officers laying down these laws had a lack of confidence in them and that they were not trusted to behave themselves, or to carry themselves with dignity when on duty.

They were being treated as children or delinquents in this respect and at the same time they were expected to do a man's job and to fight and die or survive by their own resourcefulness.

Later, when the time came to question orders (those orders sending them to Jadotville included) and the UN mandate, Quinlan would be every bit as trenchantly outspoken on his troops' behalf. It did not make him popular. It did not get him the answers he wanted either, not then and not in the years to follow.

However, in those early days in Elisabethville, the members of A Company were tourists as well as soldiers, all of them alert to the world of new experiences opening up. Donnelly, arriving in Elisabethville, thought it 'a city planners' dream':

They built it from scratch. There were Jacaranda trees down the middle of the streets, every bungalow had a swimming pool and there were good hotels. The railway marked the dividing line between blacks and whites. A thriving, living place when we arrived and yet ... [he pauses, saddened] ... and yet the week before I left the Congo in December, there was green growing in the streets and the bungalows were all empty.

The excitement of travel and new places was the battalion norm. Michael Shannon says that of the approximately 150 men who made up B Company,

...only about 15 would ever have been out of Ireland. People just didn't travel, there were no foreign holidays.

When we arrived in Elisabethville, it was to find a city of magnificent boulevards, roadside cafés, coffee shops. Their own, local made beers, Simba (lion) and Tembo (elephant) were good too. To us it was the lap of luxury, not like dreamy old Ireland with its unpainted villages.

There were even a few high-rise buildings and it was dominated by a huge slag heap which could be seen from one part of the city to the other. There was no apartheid; black and white people moved around, minding their own business. We did notice mercenary men in uniforms swaggering around, combat dress, some with rank markings. They wore bush hats. The uniforms were purchased in Europe.

We didn't go into confrontation with them anyway; that wasn't our role or function. We would in time use gas to break up crowds and restore order. The Irish service helmet, which was plastic, was totally unsuitable for service. We did a lot of patrolling, which was fine.

In Elisabethville, there were battalions of Irish, Indians [Dogra troops, later replaced by Gurkhas] and Swedes. About 2,500 men in all [there were more than 16,000 UN troops throughout the Congo]. The mercenaries were scared of the Gurkhas.

Carey enjoyed the early weeks but admits that he, 'missed butter very much. Other contingents had food supplies flown in from their home countries, including fresh rations and post and could even evacuate personnel if necessary. This was not our experience.'

Post was often delayed and 'caused much anxiety and frustration' but letters, 'sometimes many weeks old, were cherished nevertheless.' The reality of the UN situation was never too distant. Carey remembers how Elisabethville, in those early days and weeks, 'was rife with rumours. We heard daily that there were to be riots and occasionally there were incidents with UN personnel and Katangans but nothing serious occurred.'

And so they settled in.

CHAPTER 35

The more I see of this place, the more I'm convinced that the situation will never be settled. Such racketeering ... Soldiers are treated like dirt by the UN civilian branch....

Comdt P. Quinlan, July 1961, Congo

Life, on and off duty, was fairly uneventful during the early weeks of A Company's time in the Congo. The sun shone, the nights continued chilly and everyone grew accustomed to the land and its people. Duties were not onerous but they were regular and included such activities as guard duties, training, sandbagging and building a defence of their location, defending a route to their outpost.

The political situation continued volatile in Katanga. President Tshombe, seen as a puppet leader backed by Belgium, was ostensibly in charge. Godefroid Munongo, his hard-line Minister for the Interior, wielded power through the army. The UN's acknowledged 'weak mandate was further weakened when it was interpreted one way by officials in the Congo and another by strategists in the organisation's New York HQ. With the debate centred on the issue of peacekeeping and peace enforcement, Dr Conor Cruise O'Brien, the UN's representative in Elisabethville, was keen to end Katangan secession even if this meant the use of force.

Anti-UN propaganda was rife in Katanga; UN soldiers unwise enough to venture out alone were surrounded and stoned. UN vehicles too were stoned and fired at and A Company was put on alert from time to time.

Otherwise there were games and sport to divert, films three times a week, books to read and—stalwart of the 1960s—sing-songs.

Comdt Quinlan, even from these very early days, had mixed feelings about the UN's handling of the situation, and his own army's organisation. He socialised, kept a lively eye on events military and political, wrote letters home, and kept a journal in which he always questioned things.

In writing, he often revealed the life-loving, caring man behind the soldier. All his letters were tenderly started and signed off with affection. References to personal and family matters have been excluded here and only those sections of the letters relevant to his tour of duty in the Congo included. In his letters, at all times, he is anxious to reassure.

Monday, 3rd July, Elisabethville

My darling Carmel and darling children:

We were at two parties. One was given by Tshombe—a rather fabulous affair—diplomats and ministers mixed together with African women with their babies tied to their backs. Tshombe is a very charming fellow and all those we met were very nice to us.

On Saturday we were at a party given by the Swedish battalion. It was pretty good and plenty of free booze. I met and had a long talk with Conor Cruise O'Brien. His son is here on holiday with him and he is coming with me as an interpreter soon. [This last did not happen.]

We expect to open an outpost on the Rhodesian border. We also expect to go to Kamina airport—one never knows what to expect here.

Swimming pool is three miles away and football pitch is two miles away and at present we have practically no transport. All the lorries, jeeps and cars were broken up and only three or four in the whole battalion are serviceable at the moment.

Life can be dreary as darkness falls at 6 p.m. and it is a long night without some amusement. There is nowhere much to go at night except a few parties. It is not recommended, or safe, to go anywhere else … The weather too is dangerous as it gets very cold at night.

With fond love to all, Daddy

He wrote again two days later.

Wednesday, 5th July, Elisabethville

My dear Carmel:

Just back a few hours ago from a 110-mile helicopter flight to Mokambo on the Rhodesian border. I am to open an outpost there. [Arms were allegedly being smuggled from the area into Katanga. A combat group from A Company was under orders to move to Mokambo to help prevent such smuggling.]

It is a desolate, sun-baked place, desolate as could be. The White Fathers have a mission school, dispensary and church there. We landed on a football pitch and were surrounded by hundreds of children of both sexes and all ages and also by hundreds of adults. I left my gun in the helicopter and landed with a smile.

It worked and my hands were shaken by nearly everyone and some even pulled at my legs to see if I was real.

We met some Irish friends of McNamee [Lieut Col. Hugh who also went along] from across the border, also an English major. They will give us a good time when we go there but I am not happy about the living conditions for the men. I will go down for a couple of days to open the camp and then I'll visit them occasionally by helicopter.

The language is a terrible barrier. I wish I knew French. I am writing in my room and I have all of your photos in front of me.

God bless, your own, Pat

Sunday, 9th July, Elisabethville

My dear Carmel and children:

Letters from you and all the kids were very welcome. I was looking forward to getting them and all the officers and men here were looking forward to hearing from home.

I had rather a bad cold and sore throat since I came here but am ok now, thank God. Please don't worry about me;

I am in no danger and I won't let anyone creep up on me either!

We have Mass in my camp here every second morning at 0630 hrs. We have tea break at 1000 hrs, lunch at 1200 hrs and dinner at 1800 hrs. The place was a shambles when we took it over but is in some sort of shape now. The Officers' Mess is in a villa, very nice, but we are awaiting furniture.

We are looking forward to a trip to Rhodesia. I am going to Mokambo on the border by helicopter again on Wednesday and will send a platoon with Lieutenant Noel Carey down on Friday morning.

The men are really a splendid bunch and I have no problems. Of course this life here can be very monotonous and boring so I don't want to talk too soon. The stock of the company is very high and the men know it and they are proud of it too. I wish we were away on our own. [This refers to his desire to be separate from the rest of the battalion, to be somewhere on their own. It's a feeling common to commanders who have a good company and want to be independent.]

God bless, as ever, Pat

He experienced the loneliness of the leader too, mentioning it in his next letter.

Tuesday, 11th July, Elisabethville

My dear Carmel:

I'm standing just now with my company ready to move out to stop riots we expect in connection with the celebration of Katanga independence today. It may not be necessary but we are not worried even if it is. In fact the men are mad to get something to do.

I get quite lonely but then I know I cannot allow myself to feel like this. I have too much to think of here to allow myself to be unprepared. Yes, I would still come here if I had my choice again. I would not like to miss the experience.

All my love to you all, Daddy

Inevitably, sections of A Company were ordered by Battalion HQ to other duties. Quinlan was unhappy about this, not caring to have the company broken up. He mentions this in his next letter.

Wednesday, 12th July

My dear Carmel:

Lieutenant Tom Quinlan and 30 men are leaving us tomorrow for Leopoldville to act as Mess Staff for the Congolese Parliament. Our company was honoured with this but I am not pleased about it as I wanted them here. I don't like the company broken up like this as the old unit spirit could disappear.

On 13 July, the day on which Lieutenant Tom Quinlan and his platoon, which included Wally Hegarty, left for Leopoldville, OC Pat Quinlan went by helicopter for a second recce to Mokambo on the Rhodesian border. He travelled this time with Chaplain Fr Joe Clarke, Medical Officer Comdt Joe Clune, Administration Officer Capt. T. McGuinn, Lieut Noel Carey and Sgt Kevin McLoughlin. He hoped to establish an accommodation and supply base for an A Company group which had been ordered to patrol the Mokambo border area. Things, as he recorded, did not quite work out:

On this second visit, we met with blank refusals to all requests. Even the children and the natives who swarmed around us on our landing on the first day were conspicuously absent on our second trip. The accommodation which had been agreed to at the mission school was not now available. The priest in charge of our mission informed us that the Archbishop of Elisabethville had given him instructions and that all further negotiations had to be with the Archbishop.

The trip was not all negative, though, as he wrote in a letter home:

Friday, 14th July

My dear Carmel and children:

I arrived back from Mokambo after a most tiring day. I went by helicopter—I hate them. A party of six of us went to recce the place for an outpost. We crossed into Muffilera in Rhodesia. Such a contrast to the Congo. The English treated us royally, put cars at our disposal and gave us dinner.

I could sleep standing up here most of the time. I never seem to have time to go to the swimming pools etc. I have several books but every time I try to read one, I fall asleep …

I'm tip top, thank God, and I intend to enjoy my experience here.

But he was observing, too, and learning from the experience:

The more I see of this place, the more I am convinced that the situation will never be settled. Such racketeering. I never dreamed it could be so bad. The people (UN civilian staff etc.) are making fortunes and they will keep the situation going. Soldiers are treated like dirt by the civilian branch. All the big allowances for the military are gone or going by the board but the civvies are getting the full $20 and more per day.

These weeks, and until mid–August, were relatively quiet and peaceful ones for Quinlan and A Company—even if the deteriorating political situation made for an edgy alertness, a sure and certain knowledge that things as they were could not last.

The heat continued to get to Quinlan and he was plagued with continuing cold symptoms.

Sunday, 16th July

My darling Carmel and darling children:

I am dead tired just now and my laryngitis is back again. The dust plays puck [a Kerry expression, relating to Puck

Fair] with my throat. One day I am all right and the next it is back again. I could sleep any time I lie down. Everything is quiet. We were on standby most of the time for the past week but it was only all wind.

His feelings of frustration continued overnight and he wrote again the next day:

Monday, 17th July

My dear Carmel:
It is very difficult to get anything here [for the company] as all items which were handed over from the 34th Battalion were broken. We have no transport or anything. We have no cups, saucers or plates here in A Company mess. The whole UN is the greatest racket of all time. Some people are making fortunes and the soldiers are suffering. It is sickening. I went to a bog industrial exhibition for an hour yesterday. Just like the Spring Show in Dublin. Very good and very interesting. It included a dance by 40 or 50 feathered and skin-clad Balubas. A weird and stupid kind of ritual....

His frustration continued through the week.

Thursday, 20th July

My dear Carmel:
There are times here when things are frustrating and annoying and you know how annoyed I can be over inefficiency! I can tell you we have some of it here too. My company is still doing very well but unfortunately we are being split up a lot and that annoys me very much.
I had a letter from Tom Quinlan in Leopoldville. They are completely cut off from the outside world and not even allowed to write letters as far as I know. They are guarding all the TDs at the Parliament. I don't know how long it will last but the men are browned off over it. This is just a

security measure for the Congolese Parliament. [Congolese parliamentarians were meeting at Louvanium University on the outskirts of Leopoldville to form a national, and it was hoped, unifying, government.]

Things are still quiet here but it is an uneasy quiet that could change at any time. I don't know what will happen if the rest of the Congo invades Katanga.

God bless, as ever, Pat

Liam Donnelly, who with 14 men had left on 14 July on a five-day safari to Lafoi Falls, was about to get an inkling of what could happen. The objective of the safari was to check roads and local reaction—as well as to enjoy themselves. But the water they were given to carry was unusable because of a jelly or oil in the water cans. Donnelly reported this, '... in writing on conclusion of the safari, *yet water sent to Jadotville at a later date by helicopter was contaminated in the same type cans, greasy and unusable.*'

On their return journey to Elisabethville, Donnelly and his platoon passed Lufira Lake and what was left of a luxury hotel destroyed by Balubas at Independence. Its destruction, Donnelly wrote, 'was the first indication to me, at least, of the ferocity of the native and the length he would go to in destroying European property.'

Tom Quinlan and his platoon, in Leopoldville at Louvanium University since 13 July, were also experiencing the less than upbeat side of UN deployment in the Congo. His platoon was deployed cleaning bedrooms, on the daily cleaning and washing-up after 400 diners, and the cleaning and maintenance of two large dining halls, kitchens and store rooms. His platoon had, Quinlan noted, 'undoubtedly the toughest and most unpopular job in the university and carried out these rather menial tasks very willingly and cheerfully.'

Wally Hegarty took charge of canteen accounts. Tom Quinlan reports how 'particularly' well he performed: '...as usual and as excellent as I had come to expect from him.'

'Generally,' Tom Quinlan says, 'the period there was a rather trying time.'

Troops in the Congo were sent regular tapes by and on behalf of their loved ones. A note from Pat Quinlan in response to one such from his family poignantly highlights the technology depended on in 1961:

Friday, 21st July

My darling Carmel and darling children:

Last night I got the tape you sent played. It was really wonderful to hear you all talking again. Distances are no obstacle nowadays with fast aeroplanes and the tape recording is a marvellous invention.

However, he was becoming ever more cautious about their situation, and more aware of a reality he could not accept quietly.

Saturday, 22nd July

My dear Carmel:

Things are still quiet here but it seems to be a kind of uneasy calm. If Tshombe does not join the Congo Parliament, there will probably be trouble but it should not affect us. The Belgians are a rotten lot here and they really give us the cold shoulder.

There was a bit of a row here a few nights ago, some Irish involved but none of A Company, thank God. They are all very good still but I don't know how I will be able to keep them occupied as there is nowhere to go here and they are bound to get browned off looking at one another. They are all very proud of A Company and are hoping we will be sent off on our own somewhere.

I would welcome that too. I'd love to get the whole company down to Mokambo. I'm not in favour of sending a platoon and I cannot send much more as I have 31 in Leopoldville. The task in Mokambo is to try to prevent arms smuggling from Rhodesia. If we get the whole company down there, the Irish and English in Mufilera will give us a good time. [The plan to send a patrol to Mokambo was cancelled soon after this by the UN.]

    With fond love to all, Daddy

Quinlan did some socialising, which added to his growing disillusionment about the Belgian presence in the Congo.

                        Thursday, 27th July

My dear Carmel:

    I got a chance to run to Kilivu in Rhodesia yesterday so I went. Rhodesia is quite nice. People are friendly and could not do enough for us. I met a John Scully from Killarney. He is manager of a big radio and electrical store.

    We have been attending a few cocktail parties here in Elisabethville recently. The whole thing is very artificial and tension is very high at the moment. The Belgians hate us and make no attempt to hide that hate. They may be damn glad of our protection in a very short time.

    In fact, they are already trying to make friends and I think they have finally asked for UN protection. The only other thing they know how to do is to run like they did before. I find it hard to have any sympathy for them as they are a miserable lot, but we cannot stand by and see them massacred if the Congolese go on the rampage against them.

    A Company is moving out of the Factory on Monday. We will be going to Sabena Villas, near the airport, the most comfortable station of the lot. B Company is there at the moment.

    The companies will change around like this every month or so.

    Fond love and God bless you all, Pat

An outdoor concert held by A Company on location on 27 July brought diversion and embarrassment in equal measure. Donnelly tells how things went:

I remember the lack of drinking glasses and mugs being embarrassing to visiting officers that night. Mess equipment was practically nil and was the same in every company mess at the time. After five weeks we were still 'putting up' with no mess utensils. I often thought it was a pity we were Irish on visits to Swedish or Indian messes; their equipment was so much superior.

A social outing just days before they left the Factory for their billet at Sabena Villas beside the airport produced humour—but also further confirmed Quinlan's continuing disenchantment with Belgian citizens of the Congo.

Sunday, 30th July

My dear Carmel:

I was at an Italian Red Cross reception and ceremony when an Italian general arrived for the ceremony part of things. The Italians run the hospital here.

When my Company Sergeant (Jack Prendergast) and myself arrived just a few minutes before the General, the Italians and Indians thought I was the General. The whole parade was called to attention and I passed through the ranks while they were at the salute. I had a good laugh at Eddie Condon [a friend in Battalion HQ] and the other Irish officers who had to come to attention too. Of course I told them it took the Italians and Indians to recognise greatness.

Everything is very quiet here still but only on the surface. The Belgians are shivering in their boots and any day now they are ready to run again. They really are a miserable lot and I find it hard to have any sympathy for them, but I suppose we will have to try and save their rotten hides if anything happens. It is very rare to meet a likeable Belgian.

God bless you, write soon as ever, Pat

Lack of transport which, Quinlan reported, 'had a definite adverse effect on the morale of the men', hampered the move to Sabena Villas:

> I heard more caustic comments on the lack of transport than on any other apparent shortcoming. We were later to suffer heavily as a result of this lack of transport when we were stranded in Jadotville at the mercy of overwhelming numbers of the enemy. If we'd only had our minimum requirements of transport, the outcome would have been different and we would NOT have been taken prisoners.

On this occasion in July, he found, however, that by dividing the company in two, he could manage the changeover in two days.

By Tuesday, 1 August, everyone had a place in the new billet.

On 2 August, in Leopoldville, a National Government was formed with Cyrille Adoula as Premier and Antoine Gizenga as Deputy Premier.

CHAPTER 36

*We are hoping our new Brigade Commander (Brig. Gen. Raja) will
do something about improving conditions for the troops.*
                                    Comdt P. Quinlan, August 1961

Sabena Villas, Elisabethville, Katanga. August 1961

When they moved to Sabena Villas, the men of A Company were
primarily tasked with defending the road approaching Elisabethville
Airport. With turbulence and political confusion on the increase
across the Congo, the airport was particularly vulnerable.

Quinlan's correspondence increasingly reflected a growing,
impassioned unease at UN and Irish Army handling of things and at
what he saw as the second-rate treatment of Irish troops by their own
army and the UN. His concern was as much for the psychological well-
being of his troops as for their physical discomfort.

Wednesday, 2nd August

My dear Carmel and children:

We are in villas—about 12 or 14 of them—near the
airport. The only trouble is the noise of the planes every night.
We have a chaplain here with us, Fr Joe Fagan. We were very
nearly moving farther than the villas yesterday!

Because of Mobuto wanting to take over the airport
at Leopoldville, and trouble expected at Matadi, a Swedish
company was given two hours' notice to be on a plane to
Matadi, and the Indians in north Katanga got two hours'
notice to move to Leopoldville.

Then last night, as you have probably heard on the news, there was a terrible massacre at Kasai. Congolese soldiers massacred 600 men, women and children in reprisal for 25 of their soldiers who were killed in an ambush.

Now that the Indians have gone from north Katanga, the whole of the north is open to invaders from Kivu to Stanleyville.

This Congo question will never be settled and I don't think the present effort of locking up the delegates and Parliament [in Louvanium University] until they come to an agreement will have the desired results at all.

We could be moved north at short notice but I don't think it is likely because if we did move, the Gendarmerie here would seize the airport and we would then be in a bit of a fix. There are not enough UN troops here to man the whole country.

It is a great tribute to the small number of UN troops in the Congo that they are succeeding in keeping some sort of peace and law and order.

Everything is still quiet here in Elisabethville but anything could happen. The Irish companies are well prepared, except that we don't have transport.

I'm not very happy about our Battalion Plan, however. There is no coordination at Battalion level so I'm just minding my own company.

In my present position, I don't need transport too badly because I'm near the airport and we could get there quickly on foot (if anything happens). I'm in a much better position here than I was at the Factory because at the Factory everything depended on getting transport and I would simply have had to seize every vehicle I could get my hands on.

I don't think, in any event, that we will have to put our plan into action. Even if we do, I am confident of my men. They are still very good but the strain is a bit much on them. We cannot let them stray around town at night. It is dangerous now as a few from the other companies got into brawls with natives, which did not reflect credit on our fellows either.

I wrote to the Commanding Officer and told him that the lack of a decent uniform for our men was detrimental to morale and discipline. The Swedes here have a very nice khaki uniform for walking out. They also have very comfortable quarters and the best of everything in their canteen. Their own government pays for everything. As well as that, they go on trips regularly to Salisbury, Victoria Falls and other places—paid for I think by their own country. Their overseas pay is also much higher than ours.

All this gives our men, who have only the old bush uniforms which are all shapes and sizes, an inferiority complex. The result is that when they get a few drinks, they try to assert themselves in the old-fashioned Irish way—they fight. The weather here is getting very warm. At midday the sweat rolls off us and we are hanging limp without energy.

All my love to you all, Daddy

Officers like Donnelly spent the early days at the Sabena Villas selecting platoon locations and Support Platoon weapons positions. They had been there little more than a week when Jadotville, without fanfare or premonition, made its first appearance in the company's scheme of things.

Sunday, 6th–8th August

Dear Carmel:

This is a very busy airport. There are planes always overhead. The African children, especially when they are very young, are grand little things.

I'm getting ready to go on a patrol to Jadotville, which is about 80 miles north of here. This is really only a training patrol and it will be one way of spending Sunday afternoon.

We are completely tied down here because of lack of transport and we are browned off with the inactivity. The transport position is scandalous.

Please God, I will not change the views or the attitude I had coming out here. My men and the efficient operation of my unit is and will be my number one concern at all times. The men are still very good.

Things are still very quiet too and all the expected trouble may blow over.

Quinlan did more than put his disquiet down on paper. He insisted on demanding equipment and transport which wasn't there. And he asked questions too, constantly.

'He created quite a bit of fuss,' Carey remembers. 'Every time he went to a HQ meeting, he asked, "What is my mission?" and "Why am I doing this?" and "Who am I responsible to?" After a while, he became very unpopular because he was creating ripples.'

Donnelly remembers Quinlan's 'ripples' too:

In Pat's position, I'd also have been asking questions at Battalion meetings. What was our mission, exactly? What was our mandate? And more. We'd no mission, no written orders later on when it came to Jadotville. Operation Morthor too was supposedly for all the UN forces in Katanga but we in A Company hadn't any task at all in Operation Morthor, weren't even told about it.

There was support too for Quinlan's position from Indar Jit Rikhye, Military Adviser to Secretary General Dag Hammarskjöld, when he wrote:

We were not an army of occupation or an army in support of its own government in the maintenance of law and order, but a UN Peacekeeping Force with a delicate mission and a weak mandate for its ability to use force.

The weather, growing hotter and more humid, did not help the impatient side of Quinlan's personality.

Tuesday, 8th August

My dear Carmel:

For the past week I was not in the best of form and had no energy whatever. The heat is getting worse

188

every day and it saps the energy and our tempers too, I'm afraid, at times. At midday, it is very strong. I think we are perspiring a lot only we don't feel it as it dries up immediately.

The Belgians come in for another blast of criticism:

The Belgians hate the UN and boy! do they let us know it. Such boycotting and ignoring you could not beat it. Never even a look of recognition. We may as well be shadows. They are foolish because I have a feeling that before we are out of here, they will need us and need us badly. They don't worry us anyway—they merely annoy us.

I just got word that Tom Quinlan and his platoon are coming back tomorrow. We will all be delighted to have them.

We have a new Brigade Commander. An Indian Brigadier. He arrived a few days ago. He is to visit A Company on Friday.

Brigadier Kas Raja, the UN Military Commander in Katanga would, eventually, support Dr Conor Cruise O'Brien's decision to take strong measures to resolve the Katanga crisis. But he would also, when the time came and A Company was ordered to Jadotville, advise O'Brien *not* to send a company of infantry off on its own, given the circumstances of hostility with the Katangese and their European mercenaries. Dr Cruise O'Brien would fail to take his advice.

When they met, on Friday as arranged, Raja and Quinlan got on well.

Saturday, 12th August

My dear Carmel and children:

We have our new Brigade Commander here with us—Indian Brigadier General [*sic*] Raja. He is OC Katanga Command. A young man of about 42 and I would say a good soldier. He inspected my company yesterday. We are hoping that he will do something about improving conditions for the troops, which our own people and the Swedes in charge have failed miserably to do, or perhaps have not tried very hard to do.

We had dinner at Battalion HQ last night and General McKeown was present. Eddie [Comdt E. Condon, a friend] and I were together most of the time. Eddie of course is as sound as ever with both feet on the ground. We are lucky and glad to have him at Battalion HQ.

Battalion OC told me I made a big impression on the Indian General when he called here. I don't know how. He must be easily impressed. He just asked me a couple of questions about my positions in defence of the airport and I just gave him the picture in a few words and invited him to see my positions. He had a general look but was evidently satisfied.

Raja would continue 'satisfied' with Quinlan as a soldier. After Jadotville, he would issue a singular commendation on Quinlan's performance in that arena of war:

I should like to make particular mention of Comdt Quinlan, who was in command of the company that had the misfortune to suffer so much at Jadotville. This officer needs little commendation as his performance in maintaining the discipline and high morale of his men during a particularly difficult stage of Katanga operations speaks for itself. I have great personal admiration for the initiative, courage, drive and restraint of this officer and I believe that he could be held as an example for all soldiers.

But Jadotville was yet to come and there was a hot and troubled August in Elisabethville still to get through. As the month passed the halfway mark, Quinlan wrote home about an upcoming patrol duty which would, through he didn't know it, hold a sharp warning about isolating troops when major conflict was planned.

Saturday, 19th August

My dear Carmel:

We are going to a party tonight—150 invited including Tshombe. It's to be held at a private house.

I have a patrol out today on the Rhodesian border, 75 miles east of here. They are to return tomorrow.

On Wednesday, I am sending a very strong patrol to Dilolo on the Angolan border 300 miles west of here. Dermot Byrne [Comdt Byrne was A Company's Second-in-Command] will be in charge and will have three armoured cars as well. The mission is to rescue the family of a Congolese minister who have apparently been held there for the past twelve months. The patrol will take over a week to get there, search for them, find them if they can and return again.

The Dilolo Patrol, so apparently routine at this stage, would be another example of a failure by both the UN Command and Irish Army to protect the lives of soldiers by ensuring they were not left exposed and isolated in hostile territory. Quinlan wrote a second letter that day, again telling of his concern and preparations for the patrol.

Saturday, 19th August

My dear Carmel:

We are preparing for the Dilolo patrol. This is going to be a big job, miles away on the Angola border over bad roads. I wanted to take the main patrol myself but McNeill [OC at this time] would not let me go so I'm sending Dermot Byrne, as arranged.

The job is an A Company effort but I'm getting three armoured cars as well to support the patrol. It will last between 5–7 days or maybe longer.

I'm sending a connecting link patrol under Joe Leech to Kolwezi about 150 miles from here. I will also have two helicopters to keep in touch and supply any needs and evacuate anyone if necessary. So the whole company will actually be involved.

The Congolese minister in question is persona non grata in the area and his family are starving out there as they are being held as hostages of some sort.

We don't know if we can find them at all but we don't expect any trouble. The natives are quiet as far as we know but then you never know. I will be in touch with them by wireless at all times and by helicopter if necessary.

I will go to Kolwezi myself, possibly on Friday depending on the situation. I may stay there for a few days so if my letters are scarce for the next week you will understand. It will take the patrol three days to get to Dilolo and I don't know how long they will have to stay there. They may have to bring back half a tribe or again maybe nobody will want to come back with them. It will be interesting anyhow and will break the monotony for a while.

I was at conferences all day. Some of these conference are maddening—such stupidity. I wish I could get a free hand here and I'd have been gone long ago (to Dilolo) and I'd bring back somebody somehow.

Fond love and God bless you all, Pat.

And so, with an excursion or two and outings for some of the men, A Company's period of calm and relative inactivity ended. Quinlan, putting the time spent so far into context, noted:

Considering all, this was a rather pleasant period but the political situation was deteriorating rapidly and the 23rd August , the date on which Capt. Byrne's patrol set out for Dilolo, marked the end of a period of calm. Thereafter, events piled up fast and there was no time for relaxation until the company left for home on 19th December.

CHAPTER 37

As I grabbed my Gustav, I saw a hundred shadows pass on their way to God knows where....

Lieut N. Carey, August 1961

Sabena Villas, Elisabethville, Katanga. August 1961

The day after that 'period of calm' ended, Pat Quinlan wrote home about one of the more telling of the swiftly occurring events.

Thursday 24th August

My dear Carmel and children:

Dermot left at 0600 hours yesterday (for Dilolo) and the wireless has failed to keep contact. We just got a short contact at 0700 hours today and all is well. The helicopter is not available for me for some reason or other. I'm not worried as it is a very strong patrol and we do not expect any trouble. I'm going to set up a number of intermediary wireless links tomorrow. I'll probably go as far as Kolwezi tomorrow to establish personal contact. I may be away for two days.

All my love to you all, Daddy

Carey, always enthusiastic and ever ready, had been an immediate volunteer for the Dilolo patrol, motivated largely by a desire to escape the rigours of life and training insisted on by his commanding officer, Quinlan. 'He kept us on our toes in Sabena Villas,' Carey says.

...with exercises, tactical problems and the usual anti-riot drills. When A Company was asked to provide a patrol for

193

Dilolo it was an opportunity to get away from him. I jumped at the chance and immediately volunteered.

The convoy consisted of two armoured cars, two trucks and two jeeps with Capt. Dermot Byrne in charge. We also had a Swedish interpreter with us. We drove rapidly on a good, metalled road to Jadotville, then just another town to us, and continued on this metalled road to another town called Kolwezi where we stayed overnight in a disused building which some months later was to serve as our prison.

Here we set up a signals station from where they got in touch with Elisabethville, even if only sporadically.

The next morning, we headed out of the town and very soon we were travelling on dirt tracks which meant we were covered in red dust from head to toe. I was driving the front jeep and had to wear goggles in order to see ahead. The road or track had deep drains on either side to cater for monsoon floods. The track got more and more difficult as we drove into the bush and it was inevitable that we would have an accident.

As the lead armoured car rounded a bend ahead of us, it veered off the road and landed in the deep ditch. We tried desperately to pull the vehicle free but despite every effort, we failed to move the wheels and, after an hour of trying, it was decided to strip the weapons and equipment from the vehicle and abandon it.

We finally arrived at a mission school in the middle of the bush, were welcomed by the White Fathers, and, after a swim in the local river, had a really great night's rest. The following morning we headed for the village of Dilolo.

The natives on the way were very friendly and gave us bananas which grew in the fields beside the track. We could see for the first time the real Congo with mud-walled huts and native villages all along the route.

So far, so good. But when the patrol finally arrived at Dilolo, Carey, Byrne and their interpreter went into the village alone, using the armoured car and minibus for transport. Carey understates what then happened:

There was some tension as we arrived in the village but we quickly found the family and put them on board the mini-bus. Without any delay, we made our way as fast as possible to the Mission and a well-earned rest and clean-up.

With a telling flair for detail, and a young idealist's energy, he recounts the return journey:

The next morning, we bade farewell to our hosts with the intention of getting back to Kolwezi by nightfall. I was really chuffed that we had achieved our mission as this was what I felt the UN was about. The countryside was fascinating with fruits growing all alongside the roadway and, in the bush, a group of baboons swinging in the trees. Along the road, we saw sticks with pieces of paper attached and this was the local postal service.

It was also fascinating to see native huts with the door of a car for the front door or as a window, the old and the new coming together.

And then we had another accident as our truck with the rations left the road. It took up to three hours to put it right but the local people had by then removed a lot of our stores, and who could blame them?

Luckily we had no one injured but this delay meant that we were unable to reach our base by dusk. We laagered on the road [set up defensive encampment] with an armed guard for the night. I slept fitfully beside the jeep and was fascinated to hear the native chanting coming from the villages close by. I was awakened suddenly in the early hours by the sound of running feet. As I grabbed my Gustav, I saw almost a hundred shadows pass on their way to God knows where.

It was a chilling experience.

As dawn broke, we were on our way and arrived at our base in Kolwezi without incident. It was on our arrival, and as we were about to settle in, that we had orders from Comdt Quinlan to return as quickly as possible to Elisabethville. We were not told why but headed off as fast as we dared with our aging transport.

Carey and his platoon did not know why because their commanding officer had neither the equipment nor time to tell them. Quinlan related a situation which eerily anticipated A Company's later abandonment in Jadotville but seemingly impinged not at all on either UN or Battalion policy about the wisdom of leaving troops isolated and unprotected with major UN action about to take place.

Operation Rumpunch, a major UN initiative aimed at rounding up the hundreds of European officers and mercenaries still operating in Katanga, was due to start early on the morning of Monday, 28 August. Carey, Byrne and the troops on the Dilolo patrol knew nothing of this. Quinlan wrote:

> On Sunday, 27th August, when it was decided to bring Operation Rumpunch forward to the next morning, Monday 28th August, I argued at length with Battalion OC that the Dilolo patrol would be caught out on a limb and could easily be wiped out. I argued that Rumpunch should be postponed until the Dilolo patrol was back at base which was expected to be Monday evening.
>
> My arguments were to no avail and he refused to convey my view and fears to Sector B or to Conor Cruise O'Brien. He was quite satisfied that there was no danger to the patrol and gave me to understand that he considered I was overreacting. Or perhaps he may have thought I was windy.
>
> What I do know is that the reaction of the Gendarmerie and the white population was completely misunderstood by Dr Cruise O'Brien and the UN Military Command in Elisabethville.
>
> I was flabbergasted and thought very hard how to get our patrol back. We knew, or expected, that they would be arriving in Kolwezi that evening and leaving for home next morning, expected to arrive around last light.
>
> With my excellent Corporal Frank Williams, my Signal Corporal, we went on to the flat roof to the airport buildings.

With the aid of a not very accurate map and a compass we took bearings on Kolwezi from the flat roof and Cpl Williams trained his C12 wireless and mast on that bearing. He was a brilliant signalman. After a few attempts, Corporal Williams picked up the patrol wireless, manned by a private, one of Corporal Williams' signalmen. I sent a message to Capt. Dermot Byrne, Patrol commander, 'Tár abhaile láithreach. Bí cúramach faoi FCA ar an bealach.' [Come home immediately. Be careful of the FCA on the way.]

Capt. Byrne got the message as the patrol was just about to settle in for the night—dog tired after an almost non-stop three days on dirt tracks which passed for roads in that area. They had also suffered transport breakdowns and moreover were threatened. One armoured car had to be abandoned after arms were removed. The other armoured car was giving trouble also.

Fr Clarke, who was with the patrol, was insisting that he had to say Mass. In typical fashion, Dermot Byrne told him he could say all the Masses he wanted when they arrived in Elisabethville but that right now the patrol was moving out for home.

Dermot understood quite clearly from the tone of my signal that there was something up and decided to head for home.

The patrol was stopped on the Lufira Bridge by a Gendarmerie roadblock and had some questions asked before they were allowed through. The patrol arrived at Company HQ in a state of almost complete exhaustion that night. After a short rest, the members were briefed on their role in Operation Rumpunch, due to take place at 0500 hours next morning. They got about three hours' sleep and were on the job again in the morning. A Company's role in Rumpunch was the taking of the Gendarmerie HQ and holding Munongo under house arrest.

I often wonder what would have happened to that patrol if it were still at Kolwezi, which was about 150 miles from base, when Rumpunch took place next day. The reaction of the Gendarmerie and the native population to Rumpunch was violent and not at all as the UN expected.

Why UN intelligence expected Tshombe and the Gendarmerie to accept UN conditions I could never understand. My firm belief is that the patrol would not have been able to return to base. In fact, I still believe that it would have been captured and wiped out. The day was saved by our wireless technical genius—Corporal Frank Williams.

Carey's account of their return journey dovetails with this, fascinating in its clarity and perspective on the reality involved. There are no portents of things to come, just a story well told:

As we approached the Lufira Bridge outside Jadotville, we were stopped by a roadblock manned by armed Katangan troops. I went forward to the roadblock and observed troops armed and dug in on the side of the road. I spoke with a white mercenary officer and explained that we were on our way back to Elisabethville with a party of refugees.

After some time, he eventually agreed to allow us through but it was quite tense as we passed the Katangan positions and quickly headed for our camp at Sabena Villas, all the time suspecting that something was afoot.

On our arrival, tired and dishevelled as we were, the main concern, as it was Sunday, was that we must go to Mass. I reluctantly attended with my men but resented the intrusion of religion as I did on a number of occasions subsequently. I felt the chaplains were allowed interfere in military matters which were none of their business and were accorded too much authority and privilege in our army of that time.

As we reached Sabena Villas and a well-earned rest, I learned why the Katangans were on the alert when OC Quinlan briefed me on my role in the following morning's UN operation to take over Elisabethville.

I then briefed my NCOs and the platoon on our task, which would be to secure the roads into Gendarmerie HQ in the centre of Elisabethville at 5 a.m. the following morning and arrest all mercenary officers.

Quinlan and the rest of A Company had been having a lively time of it during the patrol's absence. With 54 men missing on the Dilolo patrol, Quinlan had had the problem of reorganising his company's defensive positions. But there had also been the problems caused by the arrival of a UN Indian Dogra Battalion. Hugely resented by Katangans, the Dogras were the cause of much anti-UN feeling.

On Saturday, 26 August, a large group of Gendarmerie was spotted digging in at the edge of the runway by the airport buildings, obviously intending to sabotage the arrival of the Indian Dogra battalion.

Quinlan set up listening posts, got confirmation that digging was in progress and sent out armoured cars. The digging stopped each time these approached and recommenced as soon as they had passed. When he got orders to take command of A and B Companies so as to move in and capture the digging Gendarmerie at first light, Quinlan immediately drew up a strategic plan, on which he reported later:

The operation was executed exactly as planned, and at 0600 hours the position was taken. The Gendarmerie strength was 40. Two white officers surrendered and were disarmed by B Company. We found two mortars mounted with shells fused and laid out beside the mortars, ready to fire. Two machine guns were loaded and trained on the runways. All the Gendarmerie personnel were captured with rifles, which were loaded. Their wireless set was in contact with the Gendarmerie HQ in Elisabethville.

We got instructions to release the Gendarmerie but the two white officers were held prisoner and sent by plane to Kamina later that day.

Major Mathys, a Belgian Intelligence Officer and No. 1 on our list to be captured in Operation Rumpunch, was arrested by Lieutenant Leech at the roadblock while attempting to reach the Gendarmerie at the airport.

We got orders to release him as his arrest at this stage might have jeopardised Operation Rumpunch.

CHAPTER 38

For courage mounteth with occasion.

Shakespeare, *King John*

On Saturday, 27 August, Comdt Quinlan was briefed on UN plans for Operation Rumpunch: A Company would have the job of capturing Gendarmerie HQ in the centre of Elisabethville and of placing Interior Minister Godefroid Munongo under house arrest. Dr Conor Cruise O'Brien hoped that detaining Munongo, as well as taking the post office and radio station, would minimise the risk of bloodshed. Mr Munongo would be prevented from urging resistance on either the radio or via the post office telephone exchange.

Quinlan issued final plans to his company at 0045 hours.

We would be going into action in darkness and it was absolutely essential that every man should know exactly where he was to go and what he was to do … it all took some considerable time but was well worth the effort.

Carey remembers that, after very little rest, they were 'given general absolution, which concentrated the mind on the task ahead. Then I wrote what I thought might be my last letter to my darling Angela (his fiancée).'

His commanding officer too had a letter to write, to his wife, Carmel:

28th August

My darling Carmel and darling children:

I am going into action in three hours' time. I have had no sleep for a long time and I am too tired to write—I must get rest and lead my men.

200

Just in case anything happens to me remember I love you very dearly and I thank you for being such a good wife. God bless you, sweetheart. I love you all children, Eamon (Leo), Hilary, Peter and my two small boys Michael and Pádraig.

I am confident—but just in case—I place my trust in Our Blessed Lady.

All my love to you all, Pat

Operation Rumpunch, well organised and with the date brought forward as a security precaution, took the mercenaries, Gendarmerie and Katanga's leaders completely by surprise. UN troops in Elisabethville took over Gendarmerie headquarters, the radio station and transmitter, post office and telephone exchange. Minister Munongo was placed under house arrest. There was no opposition and no serious fighting. Moise Tshombe cooperated with the UN and, by the afternoon of 28 August 1961, all foreign and mercenary officers had been arrested.

Quinlan reported that:

At 0500 hours sharp we arrived at Gendarmerie HQ. All groups got into position at exactly the same time. I dismounted and went up to the gate, intending to ask for the Duty Officer and to ask for the immediate surrender of the Garrison. I found the gate deserted, but saw the two sentries had taken up position behind trees and were covering the gateway....

Donnelly is succinct about what happened next:

The leading vehicle crashed through the entrance of the objective exactly at 0500 hours; all buildings and Gendarmerie personnel were in A Company hands by 0520 hours. The offensive was led by Comdt Quinlan.

Dr Conor Cruise O'Brien and Brigadier Raja visited the position at around 8 a.m. and expressed their appreciation of the efficiency and completeness with which the mission had been accomplished.

At noon, A Company was ordered to hand over Gendarmerie HQ and return to Sabena Villas.

When the Belgian Consul in Elisabethville undertook to take responsibility for the repatriation and travel arrangements of all of the captured officers and mercenaries, regardless of their nationality, O'Brien agreed. But the Consul did *not* repatriate the captured officers and mercenaries and, by 31 August, had given asylum in the Consulate to 90 Belgian officers. Hundreds of mercenary officers began to re-infiltrate the gendarmerie and once again to influence the military situation. The toughest of them went into hiding and began to plot. Donnelly sees this marking a point when military events escalated:

> From this moment on, events in the military field started happening one after another, and led to Jadotville, the battle of Elisabethville (Morthor) and December.
>
> I repeat the question a private asked me when we handed back Gendarmerie HQ after a well executed plan had been successful. 'Sir, why, after all the fuss and bother of such an act, which could have resulted in loss of life, do we now hand it back again?'
>
> I could not answer then, or now.

Quinlan wrote a relieved letter, giving his version of events from the digging at the airport to Rumpunch.

Tuesday, 29 August

> My dear Carmel and children:
> Am I glad to be writing this letter after the activities of the last two days!
>
> In the early hours of Sunday morning, I planned and led an attack on a group of 50 strong Gendarmerie who had dug in with mortars and machine guns covering the airport. I had B Company under my command for the job but in actual fact I only used two platoons. Not a shot fired. We just crept up and sprang on them.
>
> At 0500 yesterday (Monday), I led an attack on the Gendarmerie HQ and took it by storm.

My Company was especially selected to do this; it was the only job where real action was expected. On the success or failure of this mission depended the success or failure of the whole mission and, as Dr Cruise O'Brien and Brigadier Raja told me, perhaps the UN in the Congo.

To enable me to storm the HQ and to relieve me of my duties in the airport, an Indian company took over from me here at night.

The Swedes and Indians cordoned off the native quarters of the city and took over all post office, wireless installations etc. Two companies of Swedes blocked the big Gendarmerie barracks to prevent reinforcements coming to their HQ— which A Company was attacking. Hugh McNamee with C Company and HQ Company surrounded a big hostel where some Belgian officers were living and took them. Hugh made a terrific job of it.

I had two Swedish armoured personnel carriers under my command. Everything worked as I had planned.

I went in civvies the evening before that attack and walked around the Gendarmerie HQ a few times. Then I took Joe Leech and Tom Quinlan with me around it again and pointed out their objectives to them.

Well, how did I react in this attack on the Gendarmerie HQ?

Thank God I never felt fear and was the first man through the gate. I never even heard the first few bursts of fire. We had every building taken in about 15 minutes and Tom Quinlan stormed and took the security guard of about 20 strong. We had no idea where they were and that was the only thing I was really afraid of. Tom took his own objective quickly and like the great soldier he is he did not wait for further orders, which I could not have given him anyway, but pushed on and came to the Guard and jumped them.

There were no casualties on either side. I really expected about a dozen wounded at least but we got complete surprise and they were so shocked that they were disarmed before they realised what was happening. When all were taken, there were two further bursts of fire and I felt sick fearing that some of my men had caught it—but no, thank God. It was my men who had fired to frighten some Gendarmerie who looked as if they had some fight left in them.

In addition to taking the HQ we surrounded Munongo's residence which was across the road from the HQ and guarded by about 20–30 armed police.

Nothing that I could say here would give credit to the behaviour of my men. They were like veterans—even the young boys. Dermot remarked to me before we moved out: 'God,' he said, 'some of them are very young.' They were but not a shot was fired by accident, or through fear or through nerves. Ah, those young kids were great.

Of course they are all ten feet high today.

We got General Absolution before we set out and our poor Chaplain asked permission of me to accompany us which I readily granted. I think his prayers did it all. He never stopped—I'm sure of that.

Colonel Waern [the Swedish Brigade Commander] accompanied my company just to be in at the kill. He wanted to interview the senior Belgian officer [when captured]. He was a bit of a nuisance in many ways but I did not let him interfere....

Fond love and God bless you all, Daddy.

The 35th Battalion played a formidable role in Rumpunch across the city. Michael Shannon gives the word on his role with B Company:

My own experience and mission was to do with the airport. Fouga jets were small, lightly armed jets and we wanted to get the pilots. We got approximately 20 pilots by stealing up, breaking in their dormitory door and taking them. We were carrying out our mandate.

O'Brien sent a message to all the Irish troops:

I wish to express my profound gratitude and pride on the results of the action. The results were so spectacular that they have resounded throughout the whole world.

Later came another message that 'the courage and restraint of the troops was admirable and should be recorded.'

For Quinlan events quickly followed one another.

Wednesday, 30th August

My dear Carmel:

A jeep with four Gendarmerie drove to my HQ at Sabena Villas on the afternoon of the 28th and, by means of a sketch and gesticulation, informed me that three Belgian officers were hiding in a house near Sabena Guest House.

They wanted me to go and arrest them—so much for the loyalty of the Katanga Gendarmerie to their Belgian officers!

Well, so much for the past. Now I'm packing up and moving to Jadotville tomorrow morning, about 80 miles north of here. One Swedish company and A Company will go. A Swedish major is appointed to command the two-company group with me as 2IC [Second in Command]. I think our main job here will be to help refugees.

I don't think there will be any further action....

God bless, as ever, Pat

The refugees pouring into Elisabethville were Balubas, persecuted by the Surete (political police) and victims of propaganda spread by Minister Godefroid Munongo and Radio Free Katanga. Their leaders had been arrested and they were now seeking UN protection. By 9 September, there would be 35,000 Baluba refugees in camps around Elisabethville.

The Belgians and others of the Consular Corps had been spreading and expressing fears that the Katangan gendarmerie were on the verge of mutiny and the massacre of Europeans. They would hold the UN responsible, they said, for any incidents involving Europeans. This had led to a section of B Company of the Irish Battalion and a Swedish company under a Colonel Mide being sent to Jadotville to protect the white population in that town.

The propaganda spread by the consuls achieved its purposed, causing serious confusion and concern. Even Quinlan, in those pre-Jadotville days, took it on board and worried that there would be repercussions from the UN's rounding up of Belgian and mercenary officers during Rumpunch. He noted:

> I am not at all sure that it was the correct thing to do. I think the Belgian officers in many ways restrained the Gendarmerie and now it could easily lead to a massacre of whites here in Katanga. I don't know whether the decision to expel the Belgian officers was correct or not. I am afraid it was not and that we have started something which will take a long time to settle. However, that's the politicians' job.
>
> Many of the white officers were not Belgians. They were mercenaries, from many countries and a hard lot. I have no sympathy whatsoever for them. Already refugees are flowing in from the North… [He is referring to people of the Baluba from Kasai province.]

However, Quinlan would learn, as would his troops, that the reverse would in fact be the case. The mercenary and Belgian officers would use the Gendarmerie against the UN, would arm and have white people in the ranks of the Gendarmerie they controlled.

Between 29 and 31 August, A Company was moved from Sabena Villas to a new airport location. Sean Foley recalls one of the lighter moments during those two days. He was on airport duty when,

> …there was a rustling in the trees and I called out. A tall, African man came out in nothing but his underpants. He was a policeman and had taken off every bit of his uniform lest we shoot him when we found out what he was. He'd been posted to observe us and decided discretion was the better part of valour when we heard him!

But confusion was more the norm, together with the dangers running alongside it, as Quinlan and A Company would rediscover within days.

CHAPTER 39

He is a man of courage who does not run away, but remains at his post and fights against the enemy.

Socrates

On 31 August, Quinlan and A Company were part of a humiliating and frustrating exercise which illustrated the chaos and indecision amongst those running things for the UN in the Congo. In a gesture which struck Secretary General Dag Hammarskjöld in New York as both 'foolish and inappropriate', it was decided to provide a UN and Gendarmerie guard of honour for those of the Belgian and mercenary officers who would be seen to leave the Congo. These were men who had been captured by A Company, then freed to go to the Consulate and who would, in any event, return to the Congo by other routes. Quinlan noted the debacle in his journal:

On 31st August, when A Company was in command of the airport, it was decided to fly the captured mercenaries to Leopoldville—supposed to be on their way home to Europe. Within days they were all back in Elisabethville with double or treble their numbers. Sector B and Katanga command gave permission for a Guard of Honour of Gendarmerie to give the mercenaries and Belgian officials a send-off at the airport.

It was about 1400 hours when most of A Company personnel were having siesta and as always on such occasions wore only their underpants or football knocks.

The alarm was raised as five or six trucks loaded with Gendarmerie came at speed to the airport entrance and started to dismount in a big rush.

On the alarm being sounded, all the men were immediately at their posts—most of them, including a mounted machine-gun section on the flat roof, wearing only their underpants. The entrance was heavily reinforced and Gendarmerie started to assemble in formation.

I frantically telephoned Battalion HQ to be told in a matter-of-fact fashion that it was OK—the Gendarmerie had permission to provide a Guard of Honour (with UN troops involved too) for departing mercenaries/Belgian officers.

Battalion HQ neglected completely to inform A Company of the fact that armed Gendarmerie—more than 100 strong—would be arriving to form a Guard of Honour.

Once again the alertness, discipline and confidence of the men of A Company saved the day.

At least one member of A Company was alert in a way Quinlan hadn't bargained for: Foley had a Brownie box camera with him in the control tower at the airport. 'When the mercenaries we'd captured were being flown out, I got a few good pictures,' he says. 'They came back a few weeks later through other entry points, of course.'

Quinlan, in his journal, also highlighted the incongruity of A Company's position:

We were charged with the defence of the airport, and yet permission was given for an armed party of Gendarmerie to enter the airport without one word of this information being given to A Company.

When I protested strongly, I was met with a blank stare.

These two instances [the Dilolo patrol and the airport Gendarmerie guard of honour] give a good picture of how Operation Morthor on 13th September was viewed at Battalion HQ and why A Company at Jadotville— surrounded by hostile Gendarmerie, mercenaries and armed civilians—was NOT informed of the actions planned for the morning of 13th September.

Adding to the confusion caused by the guard-of-honour incident, the men of A Company found themselves, at the same time precisely, involved in the repercussions from a prison break-out.

> In the middle of it all, prisoners who had escaped from a local prison rushed into our position, followed by firing police, seeking asylum. So we had great fun for a while. They claimed they were political prisoners and the police claimed they were criminals.
>
> We, however, took them under our protection and gave them food and accommodation in the transit building. Some of them had bullet and other wounds. They said that 600 of them made a mass breakout when they were ordered into the forest, where they expected to be shot. Several were killed. I am sure there are many criminal prisoners among them and there is certainly a big splattering of the ANC mutineers of 1960.
>
> During the night, other escaped prisoners arrived at various times in a very exhausted condition. One of these stated he had left his brother in a collapsed state about a mile from the airport. I dispatched a party to search for this man, with the brother as a guide, but he was not found.

The chaos of lost family members, starving and wounded prisoners and Belgians trying to leave the Congo from the airport continued for days. The mercenary later captured at Jadotville, Pierre van der Wegen, was one of those seeking, and failing, to get away. Quinlan would later remember and recognise him.

Donnelly had his own involvement with an escaped prisoner to report:

> One of the prisoners got as far as a church and school on the south side of Elisabethville. A priest arrived at the airport to ask for a UN car to go to the priest's residence

and take the man away safely after dark. He had been a pupil in the school and had become interested in politics. Lieutenant Leech, Sgt Monaghan and I took him back safely in the company saloon.

And then, early in September, the up-country mining town of Jadotville became an ever-closer reality for A Company. From the beginning, it caused confusion.

Saturday, 2nd September

My dear Carmel and children:

I did not go to Jadotville after all. The order was cancelled as I was about to move out. Members of B Company, with a Swedish company, went to Jadotville but are returning today or tomorrow....

A Company is moving out of here [Sabena Villas] to a new camp where the battalion is being concentrated near the city. The Indians [Dogra Company] are taking over here. Of course that may change again as you have no idea of the confusion of orders going on.

We have thousands of refugees on our hands now. They are coming in droves. These are all Kasai Africans [Baluba tribespeople] and they are being threatened and beaten up and we hear many killed also by Munongo's outfit here.

The weather is getting terribly warm. It is just sweltering from about 1100–1600 hours.

All my love to you all, Daddy

CHAPTER 40

With the white population of Jadotville not in danger, in fact hostile
to the UN, our mission was unrealistic. I returned with my troops
to Elisabethville.
                    Major Mide to Comdt Quinlan, September 1961

Group Mide was formed on 29 August. Comprising a Swedish
company and B Company 35th Irish Infantry Battalion, it took
its name from the Swedish commander of the Group, a Major
Mide.

Even in the forming of *that* group there was confusion. A
Company had at first been mooted for the detail, but then replaced by
B Company. No explanation was given. However, unlike A Company
days later, Group Mide was given a Special Operation Order, with its
mission clearly set out in writing:

> Group Mide will maintain law and order in the Jadotville
> area and in addition provide accommodation, protection and
> transport as required for the personnel and families of those
> falling within the terms of the Security Council Resolution
> of 21st February.

A half-dozen Tasks assigned to the group were also, and clearly,
outlined.

An assembly centre was to be set up in Jadotville for white
military personnel and their families. Protection, as well as transport to
Elisabethville, was to be provided, if necessary, for military personnel
and their families. Group Mide was to look after internal security
operations and maintain peace in the Jadotville area. The troops
were to ensure the security of vital installations. Movements of the

211

Gendarmerie by rail and road were to be controlled and reported. The Group was also ordered to:

> Make every effort to negotiate with and explain to local Gendarmerie commanders the present situation and policy with regard to the status of Gendarmerie Forces and the necessity for their co-operation in the maintenance of law and order.

With existing hostility to the UN in the Jadotville area made worse by the arrests of mercenaries and house arrest of Godefroid Munongo during Operation Rumpunch, it was difficult to understand why troops had been sent there. Group Mide did not stay long. As Quinlan and A Company would themselves discover within days, the situation was not at all as they had been given to believe.

Group Mide found the civilian population and Union Minière very much in control of things in Jadotville—and *very* resentful of the UN presence. Major Mide reported this back to Elisabethville, firmly stating that the civilian population was *not* in danger, was in fact hostile to the UN. As a consequence, he said, he considered their mission was *not* realistic. Major Mide later confirmed all of this himself to Pat Quinlan.

Operation Morthor, already planned for 13 September, was another consideration. Swedish officers of the Katanga Command wanted all of their troops available for action in Elisabethville within ten days. They were also very aware of the dangers to a force isolated 80 miles from the Katangan capital. And so Major Mide's Swedish company was withdrawn from Jadotville on 2 September 1961. B Company followed the Swedes back to Elisabethville.

Dr Conor Cruise O'Brien has written that B Company was sent to Jadotville because of 'diplomatic and consular anxieties'. He makes no comment about the Swedish company but writes too that Brigadier Raja, 'rightly wanted the company withdrawn on military grounds ... A Company replaced it on September 3rd.'

Why *this* was militarily acceptable was not explained. What is certain, though, is that Belgian pressure for Group Mide's replacement was immediate.

Paul Henri Spaak, Belgium's Foreign Minister, demanded, directly from the UN in New York, that troops be sent to Jadotville to protect the white population. In response to this, Colonel Jonas Waern, the Swedish Brigade Commander in Elisabethville in charge of Sector B, asked both the Swedish and Indian battalions to send companies to the mining town. The commanders of both battalions refused. They wanted, they said, to keep their battalions intact for operations in Elisabethville.

Spaak persisted and General Sean McKeown, UN Force Commander in the Congo, directed the Irish Battalion in Elisabethville to send troops the 80 miles up country to the mining town.

Colonel (retired) John Terence O'Neill has written that Spaak's request 'could be seen as a means of luring UN forces into a trap, providing the Katangese with hostages and thereby frustrating UN efforts to bring an end to Katanga's defiance.'

Or, as General Indar Jit Rikhye, Military Adviser to the UN Secretary General, wrote later and with hindsight: 'The invitation was obviously a ruse to entrap UN troops.'

A Company was ordered to Jadotville on 3 September 1961. Unlike Group Mide, A Company was given no Special Operation Order. Quinlan was given a verbal order only, one which made it clear that his mission was to protect the white population of Jadotville from a supposed 'native uprising'. Donnelly, in his submission to the Chief of Staff seeking an enquiry, seriously questioned the wisdom, and real reason, for sending A Company to Jadotville:

> It is unbelievable and unacceptable that A Company, depleted as it was through lack of transport, supplies, arms and ammunition, should have been ordered to Jadotville on the return of Group Mide. What was not acceptable to the Swedish Battalion should not have been acceptable to the Irish Battalion.
>
> What is even more confusing is that Group Mide consisted of two companies: 3 Company Swedish Battalion and B Company Irish Battalion.
>
> Full transport facilities were available to the force that 'fled, 'returned' or was 'withdrawn' from Jadotville on 2nd

September 1961 [Donnelly's choice of three different terms is deliberate as no record can be found to indicate the exact term used].

The restricted transport made available to A Company for its move on 3rd and 4th September 1961 led to obvious weaknesses in the company's operation over the following three weeks.

Swedish officers later informed us that the commander of Group Mide returned with the force to Elisabethville as he would not accept the 'mission' or the 'location'.

All of this continues to beg the question—why was an unreinforced infantry company deployed at Jadotville on 3/4th September 1961?

Donnelly lays down the facts with searing precision:

A Company was deployed in a peacekeeping role, given the unreal mission of protecting a white population which resented the UN presence. The company was deployed minus 81mm mortars, minus water reserve containers, minus emergency rations and with only normal munitions. Provisions were to be obtained locally from a people who didn't want them in town. They were deployed too in a location previously procured by UN authorities and most unsuitable.

Michael Shannon, as a member of B Company, went to Jadotville when Group Mide was there. His story further corroborates events:

After Rumpunch, we got an order: B Company was to proceed to Jadotville to take over from the Swedes. We did exactly that. When we arrived, the Swedes said there was no reason for any of us to be there, that the (generally Belgian) whites were hostile.

The second night in Jadotville about 50 or 60 whites came out to demonstrate against us. Our company commander, Alo McMahon, met with them. They said we

214

shouldn't be there. Eventually they just drifted back to town. We relayed this back to Battalion HQ who took cognizance and told us to withdraw.

I was told to head back with my own patrol of about 40, to go ahead. On the way back to Elisabethville, I don't know why, I stopped at Lufira Bridge. There were two bridges in fact, a road bridge and railway bridge.

The Belgian Foreign Minister, Paul Henry Spaak, had been informed of our departure. This did not suit Belgian political objectives so Spaak put pressure on the UN in New York and it was decided to send A Company intact to Jadotville and withdraw the rest of B Company.

At Elisabethville Airport, before they left for Jadotville, I met with Pat Quinlan and Liam Donnelly and officers of A Company and told them about the incidents of whites not wanting UN troops there etc.

Pat Quinlan and the men under his command were victims of a colonial plot by the Belgians and Rhodesians. When the fighting was going in Jadotville, the British would prove their duplicity too when they wouldn't allow the Ethiopian jets land to refuel.

A Company and Quinlan, soldiers who had taken an oath to obey orders, when lawful, went as directed to Jadotville. But Quinlan, that September, loudly decried the fact that:

intelligence and information on operations in the Congo were disseminated by the army on a 'need to know' basis, interpreted at Battalion HQ as 'they don't need to know' which ended up as a 'tell them nothing' policy. This is a severe criticism but borne out in a number of instances. Whether it was a deliberate policy or downright inefficiency, it is hard to tell.

One thing certainly borne out is the fact that consequences of actions or follow-up were never considered. It is also quite clear that whatever intelligence was available was either misinterpreted or ignored.

The clear lesson of the Dilolo Patrol incident (that troops should not be left vulnerable and isolated from major action) went unlearned. The information about hostilities, brought by both the Swedish and Irish companies who had gone to Jadotville, was ignored.

Foley of A Company has an unequivocal view of things:

We were like sacrificial lambs! The Swedish were much better equipped than we were and they didn't like it there and left. B Company came back too. We were dumped there because the Belgians wanted their interests protected.

And so it would prove.

'We were sent to Jadotville on a direct order from General McKeown,' Quinlan wrote.

I found the situation exactly as Major Mide had explained it to me when he returned. I reported this several times and in detail to Battalion HQ, requesting either heavy reinforcements or to be withdrawn....

I would not dream of withdrawing without orders.

CHAPTER 41

If a two-company strong body was on military grounds rightly withdrawn [from Jadotville], it was madness to replace it with a group half that size.

Col. (retired) T. O'Neill, International Peacekeeping
It was 1100 hours, and a Sunday, when Quinlan got orders to move his company to Jadotville. His report gives the bare facts:

> B company and the Swedish company had returned from Jadotville and I was informed (by Battalion HQ) that the white population there were apprehensive and had requested UN protection. As well as my company I had under my command one section of two armoured cars under Lieut Kevin Knightly. I was told that M. Spaak, the Belgian Foreign Minister, had requested this protection for the people of Jadotville.
>
> Intelligence estimated Gendarmerie strength in the area as 150 in Jadotville itself, 1600 in nearby Shinkolobwe and 350 paratroopers in Kolwezi.
>
> As soon as I got transport from the Swedish battalion my Number 2 Platoon, with operation elements, mortars, anti-tanks, two armoured cars and elements of Company HQ, left for Jadotville under Capt. Dermot Byrne. The transport returned late that night and preparations were made to remove the remainder of the company next morning.
>
> We had two 81mm mortars on location to A Company for defence of the airport but, owing to the lack of transport to move the mortar ammunition, we had to leave these valuable weapons behind.

Possibly our worst blow was the fact that we also had to leave behind our emergency supply of American pack rations (ten days' supply, approximately) because of lack of transport.

These rations were to be sent to Jadotville as soon as transport was available but they never arrived and this had disastrous results for us later when we ran out of food during the fighting.

Donnelly, making the move to Jadotville with his Support Platoon on 4 September, was once again outraged by this lack of transport and equipment:

I should have been informed of the whereabouts of the 81mm—part of the Support Platoon weaponry—and their crew. Despite requests to Elisabethville about the whereabouts of the mortars it was only after all the fighting was over that I was told that my mortars and crew were offloaded from the trucks and flown to Kamina air base for its defence. In fact it transpired that the crew were commended and praised for their valuable contribution to the defence of Kamina.

He was infuriated too by the indignity and discomfort forced on the soldiers of A Company by especially inadequate bedding:

The platoon bedding at this stage was tattered and burst and broken, and it was little comfort to use the beds. What a waste of transport it was to carry beds complete with springs and mattresses for a company 80 miles from its base when the Swedes in such a situation would have had Li-lo beds as part of the personal kit.

I arrived at Jadotville at 2100 hours. Support Platoon was accommodated in the largest villa on the town side of the company location.

The following morning, his first in Jadotville, Donnelly reported that,

'...our presence in Jadotville does not seem to have the approval of the citizens, judging from reactions so far.'

By the afternoon, he had added the reality that, 'Each platoon is to have a guard on duty day and night at platoon accommodation.'

CHAPTER 42

'Theirs not to reason why. Theirs but to do and die.' I quoted this to Battalion HQ and said that Balaclava was over 100 years ago and attitudes to soldiers' right to information should change in like proportion.

Comdt P. Quinlan, September 1961

From the beginning in Jadotville, Quinlan, wrote to his wife, Carmel, and family, giving a reassuring slant on things. All was well, he told them, and they must not worry about him.

Jadotville. Wednesday, 6th September 1961

My darling Carmel and darling children:

Here I am in Jado since yesterday. Things are moving so fast just now that we cannot keep up with them. I'm delighted with this place. Everything is quiet and the white population are, believe it or not, friendly—at least 50% of them are. Jado is much nicer than Elisabethville. I have made contact with the Mayor/Burgermeister and all the 'Big Chiefs' and we have a perfect understanding.

It was chaos in Elisabethville when I left yesterday. About 15,000 refugees of all sorts, escaped prisoners and etc. I'm glad to be away from it.

We really did a good job in Elisabethville on Sunday and Monday and when the history of the Congo is written A Company will be high in the record.

We probably will be here for the next month or six weeks so the mail may be slow. Don't worry, we will be all right.

Don't worry, Jado is grand and very quiet....

In reality, from the beginning in Jadotville, Quinlan knew that things were not at all as they should be and that A Company was in anything but a good place. This view, and the reality of events, he faithfully recorded in a journal when it was all over:

Jadotville. Monday/Tuesday, 4th-5th September 1961
Journal entry

On arrival in Jadotville on 4th September I found villas allocated to the company on the outskirts of Jadotville on the Elisabethville road. These were the villas which the UN had taken over previously for Swedish troops and B Company, 35th Battalion. They were scattered along approximately one mile of the road at the entrance to the town with civilian villas occupied in between.

Two additional villas in isolated locations surrounded by bush were allotted for us but Capt. Byrne refused to take these over when he arrived with the company advance party. This was a stroke of luck as the company would have been in a very bad position indeed when the attack opened if we had been scattered so much.

I set up my HQ in a small building at the rear of Purfina Garage, a large, two storey building with a double garage on the ground floor and two self-contained flats overhead. (The proprietor, M. Louis Christiaens, a Belgian, rented the garage from the petrol company. This gentleman was most helpful to me at all times and suffered considerably because of his sympathy to the UN. His garage equipment and stocks were destroyed by mortaring and bombing. I understand that the Katanga Government refused compensation. He felt insecure in Katanga as the Surete Police were watching all his movements and he later left for Belgium.)

Tension was very high in Jadotville and the authorities, both white and African, were openly hostile. The owners of the villas which we were endeavouring to rent were warned that we were not to be accommodated in any way.

M. Christiaens was warned several times that he was not to supply us with petrol and that his telephone would be cut off if he allowed me to use it. [The telephone would eventually be cut on Monday, 11 September.]

Traders, shopkeepers and hoteliers were warned not to supply us. We were in a state of boycott. I tried to hire trucks as I had no transport except two jeeps and one truck which had broken down and was beyond our capability to repair plus one saloon and one ambulance.

All those whom I approached re hire of transport had the same reply—which was that they had nothing to hire. One gentleman, a Mr Hedo, a mining contractor, told me bluntly that if he hired me some of his trucks he might as well pack up and leave because Union Minière would put him out of business. He supplied mining products to Union Minière.

On my arrival in Jadotville I contacted Major Guertz. I had been given his name as a contact by UN HQ in Elisabethville. He was a native of Luxembourg and an ex-major of the British Army in East Africa. He was a lawyer and Estate Agent. He warned me of the hostility towards the UN. Through him I eventually succeeded in getting an interview with the Mayor/Burgermeister, an African named Amisi, and with the President of Union Minière.

The assistant mayor, a Belgian, refused to see me when I tried to meet him.

Quinlan continued with a chronological record of events over the days that followed.

Jadotville. Wednesday, 6th September 1961
Journal entry

I met Mayor Amisi this day, Wednesday, 6th September. He was cold and formal. He resented the presence of UN troops and said that he feared it would cause trouble as the people would not understand. I told him that the presence was especially to support him and the local authority and that we had no intention of causing any trouble.

Battalion HQ pressed me to send a patrol to Kolwezi to assure the white population there of UN protection. A Swedish company was due to arrive in Kolwezi from Kamina but their move was delayed. I used the trucks which arrived with our rear party and stores for this patrol which consisted of No. 1 Platoon, two armoured cars and elements of Liam Donnelly's Support Platoon with Lieutenant Joe Leech in charge.

It set out on this day, Wednesday 6th September, and got as far as the bridge on the Lualaba River approximately 20 miles from Kolwezi and over 100 miles from Jadotville.

A strong force of gendarmerie and paras were guarding a roadblock on this bridge and the patrol was refused permission to cross. In accordance with instructions NOT to use force, the patrol withdrew as darkness was falling and returned to Jadotville.

As a result of information gained from this patrol the move of the Swedish company to Kolwezi was cancelled.

This was a lucky break under the circumstances.

With newspapers and radio reporting the violence and growing unease in Katanga, his next letter home was predictably reassuring, giving no indication of the mounting tensions in Jadotville.

Thursday, 7th September 1961

My dear Carmel:

We are all tip top here and enjoying Jado. It is much nicer than Elisabethville and we are all hoping that we will be left here.

Don't take any notice of the papers or wireless. Things are not at all bad in Elisabethville and there is really no danger. There are several thousand refugees of all sorts but that's all, and small core demonstrating here and there....

Fond love and God bless to all. Daddy

This would be his last letter until after the fighting. His next letter was written on Tuesday, 19 September, the day after his company was taken prisoner. But his journal entries tell how things unfolded, days and events following one another in a succession so rapid that there was little time for reflective thought. Or rest.

Jadotville. Thursday, 7th September 1961.
Journal entry

From the date of our arrival in Jadotville each platoon provided its own guard and set about preparing defensive positions to meet any sudden attack. As tension grew we strengthened the defences and we had a perimeter of trenches dug with supporting weapon pits in depth. We also fortified some villas with sand bags and had further plans to use bed and mattresses leaning against window sills to give fire positions in the villas.

The same plan we put into effect when we were attacked and the villas were used as strong points to break up any attack that might succeed in over running the forward trenches in any sector. We had no barbed wire, no trip flares.

I requisitioned all these from Battalion HQ but there were none available.

I met with the President of Union Minière on this morning, Thursday, 7th September. I expected him to tell me of his fears for the white population (the reason for our presence in Jadotville) but I met with a very cold and formal reception. I was forewarned when he refused to allow Major Guertz into his office as interpreter.

I introduced myself and told him that I hoped for cordial relations with both whites and Africans in Jadotville. He remained silent. I mentioned that I thought that the white population in Jadotville were somewhat suspicious and uncooperative and that I wished for better relations.

He passed some non-committal comment to the effect that he also hoped for very good relations and hoped we would enjoy our stay in Jadotville. I waited for him to broach the subject of the threat to the lives and property of the white population in Jadotville but he remained silent.

I passed my visit off then as a courtesy call and left his office.

I was both puzzled and suspicious now as I knew that if UN troops were required in Jadotville to protect the white population that the President of Union Minière would be the man to requisition such protection as he was the all-powerful white man in Jadotville.

On our return from Union Minière HQ, Major Guertz suggested we drive to the top of the hill to see the view. This was a well-known sightseeing spot for tourists. When we got there, a barricade was up and a civilian told us that visitors were not allowed there any more.

I believe now that there was a radio station situated there and that this was the station which later continually tried to jam our signals to Battalion HQ.

I was by now very suspicious of the whole set-up. Major Guertz was very uneasy too and he told me that he was afraid for his own safety now. I returned to his office and he gave me a map of Jadotville. This was the only map of the area that I possessed.

On my return to my Company HQ, I decided to drive immediately to Elisabethville and report the situation to the Battalion OC and Dr Cruise O'Brien.

Immediately after I arrived in Elisabethville, rioting broke out there. I had a conversation with Lieut Col. McNamee and I explained the whole situation as I found it in Jadotville, and of the failure of the patrol to reach Kolwezi and my uneasiness about the position.

He undertook to talk to Dr O'Brien and Brig. General Raja and to get in touch with me. I presume the Battalion OC did explain the situation to Dr O'Brien and Brig. Gen. Raja but I received no information or decision.

I set off for Jadotville by back roads, skirting Elisabethville as I wanted to be back in Jadotville in case rioting broke out there also. I passed through the roadblock on the Lufira Bridge without incident.

Later that evening, Major Guertz was arrested at that roadblock on his way to attend a reception with Dr O'Brien in Elisabethville. He was escorted back to Jadotville by two jeep loads of Gendarmerie and, on passing through our position, he shouted to one of my men, 'Tell Major Quinlan that Major Guertz is arrested.

I notified Battalion HQ of this and got in touch with his wife. She was worried but she was confident she could secure his release.

He was released next morning, having spent an uncomfortable night lying on a cell floor. He telephoned me immediately. He had to give an undertaking not to have anything further to do with the UN. He asked me to inform Dr O'Brien of this position. I telephoned this information to Battalion HQ.

During these first days I did a recce of Jadotville with my officers. This recce was carried out disguised as sightseeing tours and we usually travelled in pairs in civilian attire.

To hold the town in the event of serious trouble was, we estimated, a job for a force of battalion strength.

I decided on a plan to hold strategic points separating the city from the native communes. These points were:

(a) Junction of Kolwezi road and road leading to native city.
(b) Railway bridge and road leading to Union Minière.
(c) Road leading to native commune (the population of this large commune was known to be hostile to the UN as all workers in Elisabethville were similarly hostile).
(d) Road junction where Elisabethville road entered the city.

To hold these points and maintain a patrolling force would leave the company very thin on the ground. All points were vital and had to be held. It was the best plan under the circumstances.

We did not at this time anticipate the overwhelming opposition of well-armed troops which later engaged us. We also expected some cooperation from the white population—after all, we were there to protect them.

As it turned out, the white population, almost to a man, took up arms against us and encouraged and led the African troops during the battle.

The following day, 8 September, Donnelly wrote a brief report stating:

> Fr Fagan joined the company in Jadotville today. Major Guertz released after signing a document that he would no longer give help or advice to UN forces. Pat Quinlan completed company defensive plans and ordered defensive positions [i.e., trenches] to be proceeded with in darkness.

Next day, Saturday, 9 September, their water supply was cut off. The company was now without either water or electricity. Quinlan got permission from Battalion HQ for two officers and two soldiers to go to Elisabethville. Ostensibly travelling there to collect mail, they would again stress the points made by Quinlan on his earlier trip to Battalion HQ: A Company should be given a new mission; A Company should be given permission to withdraw from Jadotville; A Company should be given reinforcements.

Donnelly and Clune (Medical Officer) volunteered for the trip. Quinlan wrote:

> They left by saloon car with their small escort in a jeep. Their purpose, ostensibly, was to post outgoing mail, collect incoming mail and especially to get a truck to bring rations, barbed wire and trip flares.
>
> Up to this time we were able to purchase our perishable food supplies from Elekat Stores in Jadotville, but all our non-perishable rations were to be drawn from Battalion HQ.
>
> With tension growing all the time, several truck and jeep loads of Gendarmerie were seen driving towards Elisabethville during the day. Some came back full, other trucks came back empty.
>
> At 1700 hours on this day, a jeep from A Company was held up at a barrier erected at the entrance to the town.

I sent a recce patrol on the road towards Elisabethville and discovered another roadblock set up on that road approximately one mile from our position.

This roadblock was in a very strong position at the foot of a very high hill (approximately 300 feet) covering the countryside around. The hill too was held. We also discovered, through field glasses, numbers of Gendarmerie moving around in the bush on our flanks. WE WERE SURROUNDED.

I got through by voice on the radio transmitter to Capt. Donnelly at Battalion HQ and explained the situation to him.

I told him not to attempt to come through until there was further info on the intentions of the Gendarmerie, asked him to explain the situation to Lieutenant Col. McNamee (who was not available to speak to me at that time) and gave my recommendation that the Lufira Bridge should be taken the next morning.

I later talked to Lieut Col. McNamee and we discussed the situation.

We agreed that strong action was called for and it was agreed, pending sanction of Dr O'Brien and Brigadier Raja, that a force of at least company strength (two platoons, four armed cars with 81mm mortars if possible) would take the Lufira Bridge the next day (10th September).

Later, when the Battle of Jadotville was over, Quinlan would again, and with anger, give his view that taking Lufira Bridge at that time could have been the key to establishing peace in Katanga. 'The main Katanga force was west of Lufira Bridge,' he would write, 'and that was why I got the brunt of it in Jadotville. The troops that turned the tide against the UN in Elisabethville came over the Lufira Bridge from Kolwezi. I had absolutely no task but if I had been given two hours' warning [about Operation Morthor] I could have taken the bridge and held off all the enemy and it would have been all over in Katanga that day.'

However, for now, on Saturday, 9 September, he had the realities of his troops and their defence to think about.

On this night, Saturday, 9th September, we manned some trenches and the company was on stand to. The men rested fully clothed in their villas with loaded weapons. This situation continued up to the attack on the morning of Wednesday, 13th September.

CHAPTER 43

The lack of direction, information and material support from higher authority was difficult to fathom.

Comdt (retired) L. Donnelly

Elisabethville. 9 September 1961

When Donnelly went to Elisabethville on 9 September, it was, he says, 'with the urgent requirement to brief Battalion HQ on the very serious situation in Jadotville. A Company was surrounded, had few rations and water and electricity had been cut off.'

En route, with Clune and Gunners, Privates James Murray and Charles Tomkins, he saw a 'strong Gendarmerie force at Lufira Bridge. We were not questioned or stopped. We arrived at Battalion HQ in Elisabethville at 1545 hours.' Donnelly went ahead and

> …met McNamee in the Officers' Mess and briefed him on what Pat had told me, reported on the exact situation at Jadotville: We were surrounded, we had no food, our water was dwindling, we'd no reinforcements. And why had we no transport?
>
> We'd only had a few days' rations going to Jadotville anyway.
>
> I passed on to Battalion HQ Comdt Quinlan's strong recommendations that A Company be withdrawn immediately as its stated mission at Jadotville was a complete misrepresentation of the true situation. The white people whom we were supposed to defend were overly hostile to the UN.

If the company was not to be withdrawn a new mission should be issued and strong reinforcements sent to Jadotville immediately.

I briefed the Battalion O/C and staff on the exact situation pertaining at Jadotville on that day, 9th September:

Freedom of movement denied.

Concentrated Katangese forces in the area.

No company transport.

Water supply cut off.

Electricity cut off.

Limited rations remaining, perhaps for four to six days only.

Dr Conor Cruise O'Brien, at a function that evening, was told about Donnelly's briefing to Battalion HQ staff and its commanding officer. He was told too that this included Quinlan's request either to withdraw A Company from Jadotville or to send reinforcements. O'Brien directed that A Company remain in Jadotville 'until further orders' and promised reinforcements, which would include three armoured cars.

Donnelly was advised to have an early night so as to be ready to return to Jadotville next morning, together with the reinforcements of 'personnel and armour, with adequate transport and supplies.' But next morning, Sunday, 10 September, Donnelly was given a choice:

I could stay or return to Jadotville but with no reinforcements. Lieut Shannon's platoon would escort me to the Lufira Bridge if I decided to return to Jadotville.

If they choose to return, they would have just one truck and one day's rations. Donnelly was adamant that his responsibilities were to his platoon and company. 'Lord bless us!' he says, almost amused. 'I had a platoon back there in Jadotville. If anything happened to them, it would be terrible.'

Clune saw no option too but to continue his medical role. 'There was no alternative,' he says. 'You went with your company. We knew they were surrounded so we went back in. Mick Shannon got the job of escorting us to the Lufira Bridge.'

At Lufira Bridge, Shannon and his infantry platoon ran into trouble with the Gendarmerie who would permit only the one truck (carrying limited rations) and one jeep to cross the Lufira Bridge. Leaving Quinlan's saloon car behind and escorted by troops from a Katangan para battalion, the small A Company group crossed the bridge.

'I shook hands with Mick Shannon,' Donnelly remembers, 'and said good luck and didn't see him for two months.'

Shannon remembers how, watching them go, he, 'saw them over the bridge and saw them head back to Jadotville.' Then he set up a platoon defensive position on the Elisabethville side of the bridge to wait for the return of the truck after it had offloaded the rations. Later that evening, Quinlan successfully negotiated the return of his saloon car.

Donnelly, reporting to Quinlan on the outcome of the Elisabethville trip, felt strongly that: 'The lack of direction, information and material support from higher authority was difficult to fathom. When I told Pat Quinlan we were getting nothing he said, "We've a problem here. We'd better be prepared." He got us dug in further and got us positioned. There were complaints from some of the men but he was right.'

Donnelly felt too that 'the lack of military intelligence by the Brigade regarding strength and capabilities of opposing forces was a major factor in what happened. In particular, the strength, armament and disposition of opposing forces at the Lufira Bridge and its approaches.'

Quinlan called an officers' conference and ordered that every person in the Company be dug in and protected as quickly as possible in their predetermined locations, the digging to be done under cover of darkness, if possible. According to Donnelly:

He directed that the armoured cars and support weapons be sited for mutual support and mortars to be ready for ranging rounds as quickly as possible, should hostilities begin. It was only because of such preparations that some of our positions were not overrun by the attack from the town side on the position at 0725 hours on 13th September.

His many questions remain unanswered.

Why was I not given some inkling, or pre-warning [about Operation Morthor] on my visit to Battalion HQ on 9th September?

Why was A Company left as a sitting duck?

CHAPTER 44

A man doesn't go among thorns unless a snake's after him—or he's after a snake.

African Proverb

Jadotville. 10 September 1961

Quinlan, meanwhile, had been awaiting word from Donnelly, and word from HQ about his proposed plan to take Lufira Bridge. But with the surrounding Katangans becoming ever bolder, no indication that he would be given permission to withdraw to Elisabethville, and attack seemingly inevitable, he concentrated all of A Company's efforts on a defence of their position.

> On Sunday 10th September we found the ring around us being strengthened. I again sent recce patrols to the Lufira Bridge, but they were held up.
>
> I awaited word from Battalion HQ about the plans to take the Lufira Bridge. What I did get was word from the battalion that permission had been granted by Colonel Muke (who was in charge of the Gendarmerie) for Capt. Donnelly to be allowed through to Jadotville with a patrol.
>
> The patrol was to return to Elisabethville.
>
> Capt. Donnelly arrived at the Lufira Bridge accompanied by one platoon of B Company (with Lieutenant Michael Shannon in charge) at approximately 1500 hours. He was held up and permission was refused to allow the platoon through. Colonel Muke's instruction to the guard on the bridge was to allow one truck and one jeep through.

The guard stuck to their orders and Capt. Donnelly put the platoon into a defensive position. Capt. Donnelly and Comdt Clune were then allowed through with a driver for the truck and a driver for the jeep. My saloon and three of my men were held up at the bridge. The truck was driven by Private O'Brien of B Company and Battalion HQ had ordered that the truck was to be sent back right away.

At 1640 hours the truck and jeep arrived in Jadotville escorted by a jeep load of Gendarmerie. I challenged the Lieutenant in charge of the Gendarmerie escort and succeeded in persuading him to allow my saloon and the three A Company men through.

Pte O'Brien of B Company volunteered to drive my saloon to Jadotville (as the three A Company men left behind with the saloon were not drivers) and said he would get one of the men from the platoon at the bridge to take the truck back to Elisabethville.

This was how Pte Joseph O'Brien of B company happened to fight and later get captured with A Company in Jadotville. He was an old soldier and in tribute to him I must say that he was an excellent soldier. He was most helpful and exemplary to many young men of A Company.

Monday, 11th September 1961

During this day and again next day there was much Gendarmerie activity on the road and convoys passed to and from the Elisabethville direction. The troops on the trucks each had their weapons at the ready and each truck had a machine gun on the roofs of the cabs.

I also had info on this day from my Baluba house boy, Emmanuel, that Belgian civilian employees of Union Minière and mercenaries were distributing arms to the local population and inciting them to attack us. A mass meeting was arranged for that night.

I decided that I would stop the Gendarmerie traffic through our position. I intended also to set up our own roadblocks if I was not allowed through to Jadotville.

We had no fresh food and less than two days' supply of tinned food. Tinned food on its own would not constitute a meal so it was vital that we get fresh food. I intended to demand entrance to Jadotville to purchase food.

The Gendarmerie were getting bolder and their morale was improving as they had complete freedom and our inactivity was probably seen as weakness.

I was prepared to force a showdown or call their bluff.

I informed Battalion OC accordingly and asked permission for us to use force if necessary to remove their barricades. I understood him to be in agreement with me but he instructed me to wait until he had contacted Dr O'Brien and General Raja.

Quinlan's radio messages to Battalion HQ now began to take on an added urgency. At 0900 hours, he made voice contact with McNamee to whom he 'gave a complete picture of Jadotville situation'. This picture included telling the Battalion OC that they were surrounded and their movements restricted so that they were unable to get into Jadotville for rations. When Quinlan, by way of a solution, then said he would approach the Gendarmerie barrier to demand entry to the town, McNamee said he would speak to O'Brien and Raja so as to get the Jadotville situation resolved and the Gendarmerie to call off the encirclement.

A radio message shortly afterwards seemed to indicate that moves were under way.

1025 HRS. ELISABETHVILLE: HIGH LEVEL MEETING TO TAKE PLACE WITH TSHOMBE TODAY. HOLD OFF UNTIL AFTER CONFERENCE. WILL KEEP YOU INFORMED.

1359 HRS. JADOTVILLE: HAVE YOU ANY INFO FOR ME? NO CHANGE HERE.

1400 HRS. ELISABETHVILLE: SORRY NO INFO. NO CHANGE HERE. WILL KEEP YOU INFORMED OF ANY CHANGE.

1458 HRS. ELISABETHVILLE (FROM OC):TÁ COMHDHÁIL AR SIÚL FAOI LÁTHAIR IDIR NA DAOINE MÓRA. NÍ BHEIDH AON EOLAS AG TEACHT GO DTÍ DEIRE AN COMHDHÁLA SIN. [Meeting still going on between the important people (leaders). No information until the end of the meeting.]

During the rest of that day, Quinlan 'received messages re conferences between Dr O'Brien and Tshombe to arrange calling off the blockade of Jadotville.'

Then, at 2233 hours, I received a long wireless telephone message stating that use of force now would spoil the political crisis which was at hand. This message also stated that Colonel Muke had promised to lift the Jadotville blockade next day and that the Belgian Consul was advising Mayor Amisi of Jadotville to end the whites' attitude to us.

It stated too that food supplies would be sent next day and that reinforcements were ready to move on call.

He radioed his reassurances to HQ.

2245 HRS. JADOTVILLE: YOUR MESSAGE RECEIVED. DON'T WORRY. WE WILL NOT START ANYTHING. POLITICAL SITUATION FULLY APPRECIATED. HAVE TRIED TO ARRANGE MEETING WITH OC FCA. HE REFUSED. SATISFIED SIT. IS EASING. WILL KEEP YOU INFORMED.

This message was a triumph of optimism. Incidents and unease were, in fact, mounting in Jadotville.

Earlier, at approximately 2000 hours on this night [11 September] a Belgian Dr Lecos, the local dispensary doctor, aged over 70, called to my HQ. He was very excited and ill at ease.

He started by asking if I could get any information about his houseboy's wife and family whom he said had gone to the refugee camp in Elisabethville. It was soon obvious that this was not the purpose of his visit as he could not even remember the name of the woman or the number of her children.

He came to the point after a while and said that he wanted to avoid bloodshed and suggested that I should meet Mayor Amisi to discuss matters.

I thought at the time that he had been sent to me but I am satisfied now that it was his own idea to avoid bloodshed and to help us. We got to know this man well later when we were prisoners and we had no better friend. He visited us daily despite insults and threats from the guards and he gave us any news he had. He gave up in disgust after a fortnight and left the country to return to Belgium.

He was heartbroken at the course events were taking in Katanga and said he would never return to the Congo. He introduced his successor, another Belgian doctor, and asked him to be kind to us and to visit us. That was the only time we saw his successor.

On the night of 11th September when he first called on me, he said he would try and arrange a meeting with the mayor and I agreed to meet Amisi and the OC Gendarmerie.

Next morning [Tuesday, 12 September] he arrived at my HQ early and told me he had arranged for me to met the mayor. I followed him in my car accompanied by Lieutenant Lars Fröberg. At the barrier we were stopped and Major Makito [African OC of Gendarmerie in Jadotville] came with me to see the mayor.

Makito was most suspicious and hostile and every time Mayor Amisi appeared to be in agreement with me Makito scowled and twisted in his chair. He was an impossible person that morning. He was accompanied by Capt. Tschipolo who appeared to be more genial but, as we discovered later, was an even more dangerous character.

Incidentally, we were informed later that Makito was a witch doctor and still practised his trade. I don't know if this was true but he certainly looked the part. [Lars Fröberg was infinitely philosophical about Makito who was, he says, 'one of President Tshombe's confidantes and was also a sorcerer, but that's Africa for you.']

The meeting with Makito and Tschipolo 'achieved nothing', Quinlan says.

Makito refused to lift the blockade. He said he was awaiting instructions. This was the stock answer to all questions. He said we were sent to disarm the Gendarmerie. I tried to put him at ease on this point but it was useless trying to reason with him.

We managed to meet again at 1500 hours to continue discussions. I thought if I could keep them talking, I might succeed in winning them around.

The meeting in the afternoon was much more pleasant and we were all very friendly but nothing was achieved. I asked the mayor why he had ordered the shops not to supply us with food. I got no reply but he promised to allow one jeep in that evening to one shop to get goods. Time and route had to be arranged in detail.

I realised that they did not want me to see any military preparations in the town.

I invited Makito and Tschipolo to join me for a drink at a hotel. They agreed.

When we arrived the proprietress refused to serve us until she got permission from the mayor by telephone.

Some white civilians in the hotel were openly hostile. Two Belgian women accompanied by two tough-looking African thugs arrived and looked very belligerent. They spoke in Swahili to Makito.

We later met these two ladies as Red Cross workers when we were prisoners. I have never met any more violently anti-UN people nor any women less suited to the job of Red Cross workers. One was the wife of the Managing Director of Afridk, the firm which manufactured the bombs which were used by the Fouga jet, and the other was her daughter and was married to a Belgian officer, as far as I know.

Makito and Tschipolo appeared friendly now but it was obvious that they were ill at ease with the mustering crowd. They got up to leave abruptly and we decided it was time to leave also. A group of Gendarmerie had assembled outside the hotel. Makito accompanied us to the barrier and he was friendly and shook hands. We had arranged to meet again at 1000 hours the next morning to settle all matters in a friendly way.

Despite this friendliness I got more suspicious than ever that there was a major move afoot. I ordered more trenches to be dug during the night in new positions. We also rigged up bits of wire and string along covered routes and hung tins with pebbles as a makeshift alarm system.

On this afternoon also, Pierre Marc, a Belgian who had been an observer in the RAF during WWII, drove through our position and threw a map to one of my men and told him to take it to me. I had met this gentleman and his wife on two occasions previously and I liked them. They were very definitely pro-UN although Pierre Marc's father-in-law, M. Van Habost, a divorcé who, with his second wife, owned the bus depot and a garage adjacent to our position, were violently anti-UN.

Pierre Marc had already warned me about his father-in-law and suspected that he and his wife were reporting all our moves and defence positions to the Gendarmerie.

This proved correct...

Some of the Gendarmerie positions surrounding us were marked on the map, especially the location of a heavy gun, marked on the map, 'Heavy Gun—French 75—I think trained on your HQ'. Capt. Donnelly picked up the position of this gun with field glasses and estimated the range at 1550 yards.

Some of the men had reported that they could observe Mrs Van Habost almost continually on the telephone inside the windows of her house, observing us through the window curtains.

A fleet of several buses were normally parked at this depot and I had planned to seize them in the event of trouble.

I had further info that night of the mass meeting of the white and African population in the town and sent my Baluba house boy, Emmanuel, to observe and report back. He was quite willing to go but he was very much afraid to come back through the bush late at night.

He had attended the meeting on the previous night and reported Munongo and the Mayor in attendance. Many white people spoke. Due to language difficulties I could not get the full story but it was obvious that the purpose of the meeting was to incite the local population to attack the UN along with the Gendarmerie.

Emmanuel reported too that arms were widely distributed but the African population did NOT want to fight. He gave me the names of several of the white people who spoke. All were employees of Union Minière. One was a Belgian major who was supposed to have left Katanga and returned to Belgium the previous week, according to the undertaking to send Belgian and mercenary officers home.

Quinlan, just before they were captured, destroyed all and any documents which might incriminate those who helped A Company, or contain information of use to the Gendarmerie. The list of names given him by Emmanuel was one of the documents he destroyed.

Night fell.

On this night, 12th September, I waited for the house boy to return but he did not return until next morning. When he did, he gave me some info on the meeting of the previous night but by then it was too late to be of use. In any case, due to language difficulties, I could not understand it all. The meeting appeared to be a repetition of the previous night.

Even then, at what was literally the eleventh hour, faulty transport and lack of communications dogged A Company. As Quinlan wrote:

During that afternoon [12 September] a truck with food supplies left Elisabethville for our position but broke down.

Its movements were followed by our wireless. A repair truck was sent from Battalion HQ but at 1745 hours a message from Battalion HQ recalled both trucks to Elisabethville where they arrived at 2015 hours, according to a message received at my HQ.

2015 HRS. ELISABETHVILLE: Ní FEIDIR LIOM AON SCÉAL A TABHAIRT DUIT FAOIN SUÍOMH GINERÁLTA. TÁ AN CAPALL DUBH TEACHT THAR N-AIS ANSEO. [I can't give you any news of the general situation. The black horse (ration truck) has returned here.]

The trucks had been recalled because of Operation Morthor. No word of this was conveyed to A Company, however. Quinlan was more than a little uneasy.

I was very concerned about the general situation, both political and military, at this time. I requested info from Battalion HQ and kept Battalion HQ informed of events in Jadotville but unfortunately I received no information on the political or military plans of the UN.

I sent a final message at 2335 hours expressing my grave concern and asking for immediate information. I got no reply to this message and I instructed that it be repeated hourly.

This instruction was carried out and it was repeated frequently until morning. I still got no reply. It is possible that wireless silence had been imposed late that night but had I been informed earlier of the Morthor plan I would have known what to expect next morning and could have planned accordingly.

At least one of the Jadotville messages was received, and recorded, at Battalion HQ in Elisabethville at 0005 hours, four hours before the start of Operation Morthor.

Quinlan was correct in surmising that there was a wireless telephone silence: It was put into force by UN South Katanga Command in the hours leading up to Operation Morthor. This left A

Company not only without knowledge of what was about to happen but also without the possibility of communicating with their Battalion HQ. However, word of Operation Morthor could have been given personally to Quinlan, or to Donnelly, on their visits to Elisabethville.

Quinlan was forever adamant that knowledge would have made all the difference, that forewarned would most definitely have been forearmed:

> I have no doubt that the final outcome would have been different, and that A Company would not have been captured. The whole outcome of Morthor could have ended in success. [By this he means that his plan to take the Lufira Bridge would have prevented reinforcements from getting to Elisabethville.]

A Company continued to dig trenches and prepare defences until 0100 hours on 13 September. Then, apart from skeletal crews manning vital defences, everyone retired to the villas to get some rest. Quinlan wrote:

> After dark, we had pulled back the men from roadside positions in order to avoid a surprise attack with grenades from passing vehicles. New weapon pits were dug in enfilade positions away from the road and these were manned.
>
> This was our last night of comparative peace and quiet.

PART THREE

CHAPTER 45

Had this been a fight for Ireland we would have fought on to the last drop of our blood.

Comdt P. Quinlan, Daily Mail, 21 September 1961

World news. 19–21 September 1961

In the days following Sunday, 19 September 1961, world newspaper headlines were consumed with the events of that night in the Congo.

The death of UN Secretary General Dag Hammarskjöld gave rise to much speculation. The *Irish Independent*, on Tuesday, 19 September, headlined the story of the air crash's lone survivor, Sergeant Harold Julian of the UN Security Force, who told of a series of explosions aboard the aircraft.

'Thirteen Perish in Plane Wreck' ran a second headline in the paper, over a report speculating that Mr Hammarskjöld's death, along with 'tragically complicating the Congo's troubles' would also throw 'the future of the United Nations into crisis'.

Jadotville shared this front page. A picture of an oddly empty Jadotville main street showed a couple of African women shoppers. A report (from Raymond Smith in Leopoldville) said that the soldiers of A Company were 'all safe and being well treated by the Katangese Gendarmerie who overwhelmed them after suddenly breaking a truce....'

By Thursday, 21 September, the UK's *Daily Mail*, which had throughout made something of a *cause célèbre* of A Company's stand, had got an exclusive interview with Quinlan. 'Four Days of Hell' declared the headline above the words: 'Jadotville OC tells the first full story.'

Quinlan, talking to reporter Peter Younghusband in Jadotville, said that he had made his declaration of surrender after 96 hours of continuous fighting, when his men had not slept for four days. Younghusband reported that the troops had been 'without food and water, were threatened by disease when all hope of a relieving force reaching them had faded and when they faced extermination by a numerically superior Katanga force.

Quinlan said:

It was four days of hell in which I became devoted to my men, who never failed me. They never wavered, never lost courage, and were prepared to fight on to the end.

But I was not prepared to let them die in this sort of fight and on my own responsibility, having failed to receive guidance from higher authority in Elisabethville, I took the decision to end what seemed to me to be a pointless action unrelated to what we had been assigned to in the Congo—a peaceful mission on behalf of the United Nations.

Had this been a fight for Ireland we would have fought to the last drop of our blood. But we had been continually told that we were a peace force, and that we were not to shoot unless fired upon.

These rules we tried to obey, even when we were undergoing heavy fire and provocation, until it became necessary to take heavy defensive action in which Katangese lives were lost through our mortar and machine-gun fire.

Our own troops were also under heavy fire, some of the boys were wounded, and our extermination by a numerically superior force seemed imminent...

I do not know how it was none of us were killed. We seemed to be saved by miracle after miracle. I believe it was Divine Providence. I placed myself and my men in the hands of Our Blessed Lady and it was She who brought us through four days and nights of hell, which included mortar fire, air bombardment and strafing from the air.

Elsewhere, the *Daily Mail* reported that a total of 13 UN soldiers had been killed and 63 wounded in the Katanga fighting. Seven of the dead were Indians, five Swedes and one Irish. Of the wounded, 18 were Irish.

The *Irish Independent*, on the same day, 21 September, headlined 'Katanga Ceasefire Agreed' and went on to write that President Tshombe had announced a provisional ceasefire between his troops and the United Nations force, one which included arrangements for an exchange of prisoners. The paper reported, too, that there were 'great hopes' in UN HQ 'that the ceasefire may mean the quick release of the 155 Irish prisoners in Jadotville and 26 in Elisabethville.' A couple of paragraphs later, however, there was word that the Congolese Premier, Mr Cyrille Adoula, had 'alerted his people for war to end Katanga's secession.'

'The Congo will reply to force with force,' Mr Adoula declared. 'No sacrifice will be considered too great. The Congolese Army has been put on a state of alert and from today every citizen must be ready to answer a Government call to serve in Katanga.'

Peace and the release of A Company seemed anything but assured.

CHAPTER 46

We were like sacrificial lambs! ... We were dumped there because the
Belgians wanted their interests protected.

Cpl Sean Foley

Quinlan's first letter home after the battle had ended was typically
reassuring. Dated 19 September, it reads:

I am so sorry for the terrible worry and anxiety you must
have had during the past, terrible week. I have no doubt that
it was worse for all our people at home than it was for us.
Believe me our thoughts were always with you at home too.

I'm not going into the details of the past week. God
bless my brave men (some of them still boys) who never once
wavered through four continuous days and nights without
sleep or rest, little or no food and at the end no water, without
which life cannot exist here. Believe me my decision was the
only possible one in the eyes of God, otherwise there would
have been terrible consequences.

I have no doubt but our Blessed Mother was with us all
the time and guided me in the many, many grave decisions
I had to make, the last one of which was the most difficult.

We are all very angry and bitter at the blundering fools
who left us isolated here without any indication whatever as
to the intended action in Elisabethville.

Our first indication was an attack on us as Mass started
on the morning of Wednesday 13th September. I am placing
the full facts on record and for a public enquiry.

The people of Ireland will pass judgement on whoever
was responsible for the callous disregard of 156 Irish lives.

We are very proud of the brave men who tried in vain to reach us and suffered casualties in the attempt. We don't know much of their story but we can guess. They tried hard, God bless them.

Our brave helicopter crew—a Norwegian lieutenant and a Swedish NCO—are here with us. They were really heroes. They landed in an inferno with all hell let loose. We have with us also a Swedish lieutenant—my interpreter Lars Fröberg—who is a great chap.

I hope to take all three of them with us to Ireland for a holiday. It is due to them.

The main thing now is that we are all alive and very well. Our wounded are with us and completely out of danger. We are accommodated in a hotel in Jado and we have everything we want. Mr Munongo is doing all he can to make us comfortable. We expect to be out of here very soon. Perhaps this is the best thing that ever happened and it may be God's method of solving the problems in this unhappy land.

The Katangese are good soldiers, and brave, and this is their country. I don't blame them for attacking us. The UN muddle brought it all about.

We are on very friendly terms with the Katangese troops who admire us for our brave stand. There is no bitterness. We did not come here to shoot Africans. We came to help them.

Don't worry about me and my men. The morale was never as high and all are in great spirits.

Tell Joe O'Dwyer [an army friend and neighbour in Athlone] that 5ft. trenches are protection against almost anything—that is except thirst.

All my love to you all, Pat

The freedom to write letters like this would not last. Reassurances like these could be truthfully given to his wife Carmel in the early days of captivity when A Company was, as Wally Hegarty said in a letter he wrote home to a friend, given 'great respect and privacy'.

'During our three-and-a-half week stay in Jado,' Hegarty wrote, 'we were very well treated by our former adversaries. They accorded us great respect and privacy and in no way inflicted their will on us. But then one morning, without warning....'

And so began a tale of another kind of treatment of A Company.

In the beginning, on Monday, 18 September, when A Company assembled at the Purfina Garage and marched, under guard, into captivity in the Hôtel de l'Europe in the town of Jadotville, there was dignity and heads were held high.

Sean Foley remembers how, '...when we marched into captivity, into Jadotville, we struck up whistling the tune from the *Bridge Over the River Kwai* in unison, all of us together. You could hear it back down the road, everyone the whole way back whistling. There was no such thing as heads down. Our heads were up and we marched proud.'

But some men had to suffer indignities. Noel Carey recalls:

The first indignity was to have to tell my platoon to get packed and be ready to move out by noon. As far as they were concerned, however, victory was ours and as such they had no real concept of the danger we were now in.

Next, I had to climb up into the loft in the roof of Purfina Garage and return the weapons to our mercenary captives. They shook our hands and were soon on their way to who knows where.

Then General Muke (head of the Gendarmerie) arrived with his Katangan staff to inspect our positions and weapons. His mercenary masters kept well out of sight. At noon some buses arrived and each platoon was conveyed from our defensive positions through the railway gates and into Jadotville, watched by curious natives and surrounded by milling Katangan soldiers.

The buses stopped up the street from the Hôtel de l'Europe and Comdt Quinlan gave the order to fall in, which we did.

I really felt almost nude without my personal Gustav, as the rest of our company must have felt, drawn up defenceless and glared at by hostile Katangan troops. We could see white mercenary officers in the background, directing operations, and we were then told to march to the hotel where we were to be housed.

Foley remembers that the Hôtel de l'Europe, 'was anything but a hotel!' and Carey describes it:

> The building had been unoccupied for some time, smelled of must and dust and certainly was anything but presentable, and of very ancient vintage. We arranged accommodation as best we could for our platoons, and the officers shared a few rooms, having to sleep on the floor for the first few nights. In my own case there were six officers to a room, very cramped, very few facilities. Our cooks set up a cooking area on the roof balcony of the hotel.
>
> At this time we were not guarded inside the hotel but a heavy Katangan presence was posted just across the road and this was the HQ for our guards. We were not well searched and I had my portable radio [bought in Malta on the journey to the Congo] which I hid in a sack of rice in the Quartermaster's stores. We were not permitted radios. Every night I went to the store and, while Paddy Neville and Jack O'Brien kept watch, tuned into Radio Northern Rhodesia [Zambia] for any news, sometimes relayed through BBC World Service. Anything of interest was relayed to Comdt Quinlan.
>
> Roadblocks were established all round the hotel, manned by heavily armed troops. That first night in captivity was full of uncertainty, not knowing what was to happen to us, but at the same time encouraging and reassuring our young soldiers, most of whom still thought we were the victors and were being accommodated by our Katangan hosts.
>
> Next day [Tuesday, 19 September] Quinlan quickly took over and insisted that we have a daily routine of inspections, training courses and talks to reassure our troops. He also ordered that we collect all bottles or jars, fill them with petrol from the cookers, and stuff cloth into the tops of the bottles to be lit as fuses in the event of the personnel being attacked.

Hegarty reconvened his master classes in unarmed combat. He explains:

> One of the things you don't do in a situation like that, is let the men rust. So there I was, standing outside the hotel where we were prisoners teaching the boys unarmed combat when a Gendarmerie stopped it. But Quinlan discovered a parapet on the roof which hid us from the Gendarmerie and we continued to train up there!

Private Billy Ready wrote to his mother:

> I told her what I thought she'd like to hear. She was a worrier. When a Garda, a young man, came to tell her we were prisoners he took four hours to get it out, to tell her. This was in Cavan town. She made him tea and they talked about everything and anything before he could bring himself to tell her!

During the next three weeks, Quinlan struck up a good relationship with the Katangan Guard Commander, and the food, delivered to them from the town, improved.

Carey was growing up fast. Vigorous and enthusiastic, he was learning, with the rest of A Company, about the realities of fear, responsibility and survival. Being a captive, he says, 'was not as you see it on TV or in the cinema':

> Firstly there's the uncertainty of your situation. We didn't know what was going to happen to us, whether the Katangans would single out our officers for reprisals. We had heard of war prisoners being mutilated and shot without trial. There was fear, with its gnawing feeling in the stomach.
>
> But as officers we had to give good example to our troops, who now relied on us. We were not trained for this situation and had to make it up as we went along. There was dreadful boredom, tedium, lack of privacy, but great support from fellow officers.

We quickly established a routine: morning inspections, training, courses and medical checks by our excellent Medical Officer, Dr Joe Clune. Our Chaplain, Fr Fagan, attended to our religious needs and each morning said Mass on the hotel veranda roof which was a solace to many of us.

The uneasy question of how many Katangan soldiers and mercenaries they had killed, and what reprisals they might expect, was a hovering one for A Company. Quinlan began putting together what information and facts he was able to get hold of:

During the ceasefire negotiations I was informed by one man that they had lost over 150, all of them killed. This man was one of the white advisers. He said that seven of those killed were white people.

Later, however, he contradicted this figure and said they had only one or two people killed altogether.

Dr Le Coq, a Belgian Dispensary Doctor who befriended us while we were prisoners, gave the casualty figure as 'many, many, very many'. A White Father expressed the casualty figures to Fr Fagan in the same terms.

Charlie Kearney's estimate of the casualties, when we met him again, was also about 150. He was informed too that 80 of the wounded in hospital were not expected to live and he saw 30 coffins being taken out of Union Minière. Coffins were used only for white people in that area.

We did know that three or four days after the fighting, the Katangans discovered many dead and wounded in the bush surrounding the position. These were of soldiers who had evidently fled on the Saturday.

Swedish interpreter Fröberg, on hand for every shot fired and every mortar shell which landed during the battle, speaks of 'the miracle that saw only five men wounded in A Company and so many dead among the enemy.' Gendarmerie losses varied between 150 and 250, he says, depending on the source.

Evidence that thirty of these were whites was seen in a funeral ceremony for those who died which had thirty coffins; only whites were buried in coffins. A civilian in Jadotville told me afterwards that more than 1,000 Gendarmerie had refused to go on fighting us and had deserted. I could believe this because though many of the Irish soldiers were very young, they could really shoot, so the battle must have been a hell for the Gendarmerie. When it stopped, I saw Gendarmerie with bloodshot eyes and others who were tearful.

The fear of reprisals was the cause of tense moments on the second day. Carey recounts:

When we were directed to move out onto the front porch of the hotel, Comdt Quinlan feared some reprisals. The officers remained inside on the top balcony—with Molotov cocktails at hand in case we were attacked. After waiting half an hour, tensions rising, a photographer arrived with a Katangan guard, took some photographs and to our relief the event was over.

Quinlan, too, was reasonably satisfied with the way they were looked after during their early days of captivity. Paratroopers guarding them during the first few days were, he says, 'good soldiers, professionals who did everything to make us comfortable'. He continued:

When the Gendarmerie took over, however, they were less professional and conditions deteriorated steadily. Still, for the three-and-a-half-weeks we were in Jadotville we had no real complaints. Our treatment and food were of the highest standards.

During the early days our mail was allowed in uncensored too. But later it was censored and much of it was confiscated.

Hegarty corroborated this in a letter written after they were freed—and went further:

When our 'Hosts' censored our mail only the 'good' letters were allowed out, ones which praised our captors, their food and accommodation. So at the heel of the reel the lads voluntarily decided not to write in the fear that the folks at home would think we were on holidays and that the politicians would sit down on the job.

Early on the morning of Saturday, 23 September, they were joined in their prison hotel by 32 other prisoners: 26 Irish and six Italian UN soldiers. They had all been captured in the fighting still going on in Elisabethville. The Irish officers with the group, Commandant Pat Cahalane and Lieutenant Tom Ryan, were amazed to find the men of A Company alive and relatively well. Propaganda and rumour had successfully spread the word that the company had been all but wiped out.

Cahalane himself had been wounded by anti-tank weapons during Operation Morthor and his hearing, as a result, had been damaged. Dr Joe Clune says that a kindly and helpful Belgian doctor, 'collected Cahalane in his car when I wanted him checked out because of the damage to his ear from the explosion.'

Quinlan sent off another upbeat letter the following day:

Jadotville. Sunday, 24th September

My dear Carmel and children:

We are now one week as prisoners of war. We are being treated in the best possible manner. Plenty of the best of food, beds and etc. in a hotel. We don't expect to be prisoners long more as we understand there are negotiations for an exchange of prisoners going on—and that the senseless fighting and killing is over.

We heard Jack Millar on radio last night. He paid great tribute to me and A Company. It would appear we are all considered heroes.

We get Dateline Dublin on Wednesday and Saturday so please record a message or get Jack Millar to send me a message.

We have our Chaplain, Fr Fagan, with us and have Mass and Communion every morning.

Tell all the people in Athlone that the men are in great spirits. All our wounded are almost completely recovered. God bless the brave boys of my company. Ireland can well be proud of them. Their spirit is now their crowning glory.

God bless you all, write soon as ever, Pat

What he did not write home about, but did record in his journal, was how their situation changed after a visit by the Exchange of Prisoners Commission:

Conditions altered drastically immediately the commission left. The guards became strict and somewhat belligerent and radios were taken. We managed to hide one transistor radio [Noel Carey's] and the news we received on this was not encouraging.

They set about preparing for what they half-expected might happen, determined that they would not go down without a fight if the worst came to the worst. Quinlan recorded this too, and told how the Molotov cocktails were made:

We had plans to take over the guard in the event of any attempt to relieve us. We also had plans to defend ourselves to the last in the event of any attempt on our lives. Most of the men still had jack-knives or daggers and we prepared fuel for Molotov cocktails from petrol provided for our cooker, candle grease from some candles that we had and oil from the pump of a car.

We kept the men occupied as best we could with PT, lectures [the Norwegian helicopter pilot, Bjerne Hovden, spoke about his travels in Antarctica; Fröberg told about life in Sweden, and of Swedish women, which information was, he says, well received], discussions, question-time and indoor games. We were not allowed to drill, we were forbidden unarmed combat practice and we had no facilities for outdoor games.

Again and again, his account returns to the remarkable morale of the members of A Company:

> The morale of the men was very high throughout. Even later when we got very rough treatment the morale never faltered. Every man had a deep religious feeling; our emergence from the battle with only five wounded was considered by all to be a miracle.
>
> The enemy could not believe we had no dead. On several occasions, even up to the day before our final release, we were approached on this subject by doctors, priests and others. All insisted that we had 50 dead and they wanted to know where we had buried them.
>
> They even dug up likely burial places in our defensive localities.

Fröberg remembers a different kind of digging on a Sunday when Gendarmerie began digging threateningly grave-like holes outside the hotel. 'They would come to our quarters at night too,' he says, 'armed and checking on what we were doing. They were always dangerously nervous and fearful.'

CHAPTER 47

There is no doubt that there was a violation of the local ceasefire concluded between the Irish commander and the local Katangese officer. The Irish were led into some trick or trap....
Gen. S. McKeown on Jadotville, 24 September 1961

World news. September 1961

Katanga, the miseries and horror of the war and the plight of the UN prisoners there continued to dominate world news. On 22 September, the Irish Press headlined the determination of Frank Aiken, Minister for External Affairs, to travel to Jadotville to see the prisoners there for himself. Journalist Desmond Fisher, in Leopoldville, reported:

> After the nightmare of the past week the Congo is settling into an unquiet sleep tonight. Although the ceasefire is being preserved in Katanga there is an air of uneasy tension around, as if no one is prepared to trust that it will last.

United Press International, on the same day, reported Elisabethville 'a nervous place':

> The town's white population, who have been holed up for a week, strolled along broad boulevards lined with blooming Jacaranda trees. Only yesterday the same boulevards were death traps, with flying bullets and exploding mortar shells.
> Some shops re-opened and people hurried to restock with food in case fighting starts again. That could happen at any time.
> There has not been a shot fired in anger for four hours, but both sides still have their fingers on the triggers.

The *Daily Mail*, on 23 September, carried a dramatic, half-page picture of Quinlan and A Company in captivity with, on another page, a picture of Quinlan with helicopter pilot Hovden, crewman Thors and a smiling Fröberg, pipe in hand.

On Sunday, 24 September, General Sean McKeown assured the *Sunday Independent* that the UN forces had never been in danger of defeat during the 13-day battle against President Tshombe's Katangese Army. UN troops now had the situation 'completely under control,' he said, 'and we still have what we started with—four intact battalions with armour.'

CHAPTER 48

God, my men were fine and they still have that same indomitable courage now. Ireland never reared better sons.
　　　　　Comdt P. Quinlan, Hôtel de l'Europe, September 1961

Hôtel de l'Europe, Jadotville. September 1961

Carey's transistor radio took on a role far greater than might be believed given its humble, secreted existence. Its airwaves linked the men not only to the world of political manoeuvring which would decide their fate, but also to the world of Irish sport, vital and important to all, especially Carey himself.

On Monday, 25 September, Radio Brazzaville broadcast the All-Ireland football final, played the day before in Croke Park between Offaly and Down. Carey, Donnelly and Tom Quinlan sat in their room and listened.

'We wondered,' Carey recalls, 'if all those in Croke Park even knew we were held prisoner, in a country thousands of miles from home....'

Down won the match by one point.

A Company had been in captivity more than a week when Red Cross representatives brought newspapers and letters from home. This was the first news anyone had had of their families for weeks and each prisoner was allowed write a short letter in reply, which the Red Cross representatives undertook to see delivered.

Comdt Quinlan wrote home immediately:

Jadotville. Tuesday, 26th September 1961

My darling Carmel and darling children:
　　　I have just read all your letters which Geneva Red Cross brought us today. We certainly hit the headlines. I'm very

proud that everyone thought that if anyone could get us out of that tight spot it would be me. Believe me it was someone greater than any human who got us out. It was Our Lady who did it.

I'm sorry about all the terrible press reports of 50 dead and etc. We had no dead but don't ask me why. It was just a miracle and an excellent defence with dug in trenches. I always dug in everywhere we went in the Congo, even when others were out enjoying themselves and sometimes laughing at my precautions. It paid off in grand style. I was never, thank God, taken in by the bright life. I always put my men first. It was their safety that made me make the last desperate decision.

I surrendered to Mr Munongo on written guarantee of safety of our lives and safe storage of our arms.

We are all in fine form here now and we have got fat back on us again. The paper reports were wrong. We did not have rations or water. God, my men were fine and they still have that same indomitable courage now. Ireland never reared better sons. They would have died to a man if I had decided to continue. They never wavered and my slightest sign was obeyed without question. They seemed to think that I could not go wrong. It is very heartening to have such unconditional loyalty. No man ever got the loyalty I got from those boys. When things were darkest they were always smiling. 'How are we doing, Sir?' was the usual query. Oh, God, they were great.

It's all over now and please God we will be out of here in a short time. We are being treated like special guests. We have no complaints at all. I gave a few press interviews to let the world know that we are all alive and well. All the prisoners are here with me now—Italian, Swedish, Irish etc. I'm in command and a right good bunch they are. We are delighted the Red Cross came here.

All my love to you all, Daddy

He also wrote a second, and then a third, letter on this date. How he managed to get them all delivered is not recorded.

Jadotville. Tuesday, 26th September 1961

My dear Carmel:

We have now read more of the press reports. You must have suffered terribly. God bless your stout hearts. My only worries now are for you. Don't worry about me. I'm very well and proud of my gallant men and glad to be with them. We did all that was humanly possible. I surrendered personally on a written guarantee of our safety to Mr Munongo. We have everything we want. We are very thankful to the Red Cross.

Our Government should now take immediate steps to secure our release. We expect that.

Fond love, Pat

And again:

Jadotville. Tuesday, 26th September 1961

My darling Carmel and children:

I don't want any of you to worry about me. I'm quite happy. This is the life I choose and I have no regrets. I'll be home soon please God and we will have happy times together again.

All the officers are fine. They were great stuff. I would find it difficult to say who was best, they were all just wonderful. Platoon Commanders excelled themselves.

The Company Sergeant Jack Prendergast was a tower of strength. I think Liam Donnelly is one of the finest officers I could ever meet. But then Tom Quinlan, Kevin Knightly (Armoured Car Group), Noel Carey and Joe Leech were also wonderful.

Fond love and God bless you all, Pat

Prisoners they might be, but they were also news. Following the Red Cross visit, the press came calling. Raymond Smith, a keen and faithful reporter for the *Irish Independent* on the Congo and Irish UN troops story, met with A Company in Jadotville. After an eventful journey

On the morning of Monday, 18 September 1961, Col Makito of the Gendarmerie forces in Jadotville (second from left, with hat and baton) meets with Capt Liam Donnelly (in UN beret), Capt Tom McGuinn and, on extreme right, Norwegian helicopter pilot Bjerne Hovden. The smiling face to the rear belongs to A Company's Swedish interpreter, Lieut Lars Fröberg.

President Tshombe arrives in Jadotville for his meeting with Comdt Pat Quinlan of the captive A Company, September 1961.

President Moise Tshombe of Katanga outside the Hôtel de l'Europe in Jadotville before meeting with Comdt Pat Quinlan in September 1961.

A Company officers and NCOs pictured in Custume Barracks, Athlone, in June 1961, prior to departure for the Congo. Front row, l to r: Quartermaster Sergeant Paddy Neville, OC Comdt Patrick Quinlan, Second-in-Command Capt Dermot Byrne, Company Sergeant Jack Prendergast Rear, l to r: Capt Kevin McCarthy, Capt Thomas McGuinn, Lieut Joe Leech, Capt Liam Donnelly Lieut Tom Quinlan. The shoulder just visible on the extreme right belongs to Lieut Noel Carey.

Comdt Patrick Quinlan, OC A Company (seated in foreground wearing beret), with men of A Company in the defunct Hôtel de l'Europe, Jadotville, after they were taken captive in September 1961.

Cpl Bobby Allan with young Congolese friends at A Company's camp in Elisabethville.

Comdt Pat Quinlan at his desk in Elisabethville prior to departure for Jadotville.

October 1961. Quartermaster Sergeant Paddy Neville festooned with guns he had just been given for the re-equipping of A Company after their release. The ground sheet is to protect him from the heavy rains.

Private Michael O'Sullivan in a picture taken by Sgt Walter Hegarty in Elisabethville, December 1961.

Elisabethville, November 1961, l to r: Quartermaster Sergeant Paddy Neville, Sgt Walter Hegarty (in green-coloured muslin he decided offered better camouflage than the blue UN beret), Company Sgt Jack Prendergast and, behind, Private Billy Ready.

Comdt. Pat Quinlan (left) with Private Billy Ready (right) and an unidentified man in Elisabethville during the heavy rains of November/December 1961.

Listening to radio broadcasts in Elisabethville, December 1961, l to r: Lieut Joe Leech, Lieut Tom Quinlan, Private Billy Ready, Cpl Michael Lynch and Private Bobby Bradley.

17-year-old Private John Gorman in Elisabethville during the fighting in early December 1961.

Cpls Bobby Allan, Michael Lynch and Sean Foley in the Curragh Camp before leaving for the Congo in June 1961.

The remains of the Fouga that bombed A Company in Jadotville in Elisabeth Airport after it was shot down in December 1961.

Pat Quinlan (centre) with (from left) Swedish co-pilot Eric Thors, interpreter Lars Fröberg and two Katangan guards in Kolwezi Prison camp in October 1961.

there (together with a group of other reporters), he described the meeting in his own, inimitable and evocative style:

> Entering Jadotville I felt like an explorer seeing one of the lost Inca cities … as we approached the hotel prison camp, which was ringed off with roadblocks at each end and manned by para-commandos, the Irish prisoners were sitting on the steps of the veranda. Across the road armed gendarmerie kept watch from the front of requisitioned cafés.
>
> When the prisoners saw us coming towards them they could hardly believe we were Irish. Then we greeted them with 'Céad Míle Fáilte' and they were all around us, smiling and laughing.
>
> We exchanged news and gave them the latest from the free world while they told us about their stand and how they felt as prisoners.
>
> Before leaving Jadotville we had lunch with our escort in a hotel in which I noticed that Guinness stout was for sale.
>
> 'The Irish are our friends,' said a young Katangan officer, Lieut Vicky Moujalon, 'and I want you to tell your people at home that we do not want to kill them.' He realised, he said, that the Irish troops had come to Katanga to try and help his country and he did not want to think of them as enemies. He told us that President Tshombe also thought very highly of the Irish and that was one of the reasons why he insisted on the prisoners being well treated in Jadotville and that no harm should come to them.
>
> One precious hour was all we were allowed and during that time there were interviews to be taken and scenes to be 'shot' for television. I did not feel too happy doing the interviews as a member of the Gendarmerie, with the bayonet of his gun pointing towards me, looked over my shoulder every so often and seemed to think that the shorthand outlines were some kind of secret code. But our visit, short and all though it was, brought great joy to the Irish prisoners as did the bag of mail we brought.
>
> In a bar in the native quarter we had a drink with a young Katangan officer and his commando comrade.

The tables were crowded with men and women drinking local beer. A record player with a faulty needle blared out African dance music and couples went to the special dancing platform in one corner to sway and swing to the rhythms as others clapped their hands to the beat.

But Smith's report told, too, of less reassuring behaviour on the part of others of A Company's Gendarmerie guard:

> For days after the surrender the Katangans were still bringing in their dead. Sometimes they would stop outside the building where the Irish troops were being kept and show dead bodies to the Gendarmerie on guard, something not calculated to increase the confidence of the Irish in their prospects of staying alive. The excitable Gendarmerie would then get drunk and when night fell shots were sometimes fired in the direction of the hotel prison camp. There were times when the Irish wondered if the coming of dawn would see them all massacred.

Raymond Smith spoke with Comdt Quinlan at the Hôtel de l'Europe. Discussing the 'fateful climax' of the Battle of Jadotville, Quinlan told him:

> We played a delaying game as long as we could on that Sunday, hoping against hope that reinforcements would arrive as we negotiated a definite ceasefire. I hoped that we would get a written ceasefire but soon Munongo was demanding surrender, and only surrender terms, otherwise the final onslaught would begin. I realised that our position had become hopeless and that there was no prospect of relief arriving in time. I knew too that if I continued my men would be massacred by a vastly superior force so I agreed to the terms.

Smith concluded that if Jadotville had not ended as it did, '… it would surely have resulted in heavy loss of life on the Irish side.'

Not all of Quinlan's dealings with the press were so agreeable. He was angered, and felt betrayed by Radio Éireann's John Ross to whom he entrusted a letter to be posted to his wife, Carmel, when Ross arrived back in Ireland. With the letter, Quinlan enclosed an original copy of the radio log of messages sent and received during the Jadotville battle. Ross mentioned the letter at Battalion HQ in Elisabethville and, when asked for it, handed it over. The letter was never seen again.

In October, Quinlan, incensed and unaware of the details, wrote angrily about both the Radio Éireann reporter and Battalion OC when he discovered that his letter and enclosures had not been delivered:

> John Ross is a tramp. He got explicit instructions from me that you were to get that letter. It was a complete, certified log of all messages to and from Battalion HQ and it made very interesting reading. I wanted it in your safe hands so that you could vindicate A Company and me if we did not come back. Ross gave it to the Battalion OC and although it was addressed to you I understand you never in fact got it.

Throughout all of this time, the erratic movements of the Gendarmerie continued to create tension for the prisoners. Carey gives an example of what happened early one morning:

> At first light, we heard loud shouting and vehicles pulling up at the Katangan HQ across the road from the hotel. Looking out, we saw a jeep with a coffin in the back. What was going to happen? Was it for one of us? Were the Katangans going to get their revenge on us?
>
> It got dreadfully tense as time passed, and still the vehicle remained parked outside our window. Then a number of Katangan soldiers appeared with a Katangan flag, draped it over the coffin and moved off slowly into Jadotville.
>
> Afterwards (when he was imprisoned with us in Kolwezi) Charlie Kearney explained that only officers were buried ceremonially but tension remained for days afterwards.

Moise Tshombe visited the Irish prisoners on 1 October. Notwithstanding Raymond Smith's reporting of the Katangan President's high regard for the Irish, Tshombe's meeting with Quinlan was, according to A Company's commander, anything but auspicious. He wrote:

> On the day Tshombe came to visit the prison camp at Jadotville the white population in the town fawned on him. Tshombe himself adopted a jeering attitude towards us prisoners. He asked me how we were being treated and I told him we had no complaints with regard to the food or our treatment by the guard. I protested very vigorously against the breaking of not only the verbal promises but also the written guarantees of the surrender. He refused to discuss the matter and turned his back in a sneering attitude.

Carey also felt the lash of Tshombe's derision, and wrote:

> Moise Tshombe arrived with his full retinue in a large Mercedes, surrounded by cheering natives and troops. The visit was recorded by Reuters Newsreels. Comdt Quinlan and our interpreter, Lieutenant Lars Fröberg, met Tshombe outside our hotel. We watched from our balcony as our Commanding Officer demanded our immediate release, told the President we were operating as a peacekeeping force under United Nations mandate, were entitled to freedom of movement, had been attacked completely without any provocation on our part and had only defended ourselves.
>
> Tshombe sneered at him, turned on his heels and, waving to his ecstatic supporters, disappeared in a cloud of dust back to Jadotville.

And the redoubtable Fröberg, who with justification says he was 'everywhere with Pat Quinlan and A Company' remembers the event vividly. He says that Tshombe was not

> …in a very good humour the day he came to visit us in Jadotville. His mood was not improved when Comdt

Quinlan kept him waiting. It was not one of my easier tasks as interpreter, keeping the President calm and happy while I tried to convince him that Comdt Quinlan would arrive. They didn't like each other when they met. Quinlan wanted his men freed and I was in the middle trying to make things more or less peaceful. Since Quinlan and his men were prisoners anything could have happened. It was not a good situation.

During the time A Company was imprisoned in Jadotville, all of the wireless messages were written out in chronological order. This was to ensure that there would be a record of the sequence of events during the fighting.

On 3 October, the heavens opened. 'The rains came at 15.05pm,' Quinlan noted, 'after tremendously bad thunder and lightning. It was the first rain we had seen since 21st June in Dublin.'

Concerned about the ordeal his wife and family had gone through, he wrote again and again to reassure, to give thanks for support from all at home—and to respond to newspaper reports telling how Irish troops were being used in the Congo.

Jadotville. Hôtel de l'Europe. Wednesday, 4th October

My dear Carmel:

My God, you all must have suffered. I don't know how you stood up to it with all that frightful publicity. It was far worse for you than it was for us. God bless you and all the stout-hearted wives and mothers in Ireland.

It was pretty grim here during those days. I don't know how we escaped. I am convinced there was a supernatural hand guiding us all the time. We all felt that during the battle. It is extraordinary but it is true. It must have been your prayers at home. All my decisions seemed to have been inspired. Even with the ceasefire and surrender talks, when I was tired and very weary, I got strength and surprised myself with the clarity of my mind on all the points.

Yes, perhaps I was tricked as McKeown said. But I would not have been tricked if the reinforcements had stayed at the bridge. It all hinged on that and I was helpless with no hope of more help. My only concern was for the safety of the lives of my men. Before God and their Irish mothers and wives and fathers I am satisfied that I have done my duty.

Further fighting would have achieved nothing except terrible slaughter. We would probably have taken 10 or 20-to-one or more, but we did not come here to kill Africans—we did not want to do it at any time. The result for us would have been death anyway in useless slaughter.

We are getting excellent treatment here. I really mean that. We have no complaints whatever but we would like to be out of here and at home in Ireland. The tapes were wonderful. Please thank Colonel Emphy [of Custume Barracks, Athlone] for his kind words. Those tapes were the greatest morale booster the men got.

I don't blame the Irish people for being up in arms against the misuse of Irish troops here. It is a pity that we, who never believed in the use of force, must suffer for the blunders of little dictators and stupid military leaders who thought they were here for a holiday.

God bless, as ever, Pat

Hopes of an exchange of prisoners, and A Company's release, rose over the following days. A fresh batch of letters and newspapers arrived too.

Jadotville. Thursday, 5th October 1961

My dear Carmel and children:

We are all in the best of health and spirits and hope to be out of here in a few days.

Yes, I got some of the papers. It was front page news all right. If they only knew half of it.

The Katangese are still searching the bush for their own dead and wounded. They have dug up all our positions looking for our dead. They still don't believe that we had nobody killed. If you saw the positions you would not believe it either.

Sometimes we find it hard to believe it ourselves. It was prayers at home that saved us. It was no doubt a miracle. We are told we killed 150 and wounded twice that many. [Later reports would show 300 dead.] Assure all the wives that the men are in great form.

All my love to you all, Daddy

On that day too, 5 October, the Jadotville prison hotel was visited by a UN Ceasefire Commission, made up mostly of Swedes and with the Swedish Colonel Shelgren at its head. The purpose of the visit was to view the men's conditions as POWs. Though the visit produced nothing useful by way either of information or a date for their release, the prisoners were glad to see that they were at least on an agenda somewhere.

Fröberg was glad, too, to meet countrymen, one of whom was his brother-in-law, Colonel Anders Kjellgren, and another an interpreter friend, Lieutenant Stig von Bayer. 'The helicopter crew and I, all of us Scandinavians of course, got a bottle of Scotch each. We were very glad to see those visitors.'

The prisoners were more than a little put out when the Katangan Guard, two days later, on 7 October, carried out a sudden search and appropriated all of their personal 'wireless receiver sets'. This—what Quinlan describes as 'a big blow to morale'—effectively cut their links with the outside world. Or would have, if Noel Carey's small and trusty transistor had not been safely hidden away.

Dr Hoffman, a Red Cross official, visited on Monday, 9 October. Donnelly noted that 'the guard dealt roughly with the Red Cross official'. Quinlan wrote what was to be his last letter home for two weeks, a letter that was in large part written for public, and political, consumption.

Jadotville. Monday, 9th October 1961

My dear Carmel:

The Red Cross were here today and they brought some mail. They are taking out these letters for us. All letters are subject to censorship of course, but we are still very well treated though our wireless was taken away. We miss it very much as we were able to get Irish news. We are all very well and in high spirits but of course we are tired of being hostages.

Please continue the good work at home. There is only one solution that I can see to all prisoner problems and that is to transfer us to Rhodesia, or some neutral country, at once. Please work on this immediately and by all means at your disposal. We are all depending on you on behalf of the families of all the soldiers here. It must be remembered that all the prisoners are Irish except for the two Swedes, one Norwegian and six Italians.

This should be brought forcibly home to the Irish Government. Ask them why this has happened.

Don't worry about me. We are all fine here and we have confidence in the Divine protection which we have had always with us. I think perhaps we are doing more for the peaceful solution to the problems of this unhappy land as prisoners then we did by fighting.

God bless, as ever, Pat

He did not tell Carmel Quinlan that his concerns, and desire for a transfer to Rhodesia, were the result of the visit by the Red Cross official, Dr Hoffman. 'He was worried about our safety,' Quinlan noted in a report on the incident.

He confided in me that he did not trust the Katanga authorities with regard to exchange of prisoners. He stated that these people did not want their prisoners back. He wanted to get us transferred to Rhodesia or some neutral country and he wanted me to try and contact the Irish government to work on this.

He did not want his name mentioned as he said it would appear that he was not being neutral as a Red Cross man.

Dr Hoffman was anything but neutral.

CHAPTER 49

In the last analysis, it is our conception of death which decides our answers to all the questions that life puts to us.

Dag Hammarskjöld, Diaries, 1958

World news. September–October 1961

Major Jose Denlin, the pilot of the Fouga jet which so mercilessly bombed and strafed A Company during the battle, surfaced and was given flesh in a report in the Irish Press on 28 September.

Belgian-born, he was a veteran of South Africa's Army and had fought for Katanga since that province's independence. John Kearns, the Kamina Airport Control Officer, spoke to reporter Desmond Fisher about conversations he had had with Denlin during the battles of Elisabethville and Jadotville.

> The first was when he came in using his rockets and dropped a couple of bombs. As he climbed off he signalled: 'Kamina, how was that?' I replied 'Not so good' and Denlin retorted: 'I'll be back'. He came back. This time his bombing was a little nearer and he asked: 'was that better?' I told him that he was improving and he chuckled as he said again, 'I'll be back.' He came back a third time and on this run hit and burnt a DC4 on the ground. 'How was that for shooting?' he signalled and I replied, 'Good, but anyone can have a lucky shot.' He was annoyed and said, 'I thought the least you would have done would be to congratulate me on improving so much.' I said to him, 'It is easy to hit a sitting plane. What about one flying and fighting you?'

On 30 September, reports worldwide told of how the people of the town of Uppsala, Sweden, lined the streets, weeping, at the state funeral of Dag Hammarskjöld, when the UN Secretary General was buried in a simple family grave. The mourners included the Swedish royal family, members of the Diplomatic Corps and representatives of almost every member country of the United Nations, including the Soviet Union.

On 30 September, too, the *Irish Press* carried a picture of members of A Company 'hanging out their laundry in the grounds of the Hôtel de l'Europe, in Jadotville, where they are in the custody of Katangan para-commandos.'

A few days later, on 3 October, the *Irish Press* reported Quinlan's protest about the refusal of the Katangan President to listen to his formal complaints. Quinlan told a reporter: 'You can tell the outside world that Mr Tshombe refused to listen to my formal protest against the breaking of a written surrender agreement.'

The Irish Times of the following day headlined on its front page: 'Serious Hitch Arises In Katanga Talks' over a report about Dr Conor Cruise O'Brien disclosing Mr Tshombe's refusal to allow the mixed military commission which was supervising the ceasefire to inspect Katangan troop positions in Jadotville. The commission had already visited all other UN posts in Katanga. 'The position now is that while they have seen all our positions we have seen none of theirs,' O'Brien said.

CHAPTER 50

Suddenly the villagers gathered around waving, gesticulating and making all sorts of threats, should they get their hands on us, wailing and throwing sods of grass at our windows....

Lieut N. Carey, Katanga, October 1961

Katanga. October 1961

On 11 October 1961, A Company and the other prisoners were transferred from Jadotville to Kolwezi. Their journey began when, as Hegarty describes it, '... we were without warning warned to prepare for a shift. The CO fought the thing tooth and nail but no go.'

What would be a torturous, brutalising journey, took the entire day; from 9 a.m. until nearly midnight; and is remembered by all of the men, for its various and humiliating experiences. Hegarty recalls:

We travelled all that day on water bottles, packed tight in buses to Kolwezi. On the way, we left the beaten track to go to a Gendarmerie Barracks in the bush where we spent one hour while they decided not to keep us there ... by 1930 hours we were sitting in our buses by a large building in Kolwezi, all barbed wire and heavily guarded, while a little pig of a Katangan officer called us the 'beasts of l'ONU' in French.

Next order was to take off our berets, then the dear fellow gave an impassioned speech to his satellites on how the murderers should be treated with demo. We dismounted one bus at a time, our lot first. We were personally searched, then our kits for any type of weapon, ammo, our belts, packs and in fact all ordnance down to our whistles.

Two of the lads had rounds in their kit bags for which they were struck in the face by a savage lieutenant. The CO was as white as a sheet with a liver. They even took off our boots and socks. As each bus was done the men were herded into the building to wait until all were finished. The Civvy who accompanied us from Jado was most distressed and tried time and again to get the thing hurried but to no avail. Finally, by 12 midnight it was all finished and by 0130 hours we had got cha, sandwiches and then off to a worried sleep....

Quinlan's report is entirely factual:

We had no food for the journey and very little water. All our equipment, except personal belongings, was confiscated in the morning. We were first taken to a Gendarmerie Camp at Nzilo, about 20 miles north of Kolwezi. There we were subjected to all kinds of abuse from hundreds of undisciplined Gendarmerie and women. We were, however, after some time taken back again to Kolwezi—much to our relief.

At Kolwezi prison camp we were subjected to a search which lasted for hours, during which two of our men were punched in the face by a Gendarmerie lieutenant. Very forceful protests were made by Capt. Donnelly and myself, and with the assistance of the civilian commissioner, Mr Muteba Beston, the beatings were discontinued.

Donnelly's version of events fills in some detail but dallies no longer than that of his OC on the anguish and fury experienced by the men:

Moved from Jadotville to Kolwezi via Ngilo Camp ... the tea and bread at the end of the journey was very welcome. The stop at Ngilo Camp was upsetting to us all because of the hostility of the native troops, and families. On arrival at the new prison site at Kolwezi I was extracted from the bus and a Katangan officer gave a demo with a rifle and fixed bayonet on how to deal with any UN who tried to escape.

I had many strange feelings towards that officer as I was the UN model he used for his demonstration.

A few of our men were beaten by the guards; Corporal [McAnaney] and Gnr. Peppard were definitely victims of uncalled for beatings. With the Company Commander I pleaded with the Katanga Commander to carry out his search in a soldierly fashion and eventually normal relations were resumed.

Everyone got indoors and had tea, bread as already stated and slept on the floors as our bedding from Jadotville had not yet arrived.

Tired, thirsty and upset we had little sleep that night.

And Carey, eye ever diligent to detail, gives his first-hand account:

…buses arrived, and Katangan Army vehicles, with heavily armed troops. We mounted the buses … after driving for a few hours on a main, metalled road, we pulled off into a native village and stopped. Suddenly the villagers gathered around waving, gesticulating and making all sorts of threats, should they get their hands on us, wailing and throwing sods of grass at our windows. We sat there, unarmed, defenceless, completely at their mercy and wondering what was going to happen to us. The prospects did not appear to be too pretty.

However, after an hour we finally pulled out of the village with loud screams directed at us as we withdrew. We were told later that a number of natives in the village had lost relatives during the fighting at Jadotville.

It was dark when we arrived at Kolwezi, a town about the size of Jadotville. We actually arrived at the same location that I had over-nighted during our patrol to Dilolo, about a month previously, but was now changed into a POW camp with barbed wire fences and floodlights.

The buses pulled up one by one at the main gate, manned by Katangan troops. As the first group dismounted from the bus we could hear loud roaring and some of our lads being struck and kicked around. It transpired that their bags were now being thoroughly searched and when the Katangans discovered ammo and some items of equipment like bayonets etc., they ruffed up our troops. The situation was getting really nasty until Comdt Quinlan intervened and the beatings ceased.

There was panic in our bus when a few of my platoon found ammunition and grenades in their rucksacks. I took them and as the guards had dismounted from our bus I was able to stuff them down the back seat of the bus. We were individually searched, a most humiliating experience, and finally directed into the main building.

Exhausted, shattered, tired and hungry we still had to shake out our platoons, and allot accommodation and then retire to our own area and sleep on the solid, stone floors.

But it was rest enough, or deemed so anyway by Quinlan, who had his troops up early the following morning and was insisting, Carey says, 'that we maintain a routine. I was tasked with organising a five-a-side football competition on the waste ground just outside the building. The OC himself demanded to meet the Burgermeister/Mayor, which happened, and arranged for food and bedding to be provided for the company.'

Quinlan gave a terse summary of their changed circumstances:

We had a rough time of it for two or three days with frequent searches, but eventually the situation eased. We had no beds or mattresses for two days. Eventually we got 76 mattresses and some beds. We distributed these as far as possible so that each officer and man had either a bed or a mattress.

On 13 October, Donnelly had a few drily caustic remarks to make about those beds, and the general situation:

Our beds arrive from Jadotville. They are in a poor state now. Many of us slept on the bed springs in lieu of sleeping on what appeared to be mattresses.

Generally the food is good, adequate and well prepared by an excellent company cook staff that works terribly hard to produce palatable meals.

He notes too that, 'Lieutenant Carey smuggled in a radio, a small Jap transistor which he buried in the backyard in a plastic bag. Each night that he thought it safe and secure to do so he tried to get news items at 2300 hours. "Ceasefire" talks still proceed was all we heard. About time for them to end and for us to get free was our opinion.'

Carey, for his part, was delighted to find that they were, 'supplied with Rhodesian cream butter … like manna from heaven.' He also tells about *that* transistor, how he, 'hid it in the false bottom of my rucksack where, despite a number of searches, it was not discovered. At night I could still listen to Radio Rhodesia for news.'

For Sean Foley, who says simply that the Katangans 'weren't very hospitable in Kolwezi. Some people got thumped and that wasn't right', priorities were different. He explains:

I'd a set of Highland pipes with me. They'd been my father's. I had them in my bag and a guard in Kolwezi thought they were a weapon. I told him they were for 'ceol na h-Éireann'. I told him in Irish and in French and got him to understand me. I would have died for those pipes. I wasn't going to let him have them. He understood me. I still have them and play them.

On 15 October, when the six Italian prisoners were released, the Irish prisoners were filled with a hope that their own freedom was imminent. It seemed even more likely when, on the morning of 16 October, at 0700 hours, they were given ten minutes to get ready to travel to Elisabethville (via Jadotville) where, they were told, they would be exchanged and released later in the day.

However, it was to be a bizarre, nightmare repeat of their journey between Jadotville and Kolwezi. Quinlan wrote:

We had no food to take on the journey and no water bottles, but we filled some containers with water for each bus. After a hurried breakfast we were ready but we did not leave until approx 1000 hours. We arrived in Jadotville at approx 1630 hours and were told we would have to stay there for the night as there had been a hitch in the ceasefire talks.

We got some food at approximately 1900 hours.

At 2330 hours we were ordered to get ready to move again and we left about 0300 hours. All the officers were put in one bus. We travelled by the main road to the 'Seven Sources', which was within a few miles of Elisabethville. From there we travelled by back roads and were taken to every African compound in the native city in Elisabethville where thousands of men, women and children were thronged in organised demonstrations to jeer and insult us.

We arrived at the Katangan Army HQ in Camp Massard at 0800 hours and there again hundreds of Gendarmerie, women and children were massed to jeer and insult us. We were kept on the buses until 1130 hours. Water was refused and the men were even refused permission to go to the toilet. A Gendarmerie 2nd. Lieut, aide to Colonel Muke, was in charge.

He was a sadist.

At 1130 hours we were marched between lines of fixed bayonets to the canteen. After a few minutes Mahmoud Khiary, the UN Chief of Civilian Operations in the Congo, arrived with British, American and French consuls. When they left we were marched again in groups to the buses and remained there until 1630 hours, spending all day in boiling buses in the blazing sun.

This day was a terrible exercise and I was very worried about the effects on the men. We were not allowed to communicate between buses. We were denied water and men were allowed to travel only in groups of four under heavy guard to the toilets. This was such an ordeal that they did not avail of it.

At 1630 hours we left Camp Massard and returned by the same route to repeated performances from the mobs in the native city.

On the long, long journey back to Kolwezi, again via Jadotville, comfort was minimal and, according to Hegarty, the temperature inside the buses dangerously variable:

> During the 22-hour journey I got lying space on the floor and after a while got up to stretch but in that instant another guy had dropped sleeping into the spot. It was freezing cold at night, the speed sending an icy blast down the coach. Many had their blanket pack on the baggage truck. A nightmare two days but like always the men produced secret reserves and endured the cramped space, the heat, the cold and the uncomfortable coaches without complaint.
>
> In the interim between our swap moves three Irish officers and two civilians were captured....

What Hegarty, and the rest of A Company, did not know was that the three officers, Captains McKeever, Purfield and Carroll, had been sent to Camp Massard by Battalion HQ in an attempt to see and confirm that A Company was actually at the camp. Battalion HQ had not been told of the company's movement from Kolwezi; the three officers were arrested by the Katangans as spies.

Charles Kearney and Hamish Mathieson were arrested with them. Both men were working as engineers and had earlier done what they could to keep A Company informed of moves against them. Both had also, and strongly, objected to Union Minière's supplying and financing the Katangan forces.

CHAPTER 51

I am honest and I hope that the people I am dealing with are honest.
The prisoners will not be liberated if the agreement is not approved.
President M. Tshombe, 15 October 1961

World News. October 1961

The story, and speculation about the fate, of the 184 United
Nations peacekeeping soldiers who were prisoners in Katanga
made world news for weeks. In Ireland, and because all but a
handful of the prisoners were Irish, it was headline news on an
almost daily basis.

On Monday, 16 October, the *Irish Independent* ran with the
hopeful headline, 'Prisoners Await Release' and, underneath, 'U.N.
expected to ratify pact today'. The report told readers that the
release of the Irish prisoners was 'all set for this afternoon, provided
that the agreement signed by Mr Tshombe and the U.N. negotiator
Mr. Mahmoud Khiari is ratified by the U.N. General Secretariat
in New York.' Dr Conor Cruise O'Brien was reported as saying
that he had received word from Mr Tshombe that the movement
of prisoners to Elisabethville from their compound at Kolwezi was
already under way.

Mr Tshombe, however, and in another statement, made it clear
that he would not release the 184 UN prisoners if the Secretariat
went back on the ceasefire agreement. 'I am honest and I hope the
people I am dealing with are honest,' he said. 'The prisoners will not
be liberated if the agreement is not approved.'

The same paper, next day, reported that five lorry loads of
prisoners had left the Kolwezi compound, but had not been produced
for an arranged handover. Katangan authorities, the paper said,

282

...failed to produce 184 Irish United Nations prisoners in time for a scheduled exchange yesterday [Monday, 16 October] and a tense situation appears to be building up once more.

The exchange was arranged for 4.20 p.m. local time (2.20 p.m. Irish time) on a disused airstrip built during the Second World War to ferry Katanga's uranium to make the world's first atom bomb.

An hour before the arranged time lorries drove up with 45 Katangans who were being held by the United Nations. An hour after the exchange time the prisoners held by the Katangans had not appeared and it seemed the exchange was unlikely to go through.

Trying to make sense of what had happened, the *Irish Press* on the same day said it was not clear 'whether Mr Tshombe was delaying the exchange until he had confirmation of the U.N. approval of the ceasefire agreement or if the transport arrangements had broken down as reported in Elisabethville.'

In Britain, the influential *Economist* magazine trenchantly questioned 'how Mr Tshombe got the Irishmen whom he is now using as a bargaining counter?'

The Irishmen had been sent to Jadotville at the urgent request of the Belgian Consul and his colleagues who said that Europeans there were in grave danger.

They were promptly surrounded and shelled by a much superior force, led by Belgian officers, and bombed by a jet aircraft flown from a base 100 miles away, flown by a European ...

The U.N.'s anxiety to free them is now one of the levers on which Mr Tshombe—or his even more intransigent friends—may press to secure better terms. The Katangan President's trail of broken promises is now so long that the only question left is whether he is personally responsible for all his responsibilities or is not a free agent.

And then there came the dramatic events of Wednesday, 18 October, when, as the prisoners were taken back again to Jadotville from Camp

Massard in Elisabethville, a trio of Irish UN officers and two civilians were arrested near Camp Massard.

The *Irish Independent*, on 19 October, carried an intimidating front-page picture of Katangan police, armed with machine guns, guarding Camp Massard and, alongside, a picture of a bespectacled, captured Captain Terence McKeever. The accompanying report told how three UN officers and two civilian technicians had been arrested and detained by Katangan Gendarmerie near Katanga Army headquarters (Camp Massard) in Elisabethville.

A statement from the Department of Defence named the officers as Captain Michael Purfield (38) married, 52 Laurel Park, Clondalkin, Dublin, Captain Michael A.M. Carroll, married, 32 Ballymannen Estate, Newbridge, Co. Kildare, and Captain McKeever (39) married and from Trimleston Gardens, Booterstown, Co. Dublin. A message from Leopoldville said the group had gone for a walk in Elisabethville and not returned. They had passed close to Camp Massard.

A Katangan source said that one of the men had been carrying a map of the army camp. President Tshombe said that the five men had been armed with machine guns when arrested.

Dr Conor Cruise O'Brien refused to give the names of the civilians detained. He was of the opinion that the whole affair was 'a foolish prank.' But, two days later, in the *Irish Independent* of Saturday, 21 October, Mr Tshombe claimed that the arrested group had been trying to liberate the 184 Irish UN prisoners then held at the camp.

A UN statement continued to maintain that the five had gone for a walk near the camp.

CHAPTER 52

This time we made plans. This time we determined that, if there was any hitch in arrangements, we were NOT going to become prisoners again.

Comdt P. Quinlan, October 1961

Katanga, Congo. October 1961

In Jadotville, when the prisoners got there, the Hôtel de l'Europe, was locked and chained. It was 2030 hours and Quinlan 'bought some biscuits and tins of cooked beef for the men. The Italian owner of the shop where we bought this food gave all his minerals and a lot of sweets and biscuits free of charge to the men.'

The captives slept for a few hours on the footpath where, according to Carey, 'even the Katangan Guards were exhausted and disgruntled.'

A few hours later, they left Jadotville, again, for Kolwezi, again. The journey through the chilly night and into morning took five hours. They were joined in the Kolwezi camp at 0600 hours by Commissioner Mutaba, a man Quinlan describes at 'very kind and considerate' and who made immediate arrangements to have the captives fed. Quinlan wrote:

> Mr Mutaba did everything possible to make our lot comfortable. He sent his staff on distances of about 50 miles to secure vegetables, potatoes and meat for us. I submitted a written demand to him to be given to Dr Hoffman of Geneva Red Cross, telling Hoffman of our position and asking that he be allowed visit us and bring us our mail.
>
> My demand was taken to Tshombe and he refused it.

On 19 October, at 0900 hours, there was what Donnelly calls, 'such a surprise', when they were joined by five new prisoners. Terry McKeever, Mark Carroll, Mick Purfield, Charlie Kearney and Hamish Mathieson, subject of much newspaper reporting and speculation, who had been captured near Camp Massard in Elisabethville, were brought to join them in Kolwezi. Their arrival was hugely welcomed, Carey heralding the civilian newcomers as 'invaluable' because of the 'stories they had to tell':

> They told us that Union Minière, during the battle in Jadotville, had started converting JCBs as armoured vehicles to attack us with. They also told us that we'd been surrounded by up to 3,000 troops and that we had inflicted hundreds of casualties on the Katangans.

Hegarty too was delighted with 'Charlie Kearney and a Scot by the name of Hamish Mathieson, who were particularly invaluable when it came to giving us information as both had been in Jado during the fighting. The stories they told! The five of them were captured while having a few drinks....'

Quinlan acknowledged the five as a welcome addition to Kolwezi in more prosaic fashion in his report: 'They gave us the first news of the outside world we had heard for about four weeks.' But word of these good times clearly reached the ears of President Tshombe who, the following day, ordered that the newcomers were to be isolated and taken to another camp.

This was not good. A 'civilian adviser' came to Quinlan and, 'gravely concerned' about the prospects of moving the five men, asked the OC of A Company if he could organise a way in which the five could be isolated within the Kolwezi camp. Quinlan did what he could and they were allowed stay. The civilian adviser got the situation sanctioned. Quinlan wrote:

> It was agreed as a temporary measure only but the men were never in fact transferred away from us at any time. Also, on their first night in Kolwezi, the guards took their watches and made life very unpleasant. I learned of this and made vigorous

protest immediately. Their watches were returned and the guards treated them well thereafter.

Carey, ever resilient himself, professed amazement at the fact that:

> ...within a few days [in Kolwezi] the lads [his platoon] were back to themselves. My platoon Sergeant, Kevin McLoughlin, a real father figure, did a great job restoring morale. We recommended daily inspections, training and sport such as our five-a-side soccer competition which was played with great gusto. Each morning we had open-air Mass and I still listened to my portable radio in secret. Accommodation was dreadfully cramped and privacy was nil and I was told later that my NCOs used to watch my face each day to see if things were getting more serious, or less.

Donnelly had the more commonplace discomfort of an aching tooth to contend with. On 21 October, he was escorted by Gendarmerie to a dentist in the town. The dentist wore civilian clothing, put in a temporary filling and told Donnelly to come back on the following Monday for the permanent job.

On Sunday, 22 October, the chaplain performed two wedding ceremonies for members of the Katangan guard. 'It was an unusual event in such surroundings,' Donnelly wrote, 'and helped cheer us up.' Quinlan wrote home about it, cheerfully, and more optimistically than the reality warranted:

> Kolwezi. Monday, 23rd October 1961

> My dear Carmel and children:
> Well, yesterday was a big occasion here. It was 'Propagation of the Faith' day and do you know we had two baptisms and two marriages performed by Fr Fagan. Katangan soldiers of our guard got married. One of the new wives was baptised first. The other new wife had her three-month-old daughter baptised. We gave the wedding breakfast and it was a great day.

So you see we may be doing more good here as prisoners than in any other capacity. The men of the company were godfathers and best men and etc.

Don't worry about me, I am fine. The men need my leadership now more than they ever needed it. I always pray that I won't fail them. I go to Mass and Communion every day. We now appreciate a lot of things that we took for granted before. The food here is very good and I have a small imprest with which I buy some beer and cigarettes for the men every day.

We have good accommodation in our new prison camp and just as well as the rains are here now. We had hailstones as big as marbles today.

It was a big blow to us last Tuesday when we were taken to Elisabethville to be returned to the UN but something went wrong with the talks. We don't know what happened of course as we have no contact with the outside world. We heard from Mark Carroll (Ned's brother) who had joined us here with four others, that Fianna Fáil has formed a government again.

We are all hoping that the Irish people and government have taken our cause into their own hands to secure our quick release. After all, there are 186 Irish prisoners here out of a total of 190 men.

I also wrote to Colonel Emphy and Colm Cox on 8th October and sent the letters via Dr Hoffman of the Geneva Red Cross. I have asked for Dr Hoffman to visit us here and to bring us letters but so far nothing has come of it.

I have the record player with me and we play Irish songs for the men now and again. They are in great form. God bless them, they are wonderful.

Fond love and God bless you all, Pat

On Monday, Donnelly did not make it to his appointment with the dentist. The guard commander did not understand English. The following day, he asked permission from the new guard commander and was sent to the dentist without an appointment. 'On this occasion,' Donnelly writes, 'I found the dentist splendidly garbed in Gendarmerie officers' uniform of captains' rank. He was much embarrassed and changed into civilian attire to fill my teeth. Later, with Lars Fröberg and Comdt Quinlan I attended a Press Conference at the District Commissioner's office for world press correspondents. At 2010 hours we got news that we would be freed in Elisabethville the next day.'

They were to leave at 0900 hours next morning.

Quinlan, anticipating another journey, had several days before asked for a supply of bully beef. They got this now and made sandwiches. Quinlan was not going to take anything for granted on this occasion; not even their release.

'This time we made plans,' he wrote. 'This time we determined that, if there was any hitch in arrangements, we were *not* going to become prisoners again.'

Carey explains what was planned:

> A meeting was called by our Commanding Officer Quinlan at which it was decided that if our release failed we would take over each bus by disabling our guards, driving the buses from the edge of Elisabethville, down the main road towards the Indian Dogra roadblock. It was a desperate plan, which could prove difficult to coordinate and could result in many casualties.

But if the alternative was to become prisoners again...

They left Kolwezi at 0900 on Wednesday, 25 October, and were taken along the same route as before, travelling, Carey says, 'again through Jadotville, past our old positions. We were delayed a while at Lufira Bridge while obstacles were removed, then went the sixty miles to Elisabethville again. Our hearts were literally in our mouths as we suddenly observed troops and transport lined up in what turned out to be an old, disused airport. When we saw they were UN vehicles and troops our hearts soared.'

It was 1620 and all was quiet, the protesters of the week before nowhere in evidence. Within half an hour, they had been released onto an old air strip.

'We disembarked,' Carey says, 'lined up under the command of our heroic commander Commandant Pat Quinlan and, suddenly, we were free.'

They marched, Donnelly says, 'into the Irish Battalion HQ at the 'Farm' behind the pipers' band and with a Guard of Honour to a welcoming speech by the Battalion OC. Everyone slept, and ate, and read letters and talked and felt a bit awkward to be free and happy once more.'

Everyone experienced the same confusion of emotions. Carey says:

It's impossible to describe the feeling, as it takes days and weeks before you finally realise that freedom means going when and where you wish. We were met by colleagues with great enthusiasm and excitement. I met Lieutenants Jimmy Farrell and Michael Shannon who had a very sympathetic and genuine greeting. When I learned later of their dreadful experiences at the Lufira Bridge and being ambushed on the return journey with a number of casualties we appreciated how impossible was the task given to them. There was absolutely no animosity on my part towards them.

And Quinlan met with President Tshombe, briefly. Fröberg, recalled as interpreter from a celebration of his release with the Swedish battalion, gleefully recounts what took place:

President Tshombe spoke in French and so I asked Comdt Quinlan what he wanted to say to him. He said, 'Whatever you like, Larry' and so I asked the President if he had any questions for Comdt Quinlan. Tshombe was not very nice, sneering and derisive, in fact, and told me to ask why there were so many UN prisoners and so few Katangans. I did not relate this to Quinlan but asked the President instead if he really wanted to know why this was so. He said 'yes' so I told him to go to Jadotville and dig in the ground there, where he would find his brave soldiers. He stopped grinning then. Quinlan could see I wasn't being polite and was pleased. I didn't like Tshombe's impolite sneering at Quinlan, who didn't speak French.

Quinlan wrote home, next day.

Elisabethville. Thursday, 26th October 1961

My darling Carmel and darling children:
    I am free with all my men. We were released at five
o'clock yesterday evening. I have loads of mail here but no
time to read them yet. I must get this away in the post. I will
write tomorrow as soon as I get your letters read and time to
look around. I'm in great form and so are all the men.
    With fond love to all, Pat

On the same day, Carmel Quinlan got formal word of her husband's
release. It came from the Adjutant General's Branch, Army HQ,
Dublin.

To: Mrs P. Quinlan. Re: Release of Prisoners.

A Chara,
    I am directed by An t-Árd Aidiúnach to inform you that
it gives him great pleasure to announce that your husband,
Comdt P. Quinlan, lately held prisoner at Jadotville in the
Republic of the Congo, was released on 25/10/1961. He is
fit and well and suffering no ill effects of his experience.
    Is mise, le meas,
    S. O'Beara (Ceannfort)

The *Irish Press* reported the prisoners freed 'when the ceasefire
agreement between Katanga and the United Nations came into effect'
and told how Mr Tshombe, having arrived late, 'held his hands joined
over his head in a boxer's triumphal salute as he drove along the crowd
of onlookers.'
    Freedom for the men of A Company meant what Carey called 'a
honeymoon for a week, a well earned rest and being resupplied with
weapons.' But then, very quickly, the honeymoon ended as Carey and
others began to sense 'a certain animosity developing between some
members of the Battalion and A Company because of the surrender....'

Quinlan, together with Fr Fagan, was ordered to Leopoldville by General McKeown. The pair arrived in the Congolese capital on Saturday, 28 October, and Quinlan wrote home about the visit a couple of days later. It was a letter which brought many things together, in particular Dr Hoffman's role in things.

Leopoldville. Monday, 30th October 1961

My dear Carmel:

I have spent all day yesterday and today writing a report on Jado and our prisoner of war experiences. The General is going home on holiday and wants it to take with him.

The General wanted me too to take a week and stay here if I liked but I will go back to the men on Thursday.

God but the press went to town on us. I have been completely misquoted and I have been quoted for things I never said at all.

The relief of being free is great. We are not accustomed to it yet. For the past three weeks our lives were hanging on a thread.

When I wrote that letter to you, and to Command O/C [his letters of 9 October to Col. Emphy and to Carmel Quinlan urging that they lobby for A Company's freedom or transfer to a neutral country], I did so on the advice of Dr Hoffman, Geneva Red Cross.

Hoffman confided in me that he was very worried about us prisoners. He said the Katangese did not want their prisoners back and that they would probably shoot them anyway. He felt that Tshombe would hold for impossible concessions and that the UN would have to attack him again.

If that happened we would have had it.

I do not think Dr Hoffman had any confidence in Khiari, the UN representative, either. He wanted the Irish Government to get to work with the Americans and British to have us removed to Rhodesia. He did not want his name mentioned as he would be accused of taking sides.

He also said he was going to contact Geneva and try to get other countries to take up our cause. We were hostages and we knew it.

He was not allowed to visit us again. However it is all over now thank God and all the men are fine.

We all lived on our nerves for a long time and many reactions have set in since we were released. We are operational again and pity help anyone who tries to take away our freedom again.

The Katangans still claim that we had 50 killed and they are still digging looking for the bodies. Now they say they only had two killed. We killed at the very least 150 with twice that number wounded. There were several hundred whites against us as well as 4000 Gendarmerie. Nearly every white in Jadotville, except the Greeks, took up arms.

Tell Joe [Comdt Joe O'Dwyer, a friend and neighbour] that I had a long letter written to him but burned it in case they found it on me if we were searched before release. It had too much in it for their liking. I will give him a good picture of the whole battle later.

We will be home on 18th December.

God bless, Your own, Pat

He wrote again two days later, time and distance having given him a period of reflection but little peace from growing feelings of betrayal.

Leopoldville. Wednesday, 1st November 1961

My dear Carmel and children:

I'm going back to Elisabethville at 4am tomorrow. The General has told me to stay here for a week or more if I wanted but I won't be happy until I'm with the men as things are still sticky enough. I know they want me there and I want to be with them anyhow just in case something happens.

We are all tip-top but it was a terrible strain on the nerves as we knew our lives were forfeit if anything happened between the UN and Katanga while we were prisoners.

We knew too that the Indians were only waiting for an opportunity to have another go and we did not feel that they were worried about 184 Irishmen. It was probably worse on me than on any of the others as I had a terrible responsibility to shoulder the lives of all of the men.

If they tried anything of any sort with us we were determined to sell our lives dearly. Thank God it's over.

I don't know if there will be an enquiry. I'd say the policy now is to play down Jado. Too many big shots are involved and too many heads would roll. On the other hand I don't know how they can avoid a full enquiry.

The whole thing stinks before heaven.

Thank God we saved them all. I have heard that I was to be promoted in the field but it was stopped for some reason, press reports I believe. I was misquoted and people who wanted to believe these misquotes jumped at the opportunity. I'll avoid the publicity from now on.

We certainly will march through Athlone on our return. We will have our own Battle Pennant now, battle battered but still flying proudly. We intend to present it to the Officers' Mess where we hope it will be hung in the ante room— the first Irish battle pennant. It was presented to us in the Officers' Mess before we left.

We have our own UN flag too, also very battered, which the men propose to present to me as a memento of the battle.

All these things can wait anyhow. I'm glad we are finishing the full term here. We would not like to be returned before the rest of the battalion.

All my love to you all, Pat

He went back to Elisabethville and A Company the following day.

CHAPTER 53

I believe the armchair soldiers say that we should have all died at Jadotville. I have all my men alive and that is the greatest victory I could ever hope for.

Comdt P. Quinlan, November 1961

Elisabethville. October/November 1961

With the monsoon rains pouring with a vengeance in Elisabethville, Pat Quinlan's sense of foreboding was not helped by the accommodation provided there for A Company, nor by the weapons with which they were supplied:

> The arms were unsatisfactory: No machine guns or mortars, different types of rifles using different ammunition, only five Bren guns and only one 84mm anti-tank RCL.

Their duties were heavy and included, for a couple of weeks, a guard of 20 men on Dr Conor Cruise O'Brien's house in Le Roches and, later, a similar number guarding the food for the refugee camp. Five members of the company did 24-hour guard duty for the Italian hospital. On 7 November, when B and C Companies left for Niumzo and Niemba, A Company took over responsibility for the security of the Irish camp (HQ personnel were excused all but a minor share of this because of other duties).

Quinlan was again, as he had been in the beginning, outraged at the conditions in which the men were forced to live. He railed about a disregard for their dignity, about the demoralising aspect of their accommodation, a situation which went on regardless of the serious fighting they were involved in right up until they left for home just before Christmas. He wrote:

On our return from POW Camp, the only accommodation available for A Company personnel was a large cow-byre in the shape of an open square with the inner side completely open on to a dirty paved yard. The roof was leaking all over and this was the rainy season. It was alive with mosquitoes. The men were most uncomfortable.

I considered it humiliating to billet men in such accommodation.

While the men accepted privations cheerfully during action it was difficult to understand the necessity for such accommodation at this period of peaceful co-existence with the Katangan forces. It was the only time during our tour in the Congo that morale was in danger.

When I protested, the Battalion OC and Quarter Master assured me that they were doing their best to provide alternative accommodation. They said it would be only a matter of a day or two until some of the many vacant villas in the locality were taken over.

However, this did NOT materialise, due perhaps to difficulties experience by the UN in dealing with Katanga authorities and Belgian owners of villas.

I felt that the occupation of such inferior accommodation did not enhance ideas of our living standards at home in the eyes of other UN contingents and the civilian population.

When B and C Companies left Elisabethville on 7th November A Company moved into the villas evacuated by B Company. But later, on 28th November when the advance party left for home, 50 men were again ordered back to the cow-byre.

However, when fighting broke out again within a few days, accommodation was no longer an important factor.

At this time too, all our food was tinned and an epidemic of diarrhoea broke out which lasted up to the end of our stay in the Congo. Some men were very ill and the energy and vitality of all was sapped.

Despite this, duties were unavoidably very heavy and men were at a low physical state when fighting broke out again in December.

Those duties, inevitably, brought the soldiers of A Company closer than ever to the inhumanity of war and the pain of the vulnerable. Both Donnelly and Carey tell of the distress of patrolling the Baluba camp.

'It was an upsetting duty to see such poverty,' Donnelly says, 'and such a mass of humanity enclosed in such a small area in what was the worst collection of hutments I saw anywhere in the Congo.' The rain was heavy, he says, the mosquitoes 'numerous and objectionable'.

Carey tells of 'some thirty thousand souls living in appalling poverty' and of the dangers at night when 'firing occurred on a regular basis':

Should our patrol vehicle break down we could be in extreme danger. Indeed a number of refugees were murdered in the camp. On one occasion when we were delivering supplies we were surrounded by starving refugees and I had to order my patrol to fix bayonets to protect us from being swamped by the desperate people.

November went on, a month filled with patrols and sentry duties and the endless heavy rain. Hegarty and the other wounded had X-ray and hospital checks. Afterwards, Hegarty wrote to a friend from A Company's new Elisabethville address:

The Farm. November 1961

Since my release from durance vile I've received two letters from you, one containing newspaper pictures of our hand over. Yep, that is me alright but no 'Ronnie' as you say. [He had shaved off a moustache.] The other day I had an X-ray and my bottom was found to contain several chips of shrapnel (I'll bear in mind your tip about the price of pig iron at home). However as it does not cause me inconvenience sleeping dogs pertain. All our other wounded have been found free from 'stain' (pun!)

Foley remembers a small altercation with the UN Representative in Elisabethville:

> Following our release some of us, including me, had to do sentry duty at the villa lived in by Conor Cruise O'Brien and Máire McEntee, who was visiting. There was a high wall around with a walkway inside. He [Conor Cruise O'Brien] told us we weren't to walk by when Máire McEntee was swimming in the pool. I told him that if he wanted security we'd have to patrol everywhere, all the time. That is what we did.

And then there was the day the cook got the chance to flex his culinary muscles. 'I made a great stew one day,' Bobby Allan recalls:

> It happened after an incident led to me getting lots of unexpected stores; 6–8 turkeys and a side of lamb and more. But I'd no oven to roast any of it. So I cut up the turkeys and meat and put the lot into a pot and boiled away and used powdered potatoes to thicken it. A great feed was had by all; there was nothing left for the cat that night!

But Quinlan and others of A Company were becoming increasingly aware that Jadotville, and talk of Jadotville, was *non grata*. Clune, the company's much-regarded Medical Officer, says that, 'when we were eventually released tensions prevailing about what had happened came out into the general battalion. Some people spoke out and quickly realised they shouldn't have. After that no one spoke out.'

Quinlan was troubled by what he increasingly saw as 'policy to decry Jadotville', and incensed by the view in parts of the army that A Company should have died to a man rather than surrender. He continued vexed too that his letter containing the radio log (given to reporter John Ross to post but handed over to the Battalion OC) had gone missing. He wrote home about it all.

Elisabethville. Tuesday, 7th November 1961

My dear Carmel:

There is a deliberate policy now in certain places to decry the action at Jado and to minimise it as only a skirmish in order to shift the pointed finger of responsibility from themselves.

I told you that John Ross gave Battalion OC the letter to you with my wireless message log. We have another copy of the radio log which Liam Donnelly hid in a lamp shade. The reason I wanted you to have it was in case we would not get out [of Jadotville]. I wanted the log in safe hands so as it could be used to vindicate the good name of A Company. [The mystery of the disappearing letter deepened when Carmel Quinlan, in Dublin, questioned John Ross about its whereabouts. The Radio Éireann reporter told her that when he mentioned the letter to the Battalion OC, he insisted on taking it, assuring Ross that he would send it himself to Mrs Quinlan. Mrs Quinlan's letter never turned up.]

I'm doing nothing, and saying nothing, about this until I get good advice when I go home.

I don't know how they expect to muzzle the 156 men of A Company because they will talk and tell the truth of what happened when they get home.

All in A Company are saying, 'Thank God we did not have to come through the Lufira Bridge; we could have done it but we would have suffered a lot of casualties.' I don't know, maybe we would. The bridge should have been taken on the Sunday before the fight. I begged and implored Battalion HQ to take it or to let me take it but I was refused. I was ordered to take no action and then I was left in the lurch without even a hint of the action planned in Elisabethville.

Only for our own alertness we would have been wiped out that morning on 13th September in the first attack.

I could have taken the bridge easily if only I had a clue of the job planned in Elisabethville. The whole situation in the Congo could have been fixed that day. All the Katanga forces were on my side of the bridge and I could have held them back. Instead I had to fight them in a place where it was almost impossible to defend. They had up to 600 whites—Belgians, French and other nationalities leading them and urging them to attack us. We would be there yet if we had water.

The bridge was never really attacked and luckily they [Force Kane] got home through the ambush. Several Indians were killed and about 20 wounded and eight Irish were wounded. That attack was a fiasco. They did not get within five miles of the bridge on Saturday.

We are only getting this information in bits and scraps from the junior officers and men who took part in it.

B Company are gone off to North Katanga about 800 miles away since yesterday.

They are to relieve the infantry group. This is another stupid blunder. We need every man here but please God all will be well.

If Round Two comes the 36th Battalion may have to fight it. I don't think now there will be a Round Two however. For a while I was convinced there would be but I think that Tshombe has lost his following.

Of course he is only a figurehead. It's really Union Minière, the big mining concern here, that is at the back of it all.

I believe the armchair soldiers say that we should have all died at Jadotville. For what? We have no doubts and don't think that I regret my decision. I have all my men alive and that is the greatest victory I could ever hope for.

The rainy season is well in. We are all tip top here but the mosquitoes are playing hell with us.

I had hoped to have all the company home together but I'm afraid that won't be possible now. Fifty of the company are scheduled to go home on 28th November. I requested that the company be allowed to return all together for the Athlone welcome that is to be arranged, according to the *Westmeath Independent* anyway, but my request was turned down flat.

Another deliberate effort, I think, to put a spanner in the works.

I'm in the best of form, a bit thin maybe, but I'll put the weight on again.

Fond love and God bless you all, Pat

Quinlan had much support for his view that troops should not be isolated and without support in times of conflict. Michael Shannon, whose military time with B Company in the Congo so often overlapped with that of A Company, absolutely supported Quinlan's view (then and now) about the sending of troops to Niemba and Nyunzu. According to Shannon:

> In mid-November, B Company and C Company of 35th Battalion received orders out of the blue to proceed by air from Elisabethville to Albertville en route to, in the case of B Company, Nyunzu and, in the case of C Company to Niemba.
>
> We spent about five weeks there, patrolling a vast area and to what purpose? It was to prevent groups of Gendarmerie, officered by mercenaries, from pilfering and plundering villages. A commander of one of the mercenary groups was Major 'Mad Mike' Hoare. He's still infamous. He was working for Katanga province. But what was remarkable was that, once again, Irish peacekeeping companies were sent to isolated locations, breaking the military principle of security.
>
> It all begs the question—*Did the UN and its command in Leopoldville learn anything from the debacle in Jadotville? No one shouted stop. No one said look at what we're doing here, AGAIN.*

Medical Officer Clune saw and sees the issue of the silence descending in the social and cultural context of the time: 'At the time there was a climate of sweeping everything under the carpet. Plus, if you had a tribunal of enquiry where would the heads stop rolling? Plus, you'd have taken a military situation into the political arena and never have got anywhere.'

Quinlan followed his frustrated letter of 7 November with a more reflective word to his wife the following day. He was less irate but every bit as committed to the truth of events in Jadotville and their aftermath.

Elisabethville. Wednesday, 8th November 1961

My darling Carmel:

Don't take too much notice of the steam I let off in my last letter as I was not in good humour maybe. Did you get the Red Cross letter that I sent from Kolwezi? The last part of the message for Aiken was not correct. I put that in especially for the benefit of the censors, so ignore it. [This was his letter of 23 October in which his last paragraph read: 'What I told Mr Munongo to tell Mr Aiken was that "we did our duty as Irish soldiers to the best of our ability and in keeping with the instructions of the Irish Government to shoot only in self defence".' The Irish Government would not, of course, have issued any such dictum.]

Evidently I am a controversial figure in Ireland and in other places because of the Jado effort. I am glad to see that I have plenty sensible people who are prepared to defend us against the armchair critics.

I have not been to the market here in Elisabethville since we came back. We never go out except on duty and then with an escort and armed to the teeth.

Eddie Condon [Comdt Condon was a Kerryman and good friend who was a member of HQ personnel] is gone to Leopoldville since Saturday last. He may be back tomorrow. Jado nearly killed Eddie. He was helpless to do anything of course. I think he wanted to take charge of the reinforcements. If he had he would have got through, but then again at great loss of life. So perhaps it's just as well.

Máire McEntee (Minister's daughter) is here on some special mission. She told me about it and also said to me that they realise now that newspaper reports were a deliberate policy to blacken UN.

We are all fully equipped again and operational. So don't worry about us. This is chicken feed after Jado.

All my love to you all, Pat

Political turmoil being no respecter of peacekeeping forces, tensions continued to mount in Elisabethville, and throughout Katanga, as the 35th Battalion's tour of duty drew to an end and the 36th Battalion, with an advance party, made ready to replace them. It was becoming clear also, as Quinlan had feared, that A Company would definitely not be departing for home as a single unit. Donnelly's Support Platoon and Carey's No. 3 Platoon were told they would leave the Congo on 2 November. The rest of the company would follow in December. Carey created the following pen-picture of how things were during the weeks before they left for home:

> The monsoon rains bucketed down at times, tension was rising in the city as Katanga still hadn't agreed to discontinue its separation from the Congo Republic, UN personnel were put under pressure and we were instructed to carry arms on our location at The Farm. It was a regular occurrence to come under small arms fire coming and going to meals.
>
> A Mr Joe Kalleal, who supplied goods to the UN, was kind enough to let us have the use of his private swimming pool, which was most welcome in the intense heat and humidity. We travelled to and fro for swims fully armed, even in civilian attire.

His commanding officer, Quinlan, continued to write home, more aware as the days passed that what was already being called 'The Jadotville Affair' was to be airbrushed from history and his men sidelined. He had also made the disillusioning discovery that Dr Hoffman, their Red Cross visitor in Jadotville, had not been all that he had seemed to be:

Elisabethville. Saturday, 11th November 1961

My dear Carmel:

You are sharp to have suspected Hoffman! You were right. Of course our unfortunate position at that time was exploited by every bastard who came our way.

I had already written to G. Bartley [Minister for Defence] and explained re Hoffman before I got your letter. Fr Clarke (a Chaplain) had long ago suspected the same Hoffman. His methods were exactly the same as those employed by the Belgians but we did not know it at the time.

Fr Clarke and Fr Fagan have written to the Head Chaplain and given a full report of it all. They are with me 100% in everything.

As to Jadotville ... I must wait until I have an opportunity of giving the facts and then let people judge for themselves.

All in the UN here made a complete mess of things including UN HQ in Leopoldville, so the cards are stacked against me. All Tshombe had was us Irish prisoners and that was organised by the Belgian Government before anything happened. Katanga and Belgium knew that Operation Morthor was planned for Elisabethville through informers within the UN. We were lured to Jadotville supposedly to protect the white people and we ended up as hostages. So you see what I am up against.

We are all safe and alive thank God and the affair between the Battalion OC and myself is only a small part of the whole effort. Everyone knew about the plans for Elisabethville on 13th September except my unit.

If I had known I would have taken the Lufira Bridge that morning and all would have been over in Katanga because they had 90% of their forces on my side of the bridge. I held them for four days and nights in a position that was almost impossible to defend. If I knew and took the bridge and with a river to my front I would hold them for the next year and all would be over in Katanga.

The UN made a complete mess and A Company's stand is the only bright light in the whole effort. There was more shot and shell in one day in Jadotville than was fired in all the fighting in Elisabethville.

People think that because there were none of us killed there was no fighting. It is a new slant on things for me. If you have men killed you have a victory but if you save your men and have a good defence it is a defeat.

Believe me, our enemies expected an easy victory and got the land of a lifetime. We were so few against so many they thought that all they had to do was come and take us. The Director of the firm which made the tank they were getting ready to attack us with said drily to me when it was all over, 'We were lucky there were not 1,000 Irishmen up there'.

God bless, as ever, Pat

Foley, together with all of those under his command in Jadotville, is staunch in Quinlan's defence in these matters. Telling how he saw things in Jadotville, he adds to his own corner of the story:

Pat Quinlan was betrayed by the people in Jadotville and by Battalion HQ not giving him any help. Some of us were planning a breakout two nights before the end. Most fellows in our group were very fit from cross-country running and we'd have been able to navigate the river up and down. But some wouldn't have made it so we didn't go.

Pat Quinlan saved more lives by doing what he did in the long term. What happened to him would have broken any soldier's heart. He was a committed leader and loved by the men. Everyone could see the fruits of his labours when the fighting broke out. The practice training had been great, no one was afraid. We felt superior, there were thousands milling around about us but that, as far as we were concerned, was as close as they were ever going to get!

CHAPTER 54

Wars begin in the minds of men, and in those minds love and compassion would have built the defences of peace.

U Thant, UN Secretary General

World news. November 1961

'The situation in the Congo' covered acres of news space throughout the month of November. It had, as the Irish Press said in an editorial on 17 November, 'gone from bad to worse ... and now there is the news that Italian airmen captured by mutinous Congolese troops at Kindu were done to death.'

'Such deeds,' the paper thundered, 'may be explained as the outcome of ignorant savagery but the Congolese political and military leaders' share of the blame cannot be so easily condoned or excused.'

The *Irish Press* report on the death of the Italian airmen quoted a UN spokesman as saying that, 'the unarmed fliers were shot by unruly troops shortly after their arrest. Some of their bodies were dismembered and hurled into the Congo river by soldiers who apparently suspected them of being Belgian paratroopers.'

Earlier in the month, U Thant of Burma had been appointed Acting Secretary General of the United Nations. The first Asian to hold the post, U Thant was 52, a socialist and a Buddhist. He was considered a 'moderate' and had been a teacher and journalist before becoming a diplomat.

Earlier in the month, too, on 4 November, the *Irish Independent* reported on a UN warning to Katangan authorities that their planes would be 'shot down by UN jets if they continued bombing attacks against troops of the Central Congolese Government in Kasai Province.'

President Tshombe, pictured in a variety of papers with his family in Geneva where he was seeing Swiss doctors, continued to give press conferences on the situation in his homeland, accusing the UN of assisting the Central Congolese Government to attack Katanga.

CHAPTER 55

The Irish troops in Jadotville were magnificent and Comdt Quinlan,
the Irish commander, would, in the Indian Army, be awarded the
highest military award for gallantry.

Brig. Gen. Raja, November 1961

Elisabethville. November 1961

November, according to Donnelly, was 'a period of normal duties,
everyone more or less confined to The Farm area except for outside
duties. Baluba Camp was the big problem, constant shootings in
the area of the camp.' He too talks about the diarrhoea which
'swept' through the company and which 'had a severe effect on a
number of persons' and in common with everyone, he talks about
the rain.

Quinlan did not at all reconcile to the decision to send Carey
and Donnelly and 56 men from their platoons back to Ireland on the
Globemaster bringing an advance party of 36th Battalion men to the
Congo. He wrote that he,

> ...raised repeated objections to the sending home of this
> advance party as it weakened our strength by almost 50% and
> left A Company non-operational for all practical purposes.
> The only other Irish troops in Elisabethville was HQ
> Company which was NOT organised as a fighting unit in
> the full sense.

The issue of Dr Hoffman continued to vex him, too.

Elisabethville. Monday, 13th November 1961

My dear Carmel:

It is funny that you should all tumble to the position about Hoffman. Fr Clarke suspected him from the very start and I think there is plenty of proof that he is anti-UN. Fr Fagan has written a very long letter to the Head Chaplain that will be given to the Government. He wrote it himself immediately after we were released: Fr Clarke told me.

What happened in Jado was not McNamee's fault, by any means. There is so much involved here that it is dynamite to say anything to anyone.

Chief of Staff Powell is arriving here on Thursday. It will be interesting to hear what he has to say.

We are all back to normal again. I was very much down in the dumps and so were we all for the last couple of weeks. We were in better spirits when we were prisoners—but now we are all in top form again and fighting fit.

We are very busy these days making out recommendations for awards of gallantry in battle. Our trouble is that all our men were so good in Jadotville that it is very difficult to single them out. We all missed death by inches on hundreds of occasions. We were nearly laughing at the situation in the end.

We are all looking forward to the reception in Athlone but if we cannot go back together it will spoil it. None of the men want to go back until we are all together but it can't be helped. Maybe it will be changed.

We are all alive and that is the main thing. I am also prepared to forgive and forget. I'm not bitter anymore. It would be very wrong and unworthy of us who were saved by prayer.

Many of the NCOs' wives are writing and telling their husbands how good you were in visiting them during the trouble.

God bless you, write soon as ever, Pat

The prospect of action cheered Pat Quinlan up enormously. His rising spirits were apparent in a letter written midway through the month.

Elisabethville. Friday, 17th November 1961

My darling Carmel and darling children:

We expect to be going to Kamina very early in December, on 2nd or 3rd. I'm really in great form now. I was feeling miserable after the mosquitoes attacked me but I am okay again.

The post is very bad. You should have about six letters from me since I was released. Post comes here only about once per week. Belgium is holding it up in Brussels, we're told, and probably doing the same with the letters from here to Ireland.

All my love to you all, Daddy

But his impatient temperament, and a refusal to tolerate either dishonesty or incompetence, soon had him storming again at UN inadequacies.

Elisabethville. Sunday, 19th November 1961

My dear Carmel:

I'm afraid the postal service is gone haywire. While suspicions are that Brussels is responsible our own postal service in Leopoldville is just as inefficient as all the other UN services. Believe me there is no more disorganised or incompetent body in the world today than our UN. It is sinful for our Irish government to commit our Irish soldiers to the whims and fancies of that crowd of parasites.

Now don't worry about me. I'm not sick or anything. I'm in the best of form. We all suffer occasionally from bad diarrhoea but it is not so bad. The mosquitoes gave me two bad bitings and I was sick for two days each time.

Don't think Jado has changed me—it has not. I'm just the same as ever only perhaps I am bitter, sometimes. I can't help that but I'll get over it. All the men feel the same. All realise there is an effort to play down our efforts and now they even suggest we were not even attacked and that the enemy only fired on us. They are pretty well ashamed of themselves—that is those who have shame.

　　With fond love to you all, Pat

Next day he had thoughts and hopes about getting a hearing from the army's Chief of Staff.

Elisabethville. Monday, 20th November 1961

My dear Carmel:

　　Collins Powell is due to arrive here in a few hours and I will let you know what he has to say.

　　[He continued this letter later that day] Collins Powell has arrived with Colonel Tom Canole and Comdt Steve Leech. He is being taken on a tour so apart from his address to us all in very glowing terms we have had no chat with him yet.

　　I lost a lot of weight during the fighting—we all did—but I am almost back to normal.

　　God bless, as ever, Pat

A dinner, large and formal, was given for Major General Sean Collins Powell. UN dignitaries and military leaders all attended, and speeches were made. Quinlan wrote home after the event.

Elisabethville. Thursday, 23rd November 1961

My dear Carmel and children:

　　We had a big dinner here with Powell. He never said a word to me except that he was sure that I was glad to be back.

　　Brigadier Raja, the UN General in charge of Katanga, gave a speech and said: 'As for the Irish troops in Jadotville, they were magnificent and Comdt Quinlan, the Irish commander, would, in the Indian Army, be awarded the highest military award for gallantry.' The officers cheered and Powell said afterwards that it was well deserved.

Powell is being neutral, as I knew he would be, but he took a copy of my report home with him.

We hope to be concentrating in Kamina (airbase) around the 2nd–4th December in preparation for going home and it seems now that we will all be home together. We hope to leave between 9th–12th December. A Company will be on the first three planes with Mac and some of HQ staff on No. 1. I will travel on No. 2.

Don't worry now—we will be out of here I think before anything happens again.

O'Brien has got the sack, as has his assistant. You'll have seen this in the papers—real reasons covered up of course. They made a complete mess of the Congo.

It's terrible about those 13 Italians. Any law and order that existed in the Congo was in Katanga until O'Brien and the UN destroyed it.

The whole question is so mixed up that I don't know where the answer is now. The UN had the remedy in July 1960 when the 32nd Battalion came out. That was the time to disarm all the Congolese troops and stop the messing. Now the French paratroopers who revolted in Algeria earlier this year are in the Katangan Army. They led the attack on A Company but we taught them a lesson they won't forget in a hurry. We killed their commander (a French major) the first day and we cut the leg off another senior officer about five minutes before the ceasefire.

The Belgian officer who shot Patrice Lumumba was Second-in-Command operations against us and a French paratroop colonel was In-Command of the whole operation against us.

So you see, we did not do too badly at all considering the military brains and might against us. Without boasting I think our defence was one of the epic defences in the history of war.

All my love to you all, Pat

Carey found excitement, and his own priorities, in some of the month's events:

> Our Chief of Staff, Gen. Collins Powell, came out from Ireland on a visit and A Company paraded with pride with the Battalion to receive our UN medals. This was a great experience, after all the frustrations and disappointments. The postponed Katangan UN soccer final was played in unusual circumstances with UN armoured cars positioned at each side of the soccer pitch and the Swedish and Irish soldier/spectators fully armed. Unfortunately, we lost by two goals to one. But as captain of the Irish UN team I was presented with a medal at a subsequent presentation at UN HQ.

Donnelly, in a comment on the period, wrote:

> As November came to an end tensions rose further in Elisabethville and the city was put out of bounds to all personnel. The first advance party of the relieving 36th Battalion arrived at Elisabethville Airport.

And Quinlan, still convinced he and his company would travel intact and together to Ireland, wrote:

> Elisabethville. Sunday, 26th November

> My dear Carmel:
>   On 5th December we leave here for Leopoldville and on 7th December we leave Leopoldville for Dublin.
>   There is still a possibility that an advance party of fifty A Company personnel will fly out of here on Wednesday next, 29th November. Of course arrangements change every hour so we cannot be definite of anything. It is reasonable however to expect that we will arrive in Dublin on 10th December or maybe a day or two later depending on flying conditions.

> We had a big party last night given by the Swedes—
> our heads are not too good today. We are having another
> tomorrow night—Indian Dogra Battalion, and one on
> Wednesday night—Indian Gurkha Battalion. So it's just as
> well we are going home, as we could never stick the pace.

His protestations about the inadvisability of breaking up the company
were of no avail, however, and preparations for the return home of an
advance party of A Company went ahead apace. But not without a
hitch. Carey describes what happened.

> One evening we were called to a company conference, where
> Comdt Quinlan announced that a UN Globemaster with a
> party of 36th Infantry Battalion would arrive in the next two
> days and one of our platoons had been selected to leave for
> Ireland on that aircraft.
>
> After long discussions the others agreed that as I was
> getting married in January I should go. I was reluctant, being
> the junior officer, but after further discussion the decision
> was made; also, that Capt. Donnelly was to accompany me
> and my platoon.
>
> When I informed No. 3 Platoon they were thrilled, bags
> were packed and next day all items were weighed and checked
> ready for our departure on the morn. Time passed slowly that
> day as we made our final arrangements for departure.
>
> Then, out of the blue, I received a call from Operations
> to report immediately to the Operations Officer.
>
> On my reporting I was instructed to prepare my platoon to
> move out at 2000 hours and move into Elisabethville to rescue
> Conor Cruise O'Brien, Máire McEntee and their driver. I was
> told they had been captured by Katangan Gendarmerie.
>
> As it happened, Máire McEntee and a UN official had
> been arrested, the official badly beaten and, only for the
> intervention of the Ambassador of the United States, could
> have been in mortal danger.
>
> I felt like saying 'Sorry, I'm leaving tomorrow' but duty
> called and I alerted my not too pleased platoon. I had no idea

where I was going, how I was to get there, nor what I would find if I ever did find Conor Cruise O'Brien.

The platoon was fully armed and standing to, ready for departure, as I literally counted the minutes to 2000 hours. Time passed, I kept glancing anxiously at my watch. I wasn't relishing this task at all, especially having survived thus far. Then I received a message to report to Operations immediately.

This was it. We were off.

But to my great relief I was informed we would not be required. Conor Cruise O'Brien and Miss McEntee and the driver were safe.

I didn't argue—and what a reception I got when I stood down my platoon.

Next morning bright and early we hurriedly finished packing our trucks. We bade a fond farewell to Comdt Pat Quinlan, Captains Dermot Byrne and Tom McGuinn, Lieuts Joe Leech and Tom Quinlan, mounted the trucks and quickly speeded from The Farm onto the main road to the airport. It was still fascinating to see so many Katangese walking along the side of the road, the colourfully dressed women with baskets and plastic drums on their heads.

The Globemaster was parked beside a massive hangar. We disembarked, moved our equipment and army boxes into the giant hold of the plane, were issued with pack rations for the journey and were soon trundling down the runway and into the bright sunlit sky over Elisabethville. With little or no regret, apart from the fact that we were leaving some of our comrades behind, we bade farewell to Katanga.

That evening we landed in Leopoldville and then continued our journey to Wheelus Air Base in Tripoli where we had the freedom of the American canteen, with fabulous meals and crates of ice cream. We visited the PX and I purchased some souvenirs, records and a model aeroplane for my younger brother.

We flew out that night, exhausted, elated, swapping yarns, desperately drained, not believing our good fortune that we were on our way home. It was extremely uncomfortable as we flew for some ten hours to Dublin. Some slept on the metal floor of the Globemaster while others dozed off in the strapped seats along the side of the plane.

Suddenly it was all over, as we bumped onto the rain-soaked runway at Dublin Airport. The huge doors swung open as we were met by a blast of winter air and drenching rain.

I bade farewell to Sergeant Kevin McLaughlin and my heroic platoon. This was the last time I ever met my full platoon.

CHAPTER 56

I have become a controversial figure during my six-month assignment
to Elisabethville and have been exposed to unwarranted attacks.

Dr Conor Cruise O'Brien,
resigning from UN, December 1961

World news. November–December 1961
Newspapers in Ireland were filled with news of troops returning from, and going to, the Congo. The Irish Press, on 1 December, gloried in the return of soldiers, 'bronzed from an equatorial sun and looking fit despite their long plane journey'. This was the advance party of 73 soldiers of the 'Fighting 35th' Infantry Battalion, arriving into Dublin Airport on a US Globemaster 'after six months in the turbulent Congo' with, amongst them, '50 of the heroes of the Jadotville fighting.'

The newspaper spoke to Donnelly, who praised the courage of A Company's soldiers in the conditions in which they were forced to fight. John Manning described how he was injured:

> It was about 10.30 at night. I was behind a fence, half-kneeling at the time. There was a burst of fire and I happened to catch an FN rifle bullet on the right shoulder.
> The shot was fired from about 40 yards away.

Manning, a rifle marksman, went on to say that he regarded himself lucky to escape with a flesh wound and, pressed by the paper, said that if the positions were reversed, he probably would have been more accurate than his adversary.

The pages of all three national dailies were filled with pictures of relaxed-looking UN-bereted soldiers, skins unseasonably glowing. Private W. Duffy of A Company was caught with a forkful of a Full Irish halfway to his mouth. He looked all of 16 years old.

Tension, murder and beatings continued to be reported from the Congo. Two senior UN officials, Brian Urquhart and Dr Sture Linner, were brutally beaten by Katangan paratroopers. An 18-year-old Gurkha soldier was knifed and shot to death in a park near President Tshombe's palace. Major-General Norbert Moke, of the Katangan Army, was reported in the world's papers promising an enquiry into both tragedies. Godefroid Munongo was reported to be personally directing the search for a Sikh officer who had been with the murdered Gurkha and was now missing.

The *Irish Independent*, on 2 December, reported from the first press conference given by the UN's Acting Secretary General. U Thant described Tshombe as 'a very unstable man' who was 'incapable of making any statements' and said he would be putting forward a plan for ousting foreign mercenaries from the Congo.

And, on the same day, Dr Conor Cruise O'Brien announced that he would be leaving the United Nations and would not be returning to his job in the Department of External Affairs in Dublin. O'Brien, according to the *Irish Press*, had asked to be relieved of his UN duties because he had become 'a controversial figure during his six-month assignment to Elisabethville and had been exposed to unwarranted attacks.' Critics accused him of pursuing his own tactics without authority, 'particularly in the abortive 13th September UN Operation Morthor that led to eight days' fighting between UN and Katangan forces'.

The paper said that 'in view of the controversy surrounding him Dr O'Brien thought it inadvisable for him to return to the Congo'. He was also reported as saying that he was 'not optimistic' about UN efforts to end Mr Tshombe's secession from the Central Congolese Government. The paper also carried the report of the resignation of Máire McEntee from the Department of External Affairs.

On 3 December, in the *Sunday Independent*, there was news of the beginning of what would become 'The December Campaign' in Elisabethville—though fighting in earnest did not break out until 1400 hours, two days later, on Tuesday, 5 December. Sunday's report told of a clash between Indian UN troops and Katangan Gendarmerie at Elisabethville Airport. Gunfire was exchanged for thirty minutes and roadblocks erected in the city by both the Katangan and UN forces.

CHAPTER 57

At first it was infiltration and sporadic firing. Then the volume of fire was built up. This was an old game. A Company were quite used to it from Jadotville.

Pat Quinlan, December 1961

Tensions rose steadily in Elisabethville. With a body of his company departed, Comdt Quinlan protested the transfer to Albertville of heavy weapons and ammunition in preparation for the handover to 36th Battalion, which was to be stationed in that area:

> Given the situation I considered the transfer of our heavy-duty weapons and ammunition reserve very unwise, and endeavoured to get it halted. But without success.
>
> The result was that when hostilities commenced on 5th December we had only approximately 2,600 rounds of rifle ammunition, 3,000 rounds light automatic ammunition, three Bren guns, one 84mm RCL [recoilless rifle] with ten rounds. We got hold of one 81mm mortar which was still awaiting to be transferred to Albertville. Approximately 200 mortar bombs were available but only 50 fuses. We had NO signal equipment whatever and proper mortar fire control was impossible.
>
> When it appeared likely that hostilities were about to commence on 5th December I borrowed one 84mm RCL and 30 rounds from the Swedish Battalion. The 84mm RCLs were extensively used in the fighting which followed. They were our only heavy weapons. The Swedish Battalion was, at this time, in the process of repatriation also and only two companies were available in Elisabethville.

In fact at least one troop plane en route home with Swedish troops was ordered back to Elisabethville.

It was now, as the year and A Company's time in Katanga drew to a close, that the location of another notorious conflict first became part of the A Company story. The Tunnel, a strategic railway underpass near the centre of Elisabethville, would soon to be the scene of savage fighting and many deaths. On 2 December, when it became a 'strategically hostile location', Quinlan wrote:

> The Katangese forces under the command of mercenary officers set up a series of roadblocks in and around Elisabethville. One such roadblock was at The Tunnel, blocking the route from Irish and Swedish camp to Elisabethville. This was a dangerous situation for us.
>
> During this night and again on 3rd December a total of fourteen UN officers and men—ten Swedes, four Norwegians—were kidnapped by Katangan forces. In addition an Indian Major and his driver were killed.
>
> A Company, which was due to leave Elisabethville for home on 4th December, now set to with renewed vigour to put the defences in order again. New trenches and weapon pits were prepared and manned by night and day. There were one or two alerts, there was little sleep or rest.

Even as all of this went on, he managed to write home, reassuring as always.

Elisabethville. 4th December 1961

My dear Carmel and children:

The advance party of A Company are home now and I am sure you have heard a lot of news from them.

We were to leave here tomorrow and go to Leopoldville and from there on Thursday to arrive in Dublin on Friday. However that is all changed because of the tenseness of the situation here. We will not leave now until at least two companies of the 36th Battalion arrive. We expect them on Saturday next at the latest.

It is very difficult to understand the situation here. It looks as if the big shots in the Katanga Government with their army are getting out of hand. None of the Irish here have been involved in the incidents reported in the radio and press. This may blow over in a day or two. UN here is exercising tremendous restraint.

I'm very sorry for the Swedes. They are fine soldiers and I think they act the same way as the Irish. We have great admiration for one another. Now they have one killed, three wounded and seven taken prisoner in the last two days. We are hoping and praying that the prisoners are alive. There are also two Norwegians taken prisoner. The Swedes were due out tomorrow but it was cancelled. We expect another Swedish Battalion to replace them tomorrow.

Don't worry about us as we will be home next week, please God. It only means postponement for a few days. We are taking absolutely no chances so don't worry.

We hear that Dr O'Brien has been fired or resigned. There is also a rumour that McKeown is not coming back— we don't know if this is true or not.

I may be home as soon as this letter but if I'm not don't worry because we are confident that all will be well.

I'm sure that the men who have gone home have mixed feelings now and that they would rather be with us if anything happens again.

With fond love to all, Daddy

Something *did* happen, as history (and Quinlan) records. What would be one of the bloodiest, most viciously fought, tragically fatal (for both sides) and longest exchanges between UN troops and Katangan Gendarmerie began on Monday, 4 December.

It started when the Gendarmerie set up a roadblock on the main road between Elisabethville and the airport. Using a company-strong force of men, they placed the blockage at the crucial roundabout, effectively separating and splitting the UN forces. Irish troops were at the time located at Leopold Farm. The Swedes were billeted at the refugee camp. The Indian Gurkha Battalion was at UN HQ at Avenue Stanley in Elisabethville and the Indian Dogra Battalion located at the airport.

The Gendarmerie roadblock meant that the only way into the airport was via a bad, uneven road called Charlie. 'There was every evidence,' Quinlan wrote, 'that Katangan forces intended to cut off this route also.' Keeping Route Charlie open became a necessity. On 5 December, Tom Quinlan, so fearless in Jadotville, was ordered to take No. 2 Platoon and two Irish armoured cars to secure White Piers Crossroads on Route Charlie. They dug in there at 1400 hours. Seven hours later, when a unit of Indian Dogra troops took over from them, the Katangan authorities promised to lift the roadblock set up at the roundabout.

Instead, they strengthened it during the night. Quinlan wrote of how events unfolded:

> Plans were made to remove this roadblock by force. An ultimatum was sent to the Katangan forces to vacate the position. The plan was to attack by Gurkha Battalion from Avenue Stanley with a holding attack from the Airport Road.

The force for this attack was made up of a 20-strong platoon of Gurkhas, A Company's No. 2 Platoon under Lieut Tom Quinlan, a couple of Irish armoured cars commanded by Captain Art McGuinness and a Swedish armoured personnel carrier. The overall officer in command was Indian, a Captain Salaria.

Private Billy Ready, the first man wounded in Jadotville and back in action twice in December, was also part of the patrol. 'The Gurkhas fought mainly in the open,' he remembers, 'so they were at risk and were shot. We had to give them covering fire for a bayonet charge— I'd only ever seen bayonet charges in the films before that!'

Pat Quinlan wrote:

> The UN force left the Irish camp at 1330 hours and was ambushed about a half mile from the Roundabout at the old Sabena air strip. The UN force counter-attacked and

the one-company Katangan force was routed. Corporal McManus with Pte Feery destroyed an enemy armoured car in the attack. At least 22 dead were left behind.

Capt. Salaria was killed. Eight Indians and one Irish soldier, Pte Roche, were wounded.

Tom Quinlan fills in the fine detail of what became a brutal and tragically fatal exchange:

When the armoured patrol carrier arrived at a point on the road at the old airfield it found the road blocked by barrels. The Gendarmerie had an armed car on the right of the road. The enemy and car opened fire, which fire was immediately returned. The two platoons took cover, the Gurkha platoon along a deep trench on the side of the road, where they had dismounted, and the Irish platoon along a ridge near the airstrip opposite the enemy position....

He describes how a Gendarmerie company was 'dug in along the ridge with a number of weapon pits to our right with a light artillery in at least one of these', how sniper fire came from the left side of the road and how two corporals, McManus and Feery, 'knocked out' the Katangan armoured car. Fifteen minutes of heavy mortar fire ensued. Lieut Quinlan continues:

Capt. Saleria then decided to assault the enemy position with the Irish armoured cars, giving covering fire from the roadway, and with the Irish platoon covering the assault from the opposite ridge ... The initial objective of the assault was an ant hill some 100 yards beyond the enemy armoured car. Once this was captured the Irish platoon would move forward and support the next assault ... The armoured cars would support by moving up the airstrip.

Capt Saleria was killed and a number of Gurkhas wounded in the assault.

Capt. Art McGuinness, who was in charge of the Irish Armoured Car section, took command but, because of the language difficulties, could not get the Gurkhas to understand him. They seemed too to have lost heart a little due to the death of their own officer.

Capt. McGuinness then decided to put the Irish platoon into the assault and allow the Gurkhas and armed cars to support.

The assault was to begin at 1745 hours but Capt. R. Pundit of the Dogra Battalion arrived with instructions to take command and withdraw if he deemed it necessary.

The Irish platoon were told to dig in on their position as it was now dark. But as there was now no firing from the enemy Capt. Pundit decided to withdraw back to camp at 1900 hours.

The following day the scene of the ambush was visited by a Dogra contingent. They found 22 Katanga dead and the armoured car.

The airstrip and all its surroundings were quiet; what remained of the enemy had fled.

Pat Quinlan gives terse details of another attack on the night of the ambush:

Battalion HQ got information through an intercepted wireless message that an attack on the Irish Camp was planned for 2300 hours. All necessary preparations were made for a fitting reception. The attack came, half-hearted, from Avenue Tulipiers as planned but met with heavy fire and was short lived. We suspected, however, that another attack might come on our left flank from Avenue Katanga. This was the vulnerable flank as it could cut off the Irish from the Swedish Battalion.

I had A Company man this flank throughout.

At 0200 hours a sudden attack was launched on this flank. Much heavier than the earlier attack, which I suspected to be a diversion at best. A Company was in position and ready. The action lasted for just over one hour but the enemy did not succeed in gaining access to our position at any point. The concentrated fire of our three light automatics, two armoured cars and two 84mm anti-tank recoilless rifles broke up this attack without loss to our own forces.

We never learned of the enemy casualties in this attack.

Enemy sniping from houses and trees continued throughout the night and all next morning.

The Swedes moved assertively now, bombarding the Katangans with mortars. In an effort to clear the area between the Irish and Swedish camps they also launched an attack on the Tunnel. But when they withdrew to their camp, they found that the Gendarmerie, in even greater strength than before, had immediately re-occupied their former positions. Quinlan explained:

These forces then infiltrated in strength into the wooded and built-up area immediately opposite A Company's position. Enemy posts were set up from 50 to 200 yards from A Company's position, in a triangle contained between Avenue Savoniers—Kasenga and the Police Barracks.

At first it was infiltration and sporadic firing. Then the volume of fire was built up as further enemy forces came in.

This was an old game. A Company were quite used to it from Jadotville.

First a few of them would infiltrate and engage our positions. Then the remainder, encouraged by the 'success' of their brave comrades, would come up to add to the volume of fire.

If left undisturbed long enough a very strong force of enemy would be built up.

On this occasion we held fire until we estimated the enemy force warranted our special attention. On a given signal the whole area was raked by fire from all of our weapons.

The armoured cars and company light automatics raked the area systematically from right to left and back again, paying particular attention to windows and midway up the trees.

Except for sporadic machine-gun and sniper fire the remainder of the night was quiet. I expect that Katangan forces had second thoughts about their attack after that.

We do not know of enemy casualties. Some dead bodies were found in the area a few days later when this ground was captured.

And so the battle for Katanga went on. On 6 December, late in the evening, a company of incoming 36th Battalion members arrived in Elisabethville. When a platoon, commanded by Lieutenant Feeley, was put under Comdt Quinlan's command he decided to deploy the men in trenches with men of his own company, 'in order to get them battle inoculated':

It was a very rude shock to these raw troops just arrived from Ireland with no previous experience of being under fire.

I was very impressed by their courage and the willingness and keenness to do their part and to give of their best. (These same men were later, on 16th December, to acquit themselves with valour in the 36th Battalion attack on The Tunnel).

Next day, 7th December, when Lieutenant Joe Leech took No. 1 Platoon, and the support of Lieutenant Kevin Knightly's armoured car and crew, to reconnoitre Avenue Kasenga towards Avenue Liège they came under heavy machine-gun and mortar fire. Pte Jimmy Redmond was seriously wounded and the patrol was ordered to withdraw around midday.

Redmond was taken to hospital with three shrapnel wounds. [He would recover to be repatriated as a patient on 19 December.]

Joe Leech reported the encounter, telling how he and Sergeant James Rea searched an empty night club, then searched houses opposite a police camp, before returning to

…the Police Camp side (a large area of concrete huts) where Corporal Pat Burke and Pte Jimmy Redmond were on an ant hill overlooking a large area of the camp. They had contacted some of the police, who appeared to be unarmed and quite scared.

A Swedish patrol of platoon strength arrived and, within ten minutes, a salvo of mortar bombs raked the road.

Pte Jimmy Redmond handed me some shrapnel that had blown into the drainage channel beside him. This was the first accurate fire on the platoon; earlier we had experienced wildly inaccurate rifle fire. Extremely heavy rifle and light machine-gun fire opened on us. The Swedes and ourselves replied.

When I saw a Swedish light machine gun withdrawing I whistled for my advance elements to withdraw.

At this stage, while lying on the roadside near a bank after a heavy mortaring, I saw Pte Redmond crawling down the drainage culvert dragging his rifle in the mud. He was bleeding. Pte Michael Brennan handed him out of the culvert to Sgt James Rea and myself who placed him on the platform of the Armoured Car. They reversed on to the road to fire and we had him evacuated in five minutes. He had three wounds in his back.

We received orders from Battalion HQ to withdraw but I requested permission to see the Swedes back through us. The Swedish patrol withdrew without casualties though the mortar fire and small arms fire continued.

There were no further casualties.

The fighting was relentless, and would go on for days without cease. Even then, not long after Leech and his patrol had returned to base, a Katangan armoured car, supported by infantry, rushed the Irish Camp. Corporal John McManus and Private James Feery were in an anti-tank position in front of the officers' mess and came under fire when the Mess was attacked. The armoured car kept going but was badly damaged when supporting infantry attacked from cover provided by gardens and villas.

The Katangan forces proceeded to build up their numbers around the concrete huts of the police camp, some 400 yards from the Irish camp which was by now under continual, heavy mortar and machine gun fire.

Corporal Fallon, recently arrived with 36th Battalion, was killed. Others of the 36th Battalion were wounded, as was A Company member, Private John McDonagh. The Gendarmerie continued to build up their numbers in the police camp, to infiltrate the triangle to the front of the Irish camp and to fire on the Irish.

Irish troops remorselessly returned all fire. For A Company this was a wider arena of war than Jadotville. Pat Quinlan described how it developed:

> A Globemaster, carrying members of 36th Battalion, circled wide and low over the city before landing. We watched horrified as every enemy weapon in Elisabethville kept up a continuous fire on the plane. The plane was hit. Black smoke streamed from one engine. It landed safely however and no one was wounded.
>
> The UN jets were not in the sky at this time to give assistance.
>
> UN jets came over on 7th December but did NOT attack ground positions. From 8th December on, however, Swedish SAABs and Indian Canberras were nearly always in the air, strafing enemy positions.
>
> It was very good for the morale of A Company to see the jets diving on targets. We all had very vivid memories of the Katangan Fouga jet which had bombed and strafed us without interference in Jadotville in September.

When a group of 36th Battalion cavalry soldiers were put under Quinlan's command, he used them as infantry, gave them an 84mm anti-tank recoilless rifle and used them to hold a route between A Company and Swedes leading to the Irish position. He was convinced, because of the build-up in Katangan numbers, that an attack along this route would happen that night.

It was 7 December. The word SUGAR was to be the SOS code if and when the attack happened. But the men of A Company were tired, and Quinlan worried about them:

They were very fatigued at this time, having been continually in action since early on 5th December and with very little rest since 2nd December. Most of them had been in action either with Lieut Tom Quinlan on the old airstrip or with Lieut Joe Leech's patrol.

I now wanted to rest as many as possible as I expected heavy action next day.

Privates James Nicell and Daniel Molloy were manning an anti-tank position with 84mm recoilless rifle almost continually since 2nd December and, now that I had the cavalry unit to cover this approach, I decided to rest them in a villa beside their anti-tank position.

The gun was left loaded in its position and other members of A Company were in a trench beside it. The Katangans attacked at 0200 hours. The cavalry unit raised the alarm with SUGAR but did not fire.

Ptes Nicell and Molloy were at their post in less than two minutes and fired the 84mm recoilless rifle into the attacking force. This, coupled with concentrated light automatic and rifle fire, broke up the attack.

It was now 8th December.

At first light, as soon as we could pick out the positions from which fire had come during the night, we saturated the area with fire. I planned to clear the area this morning using all of A Company—we had sufficient members of 36th Battalion at this time to take over our defence location.

I was not permitted to launch this action however, as Sector B had planned a limited attack for later that day to drive the enemy back to the Tunnel area.

At 1300 hours, United Nations troops launched a coordinated attack against the Katangan Gendarmerie. This started when a couple of Swedish companies moved to clear the city area between Avenue Savoniers and Avenue Kasenga as far as the Tunnel. As they did this, an Irish force, commanded by Lieutenant Mick Considine of the 36th Battalion and made up of Tom Quinlan's No. 2 Platoon and a platoon of B Company

36th Battalion with two armoured cars, moved to secure the right flank of attack along Avenue Savoniers.

It worked. The UN force got to within a few hundred yards of the Tunnel and cleared the Gendarmerie out of the area. Tom Quinlan, typically low-key, describes how the UN force went about the attack:

> The 'Tunnel' was about a mile-and-half from the Irish Camp … during the advance … the Swedish armoured personnel carrier was in front followed by an Irish armoured car, then No. 2 Platoon A Company, then another Irish Armoured car; B Company brought up in the rear.
>
> Most of the firing was done by the armoured personnel carrier and armoured cars. Our main task was to protect them on the move forward. As we came to an intersection the armoured personnel carrier and armoured cars took up position and waited for the enemy to be flushed out of the houses. As they ran across the short road between the two avenues they were engaged by the armoured cars.
>
> The B Company Platoon was dropped off at the cross roads. To protect our flank and rear as we moved forward. We eventually arrived at a point about 350 yards from the entrance to the tunnel.

Initially, Lieut Quinlan says, the plan was to, 'hold the area that night and to press on and capture the Tunnel next morning.' For this reason, he got the remaining members of A Company ready to move up to occupy the right flank. But the plan changed and the attacking force was ordered back to camp—fortuitously, as two A Company members collapsed from fatigue when they got back to camp. Medical Officer Joe Clune, seriously worried, told both the Battalion OC and Pat Quinlan that 'physical and mental exhaustion would take its toll in casualties' unless the men got rest. This was not easy, as Quinlan explains:

> Conditions in our defence position were most uncomfortable also as the trenches were filled with water owing to the heavy rains. Rest in the trenches was impossible. Despite this we were again ordered to have a platoon ready to repeat the same action at first light next morning, 9th December.

CHAPTER 58

The British Government, influenced by right-wing elements with interests in Katanga, is doing its utmost to bring the United Nations operation to nothing.

Dr Conor Cruise O'Brien, December 1961

World news. December 1961

As the fighting escalated in Katanga, and hopes of peace retreated to a far horizon, Dr Conor Cruise O'Brien, now a former UN Representative in Katanga, grabbed world headlines with views expressed at an informal press conference in his New York hotel room. The Irish Press, on 6 December, reported that O'Brien had 'charged the British and Rhodesian Governments, together with "the gutter millionaires of the press" with attempting to sabotage the UN Congo operation.'

O'Brien went on to say that the British Government, 'influenced by right-wing elements with interests in Katanga', was doing its utmost to bring the United Nations operation to nothing. Their goal, he said, was to 'gain time for the Katangan President, Moise Tshombe, so that he could set up a *de facto* separate state'.

He accused the 'gutter press', led by Lord Beaverbrook, of conducting a hate campaign against him because his actions in Katanga 'thwarted the interests of British capitalists'. Others accused by O'Brien of obstructing the UN in Katanga included Captain Charles Waterhouse, 'copper king' and former Conservative MP, Sir Roy Welensky, Rhodesian Prime Minister, and the British Prime Minister, Harold Macmillan. He said that he didn't know 'in which order to place them'.

Frank Aiken, Ireland's Minister for External Affairs, was also in New York and said that O'Brien's statement could not 'in any sense be taken as representing my views.'

In a separate report, but also in New York, O'Brien blamed white civilians for the attack on Irish troops in Jadotville. He said that these white residents 'en masse led the attack'.

And in Paris, Moise Tshombe held a press conference in which, the *Irish Press* reported, the Katangan President 'rejoiced' that O'Brien 'had quit' his UN position. 'He should be brought before a tribunal,' Mr Tshombe said, 'because he has many deaths on his conscience as a result of the UN adventure of 13th September.'

On 7 December, again in the *Irish Press*, UN fighter jets were reported going into action in Katanga. 'Planes in the service of Tshombe's forces were crippled yesterday in an attack by UN Indian Canberra jets on the war-torn provinces base at Kolwezi,' the paper said.

On Friday, 8 December, the *Irish Independent* headlined the story of the battle raging in Elisabethville. 'Heavy fighting raged on the outskirts of Elisabethville yesterday,' it reported, 'with the fate of the town still at stake on the third day of the battle between UN and Katangan forces.'

President Tshombe, arriving back in Africa from Paris, told newspapers, as reported in the *Irish Independent*: 'As long as the UN continue to attack us we will fight back. The battle goes on.' The paper reported that the fighting in Elisabethville was:

> at three main points—a road tunnel between the city and the Swedish camp, a roundabout on the road to the airport and the area of the U.N. headquarters and the adjoining Indian camp.
>
> Gurkhas with brens, stens, mortars and grenades drove the Katangans from around the tunnel, which is now no man's land.

The paper said that there was 'no news of the position of the Irish troops'.

While their comrades fought around the Tunnel and airport road roundabout, the returned members of A Company were being given what the *Irish Independent* elsewhere described as 'a stirring welcome on their return to Athlone':

A civic welcome from Athlone Urban Council was given them at Custume Barracks, where they were brought by army transport from the railway station and immediately taken into the warmth of the new dining hall.

On 11 December, the *Irish Press* gave General Sean McKeown's view that President Tshombe was no longer in control. In front-page headlines McKeown predicted that the 'dirty war' in Katanga would end in 'a matter of days' unless Katangan soldiers started guerrilla warfare from the bush. If that happened, he said, the UN action in the Congo would become an indefinite campaign. The secession campaign in Katanga was 'now in the hands of foreign mercenaries' he said, 'who were working in the interest of financial concerns in Katanga.'

It would, in fact, be two years before Katangan secession ended, in January 1963. Moise Tshombe, who would depart the Congo at that time, was dismissed as President in November 1965, when Joseph Mobutu took power, became President of the Congo and changed the country's name to Zaire.

CHAPTER 59

We travelled across nearly a mile of terrible swamp, up to our waists and sometimes our necks—and we got to within 100 yards of the objective and we blew up every single tank.

Comdt P. Quinlan, Elisabethville, December 1961

Elisabethville, Katanga. December 1961

Somehow, throughout the battle of Elisabethville, Quinlan kept his usual, detached eye on things and wrote home with news.

Elisabethville. Friday, 8th December 1961

My dear Carmel:

This is the day we were to land in Dublin but the turn of events here put a stop to that. We have had some very heavy and rather bitter fighting here since Tuesday. The Kats built up strong forces over the last few weeks then started to hem us in.

A Company were again to the forefront in the very first attack on the enemy.

Tom Quinlan, with armoured cars and a Gurkha platoon was ambushed on the way to attack a roadblock. However, they evened up our score from Jadotville and practically wiped out the entire enemy. One Gurkha captain was killed in that attack. Thank God Tom and the boys came home safe.

Yesterday my orderly, young Jimmy Redmond from Athlone, was wounded. Three bullet wounds—one in the right lung—but he will be all right. I'm going to the hospital to see him today.

I want you to call on his mother and tell her he is all right. He is a fine young lad of 18. He was my orderly and I am mad as hell over it.

A Company 36th Battalion and some of HQ flew in yesterday to a very hot reception. It was hell for those lads but they are learning. There are rumours of extending our service here and that we may have to go to Albertville today or tomorrow. There is no fighting there.

It will be all over in a couple of days. We are expecting an air strike on the enemy this morning—within the next few minutes—and I think that will finish them off. Don't worry about us, we are quite all right, and we will soon put a finish to it all. UN casualties are quite light.

Air strikes apart it is great to see the Swedish and Indian jets diving in the attack. We were on the receiving end of the Katangese jet long enough and we know what it is like. Sometimes I feel sorry for them but they asked for it.

B and C Companies are up in Niumza away from it all. They are lucky.

There is a fierce mortar bombardment on now. I think it is the enemy counter attacking an Ethiopian unit which captured a big hospital yesterday where they killed a lot of mercenaries and blacks.

I see in the papers that O'Brien has resigned and is telling his story. If I cared to resign I could tell a good story too.

One other Irish lad (not A Company) was wounded slightly by anti-tank fire in the action on Tuesday. Corporal McManus of A Company knocked out an enemy armoured car that day also.

Now all is quiet. There is not even a shot being fired at the moment. UN is building up forces here very fast. We have the 36th Battalion, an Ethiopian Battalion and an Indian and Swedish Battalion on their way. All should be completed by tomorrow. So you have nothing to worry about. We are very strong. This is not Jado and we have air superiority also.

I am glad we are here at the finish. I would consider it a half-finished job otherwise. Now, I'm not bloodthirsty but these people have asked for it and now they are getting it good and hard and no punches pulled.

I'm hoping we will be home for Christmas.

All my love, as ever, Pat

But Christmas was the last thing on Quinlan's mind, or the mind of anyone else in Katanga, during the days that followed. The 36th Battalion continued to arrive, and fighting became ever more fierce and vicious. Quinlan noted:

By 9th December, two complete companies plus HQ company of 36th Battalion had arrived in Elisabethville and the Irish position was much stronger. The position was also enlarged to take in a triangular area and villas adjoining Police Camp along Avenue Savoniers.

Only sporadic long-range machine-gun and rifle fire came into our position on the 9th.

An Ethiopian Battalion had also arrived and had taken Sabena Guest House area. The new Swedish Battalion was also in Elisabethville and plans were prepared for the final attack to clear the Katangan forces from Elisabethville.

This was the position when, on Sunday, 10 December, the 35th Battalion was moved into reserve at a location called Rousseau Farm on Route Charlie. With their work load now shared, the men of A Company had some rest time—though not half as much as Quinlan would have liked for them.

A new posting was set up and given the name Shop. Its purpose was to protect the refugee camp from attack and prevent any mass break-out of Jeunesse terrorists who were being held in that same refugee camp. Numbers 1 and 2 Platoons were rotated every 48 hours on this duty which, Quinlan wrote, 'was a most uncomfortable and unpleasant post from every point of view'.

It was isolated, in a filthy condition and dangerous. (Pte James Scally was seriously wounded in this post at 1030 hours on 18th. December. The bullet passed through his lung. It is uncertain whether he was wounded by enemy fire or by fire from Swedish troops holding a similar post about 500 yards away).

Our first task at the Rousseau Farm and Shop locations was to dig new trenches; NOT a welcome task for fatigued men but no man complained. The spirit with which the men went about all their heavy duties was of the highest order.

In what was now an all-out war between the UN and Katangan forces, Gendarmerie numbers steadily grew in the surrounding areas. When the Irish camp and Baluba refugee camp were mortared, it was thought that the firing had come from the village of Ruashi, which overlooked the Irish and Swedish camps. With UN intelligence, never very good, indicating that there was a Katangan force of company strength in Ruashi, Tom Quinlan, with members of his platoon and a Swedish patrol, went along to recce the situation.

Lieut Quinlan describes how they 'took a circuitous route through the bush' to the village perimeter where 'the Swedes observed the village from an ant hill'. A large empty school was deemed a likely enemy billeting location. This was fired on with mortars before they went in and carefully searched the village. Nothing was found. However, Tom Quinlan writes:

As we left the village, one or two riflemen got courage and came out of hiding and fired after us. As it was in the dark the patrol returned home through the bush having received no casualties.

There was the odd heart-warming occasion, as when Pat Quinlan and others of A Company came upon the burned-out hulk of the tank which had been used to attack them in Jadotville. They were, Quinlan drily commented, 'glad to see it'. He described it as

…a monstrous affair made from a converted bulldozer 22ft long and 12ft wide and 10ft high mounting two powder guns as well as light automatics with walls constructed of three sheets of steel. The space between the sheets of steel was filled with stone chippings. This was fatal as it contained the blast when hit by Indian 105mm recoilless rifles and made for easier penetration.

Despite the non-stop nature of the Battle of Elisabethville that December, Comdt Quinlan found time, somehow, to write to his wife, letters full of concern for his men and, still, annoyance at the way things were being run at Battalion HQ. On a day when he was called on and led a decisive action, he wrote, unknowingly, beforehand:

Elisabethville. Tuesday, 12th December 1961

My dear Carmel and children:

I thought I would be home with you since Friday last but such is not the case. We are all hoping that, please God, we will be home for Christmas anyhow.

We, the 35th Battalion elements, were withdrawn from the front line yesterday and are at a farm about three miles in the rear and near the airport. But I had to send Joe Leech out again last night with his platoon to occupy an outpost.

We have been in battle non-stop night and day since it started on Tuesday last. The UN is waiting to build up forces in preparation for a large-scale offensive.

We did a few sorties [attacks] to drive the enemy back from our camp out of range of small arms but they came in again last night. We were hit with mortar fire and one corporal of the 36th was killed and four others who were right beside me were wounded.

The poor lads of the 36th got a warm reception here. They have already one killed and nine wounded. Thank God we are still escaping. Young Redmond is all right. He has been transferred to Leopoldville and he is in great form. I wrote to his mother.

The fighting here was heavy but it was worse in Jadotville where we were at the receiving end of enemy heavy weapons and vastly superior forces. Those who always said that the Gendarmerie could not and would not attack, and therefore A Company was not attacked in Jadotville, have had their eyes opened now.

On Saturday night last A Company sector was rather heavily attacked but we beat it off easily. Next day Mac and Kane were talking and said the Gendarmerie was getting courageous now that they were actually making a physical attack. I said, 'What attack? I saw no attack.'

They shut up like clams.

My men are exhausted but they are wonderful and the pride of all who wish to admire them. They are even better than they were in Jadotville.

The rainy season has made a quagmire of the whole place and our trenches are full of water. We are filthy dirty with no chance to bath or even wash and not a clean uniform to put on. We will be disgraced if we do not get new uniforms before going home.

I wish I had my 58 men with me that have gone home. I saw this coming and begged HQ to leave my company intact, as we would not be operational if these lads went home.

God knows A Company has done it anyhow and we want to go home for Christmas.

We sincerely hope the Government won't be so stupid as to keep us here after our contract has expired.

Fond love and God bless you all, Pat

If he had intimations of what was to come later that day, he gave no indication in this letter. Yet, within hours, he had taken personal charge of an A Company force in a dramatic, and dramatically dangerous, attack which destroyed Soco Petrol, Katanga's main petrol storage station. It was an act of sabotage which struck a major blow against Katanga and had severe and critical effects on Gendarmerie morale.

Quinlan, bringing all his tactical genius into play, wanted to go for a surprise, night-time operation with a small raiding force. But with Sector B (the command HQ) insisting on urgency, he was forced to act in daylight. This made surprise more difficult. He asked for volunteers and, with a raiding force of 16 NCOs and men with two 84mm recoilless rifles and two light artillery teams, 'took personal command of the operation. Company Sgt Jack Prendergast accompanied me as Second in Command.' Walter Hegarty went along too.

UN forces had, before this, many times and unsuccessfully, tried to destroy the Soco Petrol station's five, very large, above-ground storage tanks, as well as those underground. Mortar fire and air attacks had been tried but the station was heavily guarded; Katangan troops had several times taken on Gurkha troops from there.

Quinlan planned to start from Rousseau Farm and, moving on foot across the high, scrub- and bush-covered ground, get as close as possible to the Soco station. He would then use anti-tank weapons to destroy the petrol storage tanks with, 'the two light artillery groups to cover my right flank which was open to the enemy and three riflemen as scouts on my left to guard against snipers or other enemy interference.'

Arriving at the end of the high ground, they found a 700-yard-wide exposed marsh separating them from the station. Quinlan then:

> Disposed the force with light automatic on the right covering the scrub area. We fired four rounds but they fell short by about 200 yards. The enemy did NOT return fire. They may have assumed it was another mortar attack.

He decided to move an anti-tank team forward. Company Sergeant W. O'Sullivan (of HQ Company) and A Company privates Nicell and Molloy all volunteered and, covered by the rest of the group, stalked forward through the scant elephant grass and fired four rounds. They hit the two nearest tanks, turned and got back to the patrol as quickly as possible.

One of the tanks went up in flames; the other (hit at a point near the top) failed to ignite. The patrol watched for a while, hoping that the huge blaze would spread to the other tanks. When this did not happen, Quinlan decided to 'go in again in darkness to complete the task' and withdrew the patrol to camp.

At 1900 hours, they moved in on the petrol station again. This time, they took a different route, crossing the swamp to a point where they could hit all of the tanks. This proved more hazardous than anticipated:

The men waded waist deep in swamp for a distance of approximately 1200 yards. Some very treacherous holes were encountered where on at least two occasions a man sank to his neck and might have been in great difficulties were it not for the prompt action of his comrade immediately behind who grabbed him.

Some 150 yards from the station, by a series of small termite mounds, Quinlan positioned the force so that there were two anti-tank rifles in the centre with a light artillery group guarding each flank.

I allotted targets to each anti-tank team and on a signal from me both guns fired and continued firing until all tanks were on fire. One round was sufficient to set each tank on fire when it was hit near the base. Each round scored a direct hit on this occasion. Thousands of tons of petrol erupted in flames which soared hundreds of feet into the night sky.

On a given signal from me the anti-tank teams withdrew to a prearranged rendezvous followed after two minutes by light automatic teams.

Unable to risk a new route, the force once more had to wade in and return to camp through the treacherous swamp. Quinlan concluded:

The enemy did NOT fire on us. If an enemy force was still there it is likely they had to run from the exploding petrol. The men behaved in their usual excellent manner. Fieldcraft was of a very high standard.

The petrol tanks burned fiercely for days, the blaze, unfortunately, lighting up the airport and making easier the task of the enemy bomber which bombed each night.

The following day, Quinlan wrote a letter home in which concern for men of the arriving battalion and A Company ran alongside his exultation at the success of the Soco Petrol operation.

Elisabethville, Wednesday 13th December 1961

My dear Carmel:

We are still here in this hole but thank God we have a lot to be thankful for. The 36th Battalion who took over the line from us are suffering a lot. They have one killed and up to 15 wounded now.

Joe Leech is still in an outpost with his platoon. They were mortared last night for about an hour but thank God no casualties. Our Blessed Lady who watched over us all along is still with us.

We are in a farm near the airport.

I led a raid yesterday with 16 men to blow up the enemy petrol storage tanks. Jet strikes and mortars had before that failed to destroy it. We succeeded in a most spectacular manner.

We went in with a daylight raid first and we hit one big tank with our 84mm anti-tank gun. There were five big tanks but we could not get near the others so we went in again last night.

We travelled across nearly a mile of terrible swamp—up to our waists and sometimes our necks—and we got to within 100 yards of the objective and we blew up every single tank. There were several thousand tons of petrol and oil stored there. It was a fantastic sight. The whole sky for miles around was lit up by flames hundreds of feet high.

At midnight last night I read a paper at four miles distance by the light from it.

Pte Nicell and Pte Molloy of my company and Company Sgt Sullivan of HQ Company were the gunners of the party. My Company Sgt Prendergast and Sgt Wally Hegarty were in my party too, of course. It made news headlines today but most news broadcasts gave credit for the job to the Swedes.

It is still burning fiercely with a pall of black smoke over the city and for several miles away to the south.

The UN completely underestimated the Gendarmerie and the financial and political resources behind them.

We expect to be going to Albertville when C Company of the 36th Battalion come here which we hope will be in a day or two. We are out of the fighting line now of course.

We are all very angry at our Government's breach of faith not getting us home for Christmas. It is only a rumour at the moment that we are not going home but we have grave doubts now if it will be possible to get home in time. They might at least make a statement and let us know one way or another.

We have had enough of this; not that we are afraid to fight but this is not our war. A Company is again in the forefront and bearing the brunt of the attacks, which we beat off in great style and, thank God, with only one casualty— young Jimmy Redmond. He is doing very well and the bullet did not lodge in his lung.

Next day, he wrote his last letter from the Congo, still not hopeful about his and the company's chances of getting home.

Elisabethville. Thursday, 14th December 1961

My dear Carmel and children:

We are very doubtful if we will be home for Christmas. We expect to go to Albertville tomorrow or Saturday. There is no fighting up there and there are no Gendarmerie there so at least we will be out of the fighting zone.

If I don't get home for Christmas I will be home for the New Year, please God.

Fond love and God bless you all, Daddy

Events between then and his company's eventual, pre-Christmas departure for Ireland moved swiftly, and with much tumult on the Battle of Elisabethville front.

A Company did not go to Albertville. The men were still in Elisabethville on Saturday, 16 December, when, as Quinlan, reported:

The UN attack went in and the 36th Battalion captured the Tunnel. The Swedes captured the Gendarmerie Camp

Massard. Gurkhas advanced towards the city centre and PO and the Ethiopians closed the northern exits from Elisabethville and the Lido Hotel.

On Monday, 18 December, Moise Tshombe sued for a ceasefire. That evening, No. 1 Platoon of A Company left Elisabethville for home.

A ceasefire came into operation with the dawn on Tuesday, 19 December, and, in the bright mid-morning, No 2 Platoon of A Company and Company HQ members left Elisabethville for home. Comdt Pat Quinlan was among them:

Weapons were unloaded just before the men boarded the Globemaster. They had their first decent wash and shave in almost three weeks when they arrived in Leopoldville six hours later.

The petrol tanks destroyed by the raiding force on 12 December were still burning on the skyline, 'a rope of black smoke drifting as far as the eye could see south over the Rhodesian border'.

CHAPTER 60

The cruellest lies are often told in silence.

Robert Louis Stevenson

Aftermath. Ireland

The last plane carrying A Company members touched down in Dublin Airport at 2200 hours on Friday, 22 December 1961. Travelling onward by train, car and bus, everyone made it home to their families for Christmas. Everyone, that is, except Private James Scally, wounded on Monday 18 December and still in hospital in Elisabethville. It was three weeks before he got home, to be hospitalised in Dublin.

In Mullingar and Galway, the men were given ecstatically warm receptions by comrades, friends and families. In Athlone, the town turned out for OC Quinlan and A Company members, fêting them through the town as a hero with heroes.

And then, all too soon, the quick silence, the pervasive denial, set in. Sometimes subtle, sometimes openly hostile, it was, immediately and for the years to come, felt by everyone in A Company.

Michael Shannon who, by virtue of serving with B Company can be accorded a certain objectivity, says:

> The core of silence which descended on the Jadotville Affair is proof positive that the military authorities in Ireland at that time wanted it to be airbrushed from memory. The personnel in A Company were non grata because of the surrender.
>
> But if your mission was to go out and fight to the last man then you'd have been given the equipment etc. to do so. Everyone knew A Company didn't have any of the necessities for a prolonged battle. The troops had no body

armour. A stray bullet in the lower chest and they were dead. Nowadays they'd have every kind of thing, facilities like sights on weapons to see in the dark.

It was a time when what happened reflected the culture of the country.

A couple of years later, in 1963, the 38th Battalion would have been equipped with mortar capacity to fire heavy mortar shells to extensive ranges. In learning they changed … [he is sage, and he is adamant] … but the mere fact of learning meant they admitted the earlier mistake. This, and equipping since then, vindicates the Pat Quinlans of this world who were sent out with weapons and equipment unsuitable to deal with their situations.

Or, as the young Leech had declared, simply, eloquently and equally adamantly in his report on Jadotville in 1961: 'Men should be properly equipped to do their duty, otherwise it is an improper use of valuable lives.'

Frustration, confusion, anger—even shame—were the emotions most strongly felt by those in A Company about the silence, innuendo and denial of Jadotville down through the years. Forty-four years, to be precise. Jadotville was denied, with some people implying that it was a question of a few shots being fired and then a shameful surrender.

The soldiers of A Company felt, and suffered, their ostracisation keenly through the years. But they always, too, felt pride and a sure knowledge that, when left without options, they had fought their battle courageously. Bill Ready says:

There was no doubt in the world that people in Jadotville gave everything, gave over and above the call of duty. Pat Quinlan was made very little of for the job he did. Any other army and he'd have been put on a pedestal, along with the other officers in Jadotville. But instead, in the officers' mess, you'd hear lots of resentment about them. There was the silence, and the slagging too, for years after. You'd always hear it. The 36th went out after us and when they came back a fellow said to me that he'd found my shirt out there, in Jadotville. A white one.

Ready says too that there were rows over the years, and fisticuffs, all brushed aside. And he feels, sadly and bitterly, that the army underestimated the men of A Company.

> Major mistakes were made at the top in the Congo and they tried to hide this. But we'd have understood the mistakes. It was the army's first time out. We were led raw, we'd have understood.

John Gorman too speaks of 'snide remarks' in the officers' mess:

> I was working as a barman in the mess, and because I was young at the time, I wasn't associated with Jadotville and they would talk in front of me. Silence would drop when the man himself, Pat Quinlan, walked in. I used to start humming 'Silence is Golden'.

Gorman says too that many of the younger men were deeply affected, resorting to drinking too much, and some developed depression.

Bobby Allan says that the 'snide remarks came from fellas who never went farther than the barracks. I went back out to the Congo: I had to to redeem my self-respect because of the remarks, the silence and the denial.'

Sean Foley returned to the Congo for precisely the same reason:

> Those of us who went back with the 38th Battalion went to grind the axe, so to speak. Bury the shame we were made to feel. There had been a lot of innuendo and casual sniping, things like 'oh, ye threw in the towel' were said to me as recently as 1986. We were never acknowledged. Medals were denied to those who deserved them and were recommended.

Noel Carey remembers how, soon after the return from Jadotville,

> Uncomplimentary remarks were being made to troops of the 6th Infantry Battalion about the surrender at Jadotville. People from A Company were tainted and, in

some cases, ostracised. Pat Quinlan himself had to live with
the perception that he should not have surrendered. In my
case I was conscious that Jadotville was being buried by
the army, that I was not to talk about it and it would be
better for my career to let it die.

Or, as Pat Quinlan himself put it, not without irony: 'If you have men
killed you have a victory but if you save your men and have a good
defence it is a defeat.'

Carey served twice afterwards in Cyprus. And he served again in
Athlone under Pat Quinlan.

I got to know him better as a commander and neighbour.
He was a courageous, brave, dedicated officer whose sole
consideration was the safety of his men, who was presented
with a dreadful decision at Jadotville: Fight to the death of
many of his men, an impossible situation, without any hope
of relief, or get an honourable peace and come home with all
his men. This proved to be a Hobson's Choice.

Although he was eventually promoted, Jadotville would
always be a blot on his career.

Carey himself, 43 years later, discovered by chance that a
recommendation for an award of merit had been in his army file
since Jadotville. The recommendation was made by Comdt Quinlan
and Carey's own platoon sergeant, Kevin McLoughlin. It was further
recommended by Battalion Commander McNamee and the Adjutant
General.

The medals board had refused the granting of the medal.

Liam Donnelly, on Carey's urging, looked up his own file. He too
had been recommended for an award. He too had been refused by the
medals board. Carey says:

I am sure that a number of NCOs and privates were also
nominated for awards. Why did no officer, NCO or private
receive recognition for outstanding bravery at Jadotville?
Was it coincidental that we were never made aware of our

nominations and that in our case the board rejected the recommendation? Was there undue influence used to make sure the board complied with instructions?

When I applied under the Freedom of Information Act for answers to these questions, I was stalled but continued. On my third attempt, I was told that they could not find any of those things 'at this remove'. I tried again and was told I should let matters drop. Liam Donnelly was in the same situation. He got no award and no joy.

But the simple fact of the discovery of the commendation made all the difference to Carey.

It took 40 yeas off my life. Just to see it written down. I regretted the fact that my Da didn't see it. It was vindication of all we'd done. It's a shame about the others who should have been recognised.

The vast majority of people in Ireland today would be behind Pat Quinlan's decision. He was ahead of his time, moving then in the direction which the army has gone since. Niemba created a mind set at the time. People said, 'Soldiers were killed there with bows and arrows so why couldn't they fight on in Jadotville?' But we weren't facing bows and arrows in Jadotville. What happened was wrong. We'd no experience, no travel. Look at the times! And why didn't they tell us about Operation Morthor?

What really upset us is that we were hung out to dry by our own, by the army. It's the old Irish thing: If it's a problem bury it, let it lie and it'll die. The Congo died in all of us. We moved on, because you do move on, but it was a living sore there all the time. It's a bonding situation within A Company.

He agrees that Jadotville should be a lesson learned for the army:

If the army had taken Jadotville, and all that happened there on board, they could have taken it as a course study for every single course question to do with consequences of decisions, etc.

Allan has memories as undiluted as his regard for his commanding officer:

> Pat Quinlan was one of the greatest soldiers ever and it was my privilege to serve under him. He was great in every way: on tactics, negotiations, as a leader, fighter—everything. Pat Quinlan should be above in Dublin where that silver pole which serves no purpose is in O'Connell Street.
>
> He was blackguarded by the army. When we came home to Ireland after Jadotville, there was always something about Jadotville.

It bothered him that Jadotville was airbrushed; the denial of what they had done bothered him enough to send him back to the Congo a year after he came home in 1961:

> I went back with the 38th Battalion. I felt there was something missing, felt I had to go back for my own self-respect. We were really let down in Jadotville.
>
> It was a fiasco. They sent reinforcements on two days and they went back both times. When I went back with the 38th we'd heavy mortars and air support and everything. We brought mortars from Mullingar.

Allan was a soldier, and young, with a natural, infectious exuberance (which he still has, in spades) that exerted itself. He remembers:

> When we were going into Jado with the 38th, I let off a burst of fire. Capt. John Boyle was in charge and he said to me, 'We'll have none of that John Wayne stuff' and I said, 'I was here before' and he said, 'You'll be here again if there's any more of that!' The Lufira Bridge was still blown when I went back. We took the whole province of Katanga that time.

Billy Ready, the first man wounded in Jadotville, is another who exudes a palpable and positive life force. He was, he says, 'lucky afterwards. I got on with my life.'

But some weren't so lucky and didn't get over it. I was a sportsman and didn't drink and had an outlet and didn't think about it.

But it disappointed me, very seriously, to know that we were left out there in Jadotville, not told about Morthor. That was wrong. Wrong. Getting us to Jadotville was intentional and it was a terrible disappointment to me that they would do that to us. If things had gone differently they could be celebrating 50 or 100 deaths every year.

For young men to be used as pawns like that was a terrible thing. I put it down to the fact of it being the first major conflict for the army and to its inexperience. But that's still not a good enough excuse. I don't believe that's the reason anyway, not now. It's not good enough, any of it. The force commander, McKeown—he was decorated for overseeing a shambles. It's a disgrace.

Ready too is adamant that, 'Pat Quinlan was one of the best officers I ever served under—and I served under a good few. He should have gone to the very top of the army but was held back by his outspokenness. He was a men's officer, not an officers' officer. He was a great man for his men.'

Foley, a member of Carey's No. 2 Platoon, also and keenly felt A Company's marginalisation on its return from the Congo. It's his belief that 'Jadotville, and much of what happened in the Congo, was a debacle and all because of having civilians in charge.'

He went back to the Congo with the 38th Battalion at the end of 1962 when, he says, 'the war took off again'.

When we came back, in May 1963, I'd a sense of failure at being poked fun at about Jadotville. There were snide remarks from fellas who'd never gone farther than Eyre Square. I left the army and went to England in 1964. When I came back I got a job on a Stud Farm and was there for four years. But I wanted to be in the army so I rejoined in 1974 and stayed until 2000. I was a Company Quartermaster Sergeant when I retired. I'd go through it all again, including Jadotville.

John Gorman, who for so long waged a brave campaign for recognition of the role played by A Company and its commanding officer in Jadotville, was, like many others, little more than a youth when there.

> I was 17 when I went to the Congo. It was only when I came home, and got a bit older, that I realised the full extent of what had happened. I didn't know where to find myself when I came back. I was just 18. I was disgusted with the way things had happened. I departed and went off AWOL to England for three years and was Court Martialled for this. I said I wanted Comdt Quinlan to defend me and he did. He fought tooth and nail for me at the Court Martial and I was fined five pounds!
>
> I was disgusted all my life afterwards seeing how people of A Company were treated. I retired in 1984, as a Corporal. I never did the interview for promotion.

He has never stopped fighting for A Company and its commander either.

John Manning and Leo Boland were not much older than John Gorman. Both were 19-year-old privates, and good friends.

Boland remained in the army after coming home. A quiet man, he is adamant that there was no option but to surrender, that it was the right thing to do:

> There was a ceasefire. Both sides agreed but the other side broke it. They broke the ceasefire. Jado was forgotten about after. Maybe because we surrendered. People said we were cowards but it never bothered me what they said. We were all young. I went back out again with the 38th Battalion and had a quiet time. Pat Quinlan was one good man. One very good man. I think there should have been an enquiry into why what happened in Jadotville happened. My friend John Manning was a good soldier....

Manning, wounded in the shoulder at Jadotville, is not alive to tell his story. His sister, Mary Lattimore-Manning tells it for him instead:

> He committed suicide in 1963. He was just coming up to 21 when he died. He was very quiet when he came home from

the Congo, not the same brother who went out. Before it, he used to go hunting, shooting at the shooting times of the year. He was tall and strong, very competitive. He won best dressed in the LDF [Local Defence Force] and Best Shot. He was well educated too. To him the Congo was another adventure.

Our Dad was in the army for 31 years. Our grandad was in the Connaught Rangers and fought in the Battle of the Somme when he was 17 years old.

When John came home, he wanted to leave the army so an uncle bought him out. He went to the UK and that's where he died. He was restless, couldn't settle. He met a girl but that didn't sort out either. He was in his flat and he turned on the gas. He'd turned it off but too late; it had gone too far. He lived like a soldier in the flat, the papers said. He died on 26 November 1963.

After Jadotville he was very nervy and there was no counselling or anything then. Really, they could have done with it.

And then there is Dr Joe Clune who, with Liam Donnelly, courageously returned to Jadotville from Elisabethville knowing that A Company was surrounded. Clune stayed on in the army and became Director of the Medical Corps. He retired in 1992. 'Everyone talks of the surrender,' he says, 'but it wasn't a surrender as such. It was a ceasefire, an agreement which was broken. The Katangese started moving closer; our water was cut off. On the basis that it was a UN problem why suffer loss of life? We were peacekeepers.'

Peacekeepers who were, he too believes with certitude, 'used as pawns in Jadotville, pawns in the Katanga/Belgian/Union Minière set up.' He shakes his head. 'They weren't innocent, the Belge. There was, of course, a political thing going on, and the political was given to the military to implement.'

Clune believes that lack of communications was a major problem in Jadotville:

Our company had communications with Battalion HQ but they didn't have onward communications with the

Indian leader of the Brigade, Gen. Raja, at the other side of Elisabethville. That's why the whole of Ireland was praying for 24 hours—because communications weren't there in Africa. Why did the Taoiseach, Seán Lemass, take his information on our deaths from BBC Rhodesia? We wondered what the hell people at home were thinking; this was the biggest worry people had in Jadotville; bullets flying overhead didn't worry half so much.

He sees what happened afterward in the context of the time:

Life was different then. You came home, went back to work, got on with it. Some people went to Cyprus later, some went back to the Congo. Some people were more vulnerable and might have wondered afterwards about what happened. It was all the luck of the draw.

He has no regrets. 'I suppose it was our education,' he says, 'to see Africa. The military side of it was education too. I've no regrets about joining the army. I might have cursed it but I enjoyed it. I never think about Jadotville. My attitude is that you're not going to get answers so it's not worth the trouble.'

But some things do change.

CHAPTER 61

Only the dead have seen the end of war.

Plato

Aftermath. Ireland

Today's army officially acknowledges and respects the rights of the individual. Enshrined in a Dignity Charter for the Defence Forces, which applies both at home and overseas, are the tenets of respect for individuality and diversity and the stricture that 'harassment in any form is NOT [*sic*] accepted by us and will NOT [*sic*] be tolerated.'

Other things too have changed. With the ill effects of stress and trauma now long and generally recognised, the Defence Forces have put supports in place for their members. Soldiers going overseas are now briefed by Defence Forces psychologists, prepared for potential psychological effects of any stress and trauma, warned of the consequences to well-being on their return and given whatever counselling they need.

Everyone gets a special-issue booklet dealing with stress exhaustion symptoms and more. It tells how to cope with the death/ loss of a comrade, gives grim and basic rules on how not to identify with bodies as human beings after a disaster and advises the soldier to wear gloves so as to avoid the lingering smell of blood and death on hands. Post Traumatic Stress Disorder (PTSD) is also covered.

Lieutenant Colonel (retired) Coleman Goggin trained as an organisational psychologist when an injury ruled out full participation in physical military activity. He practised as a psychologist in the army until retiring in 2000 and was responsible for making Relaxation Training (deep breathing and muscle relaxation aimed at overcoming anxiety) a part of the training for going overseas. He says, 'the chaplains are wonderful these days. Many have masters in counselling. The PSS [Personal Support Service] is very fine too, is in every barracks in Ireland and trained to know about Social Welfare benefits and to look out for Post Traumatic Stress.'

Goggin, who served with the 37th Battalion in the Congo in 1962, says that his experience as an infantry officer focused his interest on how psychology, 'highlighted the way an organisation developed, how insight into morale and *esprit de corps* could be used to make for a more effective organisation.'

The management of stress, he points out, 'is as old as the existence of armies themselves'. He continues:

> Stress can be a great gift, can move us to do an awful lot of things. Great leaders, going back to Alexander the Great, understood leadership and the use of stress.
>
> Pat Quinlan instinctively knew the principles involved. His style of leadership was excellent. He was doing the right thing 45 years ago and never did a psychology course in his life. He knew about man management and had instinctive insight. He would boost a fellow's morale when he was down in the dumps, would watch fellows, how they took bad news from home etc., forever keeping people up.
>
> You need food to overcome anxiety and Pat Quinlan instinctively knew this and so encouraged the men in the trenches to eat.
>
> We, in 1961, knew more about propaganda and psychological warfare than we did about everyday stress. It wasn't until the 1980s that knowledge began to break and we began to understand Post Traumatic Stress Disorder (PTSD).
>
> Arising from the Israeli action at Yom Kippur and that of the Americans in Vietnam there came insight into stress in operational service. I made contact with military psychological organisations internationally. As information came along, the British, Australians, Americans developed new insights and we all pooled our knowledge of international military service. PTSD was recognised as a medical entity in the 1980s.

A Company would have been under greatest stress, he says, 'when under intense periods of bombardment':

> 'Groundhog' it's called. The soldiers involved in Jadotville would have had to be bloody fools or psychopaths if they weren't upset. But people are at their most vulnerable when they come home. Even a door banging can startle. All a soldier wants to do is relax.
>
> Nowadays they're advised to take a month's holiday. A spouse may want to organise a holiday in Torremolinos but what the soldier actually needs is to learn how to re-establish intimacy. The month should be used to allow the high level of alertness to dissipate. Nowadays, prior to coming home, people are briefed on what to expect from themselves, how irritable they may be. They're warned that the joyful reunion may not be so joyful!

He thinks it is 'quite likely some of the men in A Company developed PTSD and didn't know it':

> They would have been afraid and ashamed to talk and would have covered up. That was the culture of the time. They would have been afraid too that they wouldn't be allowed go away again.
>
> So they soldiered on.

Their salvation, he says, lay in a quality vitally present in A Company:

> It was in the way they trusted one another. Pat Quinlan built group and unit cohesiveness. He kept the company together as much as possible before and afterwards (in Elisabethville), and he encouraged them to talk. What he did is now textbook, and he was doing it instinctively.

A subject much discussed in A Company afterwards was the special group of people who helped see the men safely through the Battle of Jadotville. That none have been acknowledged by the army and the UN has always been a source of embarrassment, anger too.

Lieut Bjerne Hovden and his crew Eric Thors were men who, Hegarty says, 'volunteered for no earthly reason, were truly brave, deserved medals and never even got a mention anywhere.'

Nor did Mme Lamonfagne, Charles Kearney, Major Guertz, Marc Pierre, Louis Christiaens and Emmanuel Kamukeji. Comdt Quinlan made every effort, afterwards, to have the help of all these people recognised, assiduously tracking down everyone's whereabouts before writing to recommend that they be given army and/or state acknowledgement or, in some cases, be given help by the UN to rebuild lives shattered as a consequence of the help given to A Company.

Of Louis Christiaens he wrote:

> I feel I personally owe him a debt of gratitude for the assistance he gave me at a very trying time at great risk to himself. I shall be very happy to know that the United Nations will reward him with suitable employment.

Writing to the army authorities, seeking 'official recognition' for Major Guertz, Pierre Marc and Mme Lamonfagne, he said that he 'especially' wanted their elderly benefactress to be recognised:

> I feel she should be awarded some official recognition for her kindness and assistance to Irish troops ... and that this official recognition be conveyed to her.

It never was, nor was any such recognition given to any of the others who helped.

Events in Jadotville have not gone entirely unexamined by members of the Defence Forces over the years. In 1993, a syndicate representing students of the 50th Command and Staff Course chose 'The Battle of Jadotville, Congo 1961' as the subject for a UN Case Study.

Their study arrived at conclusions already reached by Pat Quinlan, his officers and the men of A Company three decades earlier.

It concluded that the UN in Katanga had no intelligence service, that Operation Morthor was preplanned and that it was therefore 'inconceivable that A Company in Jadotville was not informed'. It found that placing A Company 80 miles from HQ was 'a tactical error' which 'created a hostage opportunity' and that basic necessities like transport, food and water were inadequate.

Syndicate members wondered why Force Kane 2 was ordered back by Battalion HQ when it was, in fact, a Brigade Task Force mission, and they were not at all sure the surrender was a legitimate surrender. 'It was,' they concluded, 'brought about by possible duping of the company commander into entering an agreement that Jadotville would be jointly patrolled, that they would be given water and food.' And the Study noted that, 'although there were many individual acts of bravery under fire' *no awards were made.*

The easily accessible study had little if any, impact on army attitudes, or sense of obligation, regarding Jadotville.

The present Chief of Staff, Lieutenant General Jim Sreenan, initiated a Study Group Report on Liam Donnelly's submission on 'The Jadotville Affair' in 2004. Following this, a Review Group was set up under the Director of Administration, Colonel Chris Moore, to look at the issues and review other material held by the Defence Forces.

The Review's findings led to army agreement on two out of three of Donnelly's requests. It was agreed to recognise both A Company's performance and the role of its company commander, Comdt P. Quinlan. The army's vindication of A Company did not honour the recommendations made for medals. The reasons given had to do with the time which had elapsed and with setting a precedent which might lead to others requesting medals.

Sean Foley, for one, does not understand why the medals were not awarded:

> Men like John Monaghan deserved the highest honour. He was like granite! I don't see why they can't do something like put an oak leaf on the UN medal, allow A Company have this as a distinction for themselves.

The lonely outrage and frustration of many in A Company were at last assuaged by the November 2005 unveiling in Custume Barracks, Athlone, of a commemorative plaque in their honour. Its inscription reads:

> In honour of the Officers, NCOs and men of 'A' Company 35th Infantry Battalion United Nations Force in Congo (ONUC) who had the misfortune to suffer so much at Jadotville in the province of Katanga in September 1961.
> 'A' Company took responsibility for the UN Post at Jadotville on the 3rd of September. On the 9th of September a large force of Katangese Gendarmerie surrounded them and early on the morning of the 13th September the Company came under attack. Over the coming days, until 17th September, they endured almost continuous attacks from ground and air. Despite determined leadership, courageous resistance and the sustained efforts of 35th Infantry Battalion HQ to provide assistance, 'A' Company was taken into captivity on the 17th September. By this time 'A' Company had no water or food and several men had been wounded. 'A' Company remained in captivity until finally released on 25th October 1961.
> Their sacrifices in the service of peace are remembered with pride.

The Minister for Defence, Willie O'Dea TD, the first minister for defence to acknowledge Jadotville and what happened there, spoke of 'ordinary soldiers doing extraordinary things':

> It is a true story of real people, many just out of their teens, who found themselves thousands of miles away from home and in an unfamiliar and highly dangerous situation, yet had the determination, the belief and the leadership to come safely through their ordeal.

The memorial commemorated their story and, he said, 'their courage and forbearance, their suffering and their heroism. It will serve as a lasting reminder of their remarkable achievement. Through their courage and determination they have left a proud and enduring legacy to the Irish Defence Forces.'

A portrait of Comdt Quinlan by the artist James Hanly now hangs (alongside one of Lieut Col. McNamee) in the Congo Room in the United Nations Training School in the Curragh. It will carry Brigadier Raja's appreciation:

> I should like to make particular mention of Comdt Quinlan who had the misfortune to suffer so much at Jadotville. This officer needs little commendation as his performance in maintaining the discipline and high morale of his men during a particularly difficult stage of Katanga operations speaks for itself. I have great personal admiration for the initiative, courage, drive and restraint of this officer and I believe that he could be held as an example to all soldiers.

For OC Commandant Patrick Quinlan it comes far, far too late. By the time he died in 1997, he had lived with the cover-up of his company's ordeal, and the denial of his and his troops' courage, for 36 years.

Jadotville is now living history. Lieut Gen. Jim Sreenan, army Chief of Staff, the man who finally moved to vindicate the company by initiating a Study Group Report and Review Group report, says that it was easier for him 'to stand back and take an objective position on it':

> It's quite clear to me that those in Jadotville did everything humanly possible in their situation. It's likewise clear to me that those in Elisabethville did everything possible to help.
>
> The gist of the Review Report, its conclusions, was that the people in Jadotville, under severe stress conditions, performed heroically and did all that could humanly be expected of them.

He stresses that, 'it is not my business to get into the strategic considerations which got those in Jadotville into the situation' but agrees that 'the mandate was weak, and kept changing (or being reinterpreted). The Congo operation was conducted long before there was any scientific approach to peacekeeping by the UN. Those were the very early days of the UN.'

What really happened in Jadotville had, he says, 'become obscured over the years':

> No one ever seemed familiar with the facts of the situation and when communications are bad the rumour machine takes over. Stories were told and retold, often by people who hadn't even been there.
>
> In order to establish the facts, I decided to examine the battalion itself and the operations it was involved in. It took time.
>
> We owe a lot to those men of the 1960s who went to the Congo. They were the ones who pioneered going abroad. They were brave, truly brave. They didn't even know where the Congo was, most of them. They couldn't be sure they would get back. They had a pioneering spirit and those men made the army.
>
> Before that we'd nothing to benchmark ourselves against. We were a post-emergency army, going nowhere but when men were out there, with shot and shell falling around them, they learned about things, and about reality, fast. What we have now, as a result of those pioneers, is a great amount of accumulated experience in the army over the years.
>
> While the Dignity Charter makes clear that every soldier is today entitled to his or her dignity, the soldier of yesterday is entitled to his dignity too.

Sreenan, who knew and worked with Comdt (later Colonel) Pat Quinlan in the years following Jadotville, agrees with psychologist Coleman Goggin's assessment of Quinlan as a leader:

> In today's world the people coming out of Jadotville would be strongly debriefed, given a critical stress debriefing. But in 1961, Pat Quinlan knew how to handle things afterwards: I know what he did. He kept his men together, he'd have wanted them together talking and talking and talking about

what had happened. Today they're putting science and names on what always happened, on principles good leaders always understood.

And he too believes there are lessons to be learned from what happened in Jadotville: 'Certainly, and it's a lesson which has yet to be learned by the UN itself; you always need a force in reserve to get people out of trouble.'

Or as Wally Hegarty put things, in the days of their imprisonment immediately after the battle: 'I have at least learned that a company shouldn't be separated from transport or isolated....' He spoke for every UN peacekeeping soldier who had to fight in Jadotville, and has fought in the other Jadotvilles of the world's troubled places since.

There is concern among the surviving men of A Company, and as Sean Foley makes clear, annoyance too, that the Review Group Report was drawn up without consulting, interviewing or speaking to a single member of the unit. Without any such consultation, those who wrote the Report still feel qualified to pronounce on the 'suffering' of 'all personnel involved in this incident' and on the consequences of these feelings:

The suffering manifested itself in many forms including feelings of guilt at all levels. This guilt has led to recriminations and to apportioning blame without full access to the facts.

Many closely involved with the incident, for guilt reasons or out of respect and regard for the feelings of those involved, chose a solution that involved consigning those events to memory and getting on with life. Even today it is difficult to formulate a dispassionate view of events as many of the surviving participants have differing but sincerely held views.

Some of the views passionately expressed by veterans of 35th Infantry Battalion are not informed by direct personal experience and are almost certainly not informed by reference to the available documentation. In many cases the views of the surviving members have been coloured by discussion of the events over the years.

Liam Donnelly makes just and dignified comment on this, pointing out that views were passionately expressed because of the years during which, 'higher authority neglected, airbrushed and refused to examine a military situation which called for critical examination.' He finds the wording of the Review Group Report offensive. So too, having spoken with and come to know veteran survivors, does this writer.

'The people behind the Review Board leading to the memorial weren't there, in Jadotville,' Bobby Allan says. 'They don't know what the thinking was, how things were. Pat Quinlan brought the whole lot of us home; there was no one in a coffin coming back. The men who were there should have been asked about it. No one asked me. Nor anyone else. The officers and NCOs should have been asked.'

'Where,' Donnelly asks, 'did such information have its origin?'

I don't know of any person of A Company who was ever interviewed or questioned officially regarding Jadotville over the years. Too many persons from the highest to the lowest were guilty of grave errors of leadership, political intrigue, lack of definite chains of command, lack of strategic and tactical intelligence.

In fact, over those years, the Irish Military should have used every aspect of the Jadotville affair as a case study on military courses examining all the failures and benefits.

It may happen some day.

The facts are available now, in national, army, Foreign Affairs and UN archives, in the personal written accounts of Pat Quinlan, Liam Donnelly, Noel Carey and Walter Hegarty. They are here too, in the many oral memories given by those who remembered for this book. And they are in (Colonel, retired) Dr Terence O'Neill's articles, notably in his examination of Jadotville in the journal, *International Peacekeeping*. In this, he looks at 'the problems arising from assigning military tasks to troops equipped only for peacekeeping duties'. He concludes, inter alia, that, 'failure to learn the lessons of the (Jadotville) incident led to many of the problems encountered by UN troops at Srebrenica and in Rwanda and Sierra Leone.'

He looks too, and tellingly, at how:

Events in Jadotville raise implications about the 'use of force' in terms of inflicting and sustaining casualties. It is clear that in killing and wounding large numbers of Katangese, members of A Company were acting in self-defence. But was there a point at which killing of Congolese by the peacekeepers would no longer have been considered by those conducting the operation to be justifiable or acceptable? Equally, were the besieged troops expected to fight to the last man in support of the UN effort to crush Katanga? Who was entitled to make such decisions and upon what basis? Had the framers of Security Council Resolution 161A given any thought to the consequences of moving from peacekeeping to military engagement?

It seems not.

Now, with their recognition, there is hope in A Company and beyond that there may be serious and useful discussion about the lessons of Jadotville, and its aftermath. And there is always, for the men, the bond predicted by their commander when he wrote:

Wherever they go and whenever they meet the bond of comradeship built up between officers, NCOs and men in the varied adventures of the Company in Elisabethville, Jadotville and Kolwezi and Elisabethville again will, I have no doubt, be everlasting.

The day of the memorial plaque's unveiling was wet and windy, the ceremony achingly moving. For many of the survivors, it was their first time to meet since returning from Jadotville in December 1961. Many wore their UN berets with pride. All were visibly moved. Sean Foley brought with him the bagpipes which had caused such consternation in Kolwezi prison camp. But this was Ireland, and November, and the rain saw to it that he was unable to play.

Liam Donnelly, the army having failed to honour the recommendations, gallantly presented medals of his own. In a casually graceful ceremony, he gave one of these to the Quinlan family and one each to the happily present John Monaghan, Jack Prendergast and Noel Carey.

There are still questions to be answered. But the facts are, here and now, laid down. They make clear that an apology is long overdue from Belgium, whose insistent Foreign Minister had a company of Irish soldiers dispatched into terrible danger and a certain hostage situation; and that the United Nations too must look at its role in the Jadotville Affair, at how the lack of a clear mission statement, of communications, proper transport and arms so seriously endangered the lives of 156 Irish peacekeeping soldiers.

Donnelly, in a speech at the unveiling, put all that has happened into moving perspective:

'The Jadotville Affair', so long airbrushed from army history and records may from today be talked about, written about and be the basis for real study so that that awful, sickening statement used so glibly today will have real meaning and significance—'Ensure that such an episode will never be allowed to happen again.'

The survivors of A Company had, he said, looked forward to, longed for and wondered if such a day would ever arrive. He spoke of the, 'myths and fairy tales, carefully quoted half-truths and smoke screens used to airbrush Jadotville out of Irish military history' and of his long quest seeking 'critical examination and assessment of the Jadotville Affair'.

Donnelly spoke for them all about the commanding officer who brought them through, and safely home. 'What of this man— Company Commander Pat Quinlan?' he asked.

He has permeated our lives. He was always steadfast. He took enormous pride in the accomplishment of his unit. He could be pugnacious in asserting his beliefs but he respected those who differed with him. He could be hard but not petty. His enemies were the slip-shod and the second rate. The outspoken and alleged consequences of Jadotville were an unspoken and extraordinary burden, which drained him, but he would never have admitted it.

One had to know him well to understand the manner in which he communicated. The meanings of the nudges and mumbles by which he conveyed his infinite caring came to be understood over time…

If he was here today he would be so happy. He would tell us, 'Don't look back; the future is full of exciting challenges.'

But we do look back and we do remember him with pride.

APPENDIX A

ARMY RANK SYSTEM

Lieutenant General (Chief of Staff)
Major General
Brigadier General
Colonel
Lieutenant Colonel
Commandant
Captain
Lieutenant
2nd Lieutenant
Sergeant Major
Barrack Quartermaster Sergeant
Company Sergeant
Company Quartermaster Sergeant
Company Sergeant
Corporal
Private

APPENDIX B

156 MEMBERS OF A COMPANY IN JADOTVILLE

Name	Rank	Year of Birth	From	Marital Status
Patrick Quinlan	Commandant	1919	Kerry	Married
Joseph Clune	Doctor/Commandant	1927	Clare	Married
Dermot Byrne	Captain	1923	Kildare	Married
William Donnelly	Captain	1928	Dublin	Married
Thomas McGuinn	Captain	1918	Limerick	Married
Noel Carey	Lieutenant	1937	Limerick	Single
Joseph Leech	Lieutenant	1933	Dublin	Married
Thomas Quinlan	Lieutenant	1934	Waterford	Single
Kevin Knightly	Lieutenant	1932	Dublin	Married
Joseph Fagan	Chaplain	1918	Westmeath	Single
W (Bobby) Allan	Corporal	1925	Kilkenny	Married
Gerald Battles	Private	1942	Meath	Single
Leo Boland	Private	1939	Donegal	Single
Joseph Bracken	Private	1941	Offaly	Single
Robert Bradley	Private	1938	Donegal	Single
Colm Brannigan	Corporal	1940	Kildare	Single
Michael Brennan	Private	1939	Mayo	Single
John Broderick	Private	1941	Longford	Single
Michael Broderick	Private	1943	Longford	Single
Patrick Burke	Corporal	1939	Kerry	Single
James Byrne	Private	1930	Kildare	Married
Patrick Conlon	Private	1940	Sligo	Single
Desmond Connelly	Private	1933	Westmeath	Single

Name	Rank	Year of Birth	From	Marital Status
John Conway	Private	1941	Sligo	Single
Charles Cooley	Private	1942	Longford	Single
Geoffrey Cuffe	Sergeant	1934	Westmeath	Single
Thomas Cunningham	Private	1939	Westmeath	Single
Patrick Delaney	Private	1942	Offaly	Single
Albert Dell	Private	1925	Kilkenny	Married
James Dempsey	Corporal	1934	Carlow	Single
John Devine	Corporal	1938	Longford	Single
Henry Dixon	Sergeant	1924	Dublin	Married
John Donnelly	Corporal	1939	Armagh	Single
Patrick Donnelly	Private	1941	Longford	Single
John Dowler	Private	1941	Longford	Single
Joseph Duff	Private	1924	Dublin	Married
Patrick Duffy	Corporal	1919	Monaghan	Married
William Duffy	Private	1938	Donegal	Single
Maurice Doyle	Private	1931	Wexford	Single
Patrick Dunlevy	Private	1942	Galway	Single
Anthony Dykes	Private	1941	Sligo	Single
James Feery	Private	1940	Offaly	Single
Simon Finlass	Private	1937	Westmeath	Single
Dominick Flaherty	Private	1922	Galway	Married
John Flynn	Private	1940	Westmeath	Single
John Flynn	Private	1938	Longford	Single
Thomas Flynn	Private	1942	Meath	Single
John Foley	Corporal	1940	Tipperary	Single
John Foster	Corporal	1930	Cavan	Married
Michael Galvin	Private	1942	Westmeath	Single
Patrick Gildea	Private	1917	Donegal	Single
Francis Gilsenan	Sergeant	1921	Cavan	Married
John Gorman	Private	1944	Wicklow	Single
Edward Gormley	Private	1940	Sligo	Single
Noel Graham	Private	1941	Westmeath	Single
Michael Greene	Private	1941	Longford	Single
Thomas Gunn	Private	1938	Tipperary	Married
William Hannigan	Private	1937	Tipperary	Married
Dominick Harkin	Private	1938	Tyrone	Married
James Harper	Private	1940	Donegal	Single
William Heffernan	Private	1924	Dublin	Married
Daniel Hegarty	Private	1942	Westmeath	Single
Henry Hegarty	Private	1942	Donegal	Single
Joseph Hegarty	Private	1939	Westmeath	Single
Walter Hegarty	Sergeant	1932	Galway	Single

Name	Rank	Year of Birth	From	Marital Status
Gerald Hennelly	Private	1942	Mayo	Single
Patrick Hogan	Private	1940	Westmeath	Single
Thomas Hogan	Private	1942	Tipperary	Single
William Hughes	Private	1940	Longford	Single
Patrick Joyce	Sergeant	1940	Galway	Married
William Keane	Private	1940	Galway	Single
Thomas Kelly	Sergeant	1924	Galway	Married
John Kerr	Corporal	1935	Antrim	Married
Brendan Laffere	Corporal	1938	Offaly	Single
Robert Larkin	Private	1938	Westmeath	Single
Thomas Larkin	Private	1941	Galway	Single
Kieran Lynch	Private	1935	Westmeath	Single
Michael Lynch	Corporal	1924	Galway	Married
Edward Maher	Private	1941	Tipperary	Single
Francis Malone	Private	1942	Westmeath	Single
Joseph Maloney	Private	1940	Dublin	Single
Donal Manley	Private	1941	Roscommon	Single
John Manning	Private	1941	Cork	Single
James Myler	Private	1940	Wexford	Single
Daniel Molloy	Private	1938	Kildare	Single
John Monaghan	Sergeant	1934	Offaly	Married
Patrick Monaghan	Private	1942	Longford	Single
James Murray	Private	1911	Sligo	Married
John McAnaney	Corporal	1921	Derry	Married
James McArdle	Corporal	1931	Longford	Married
Martin McCabe	Sergeant	1917	Sligo	Married
James McCourt	Private	1936	Monaghan	Single
Michael McCormack	Private	1927	Limerick	Married
Michael McDermott	Private	1940	Donegal	Single
John McDonagh	Corporal	1924	Galway	Married
Thomas McDonagh	Private	1942	Galway	Single
Thomas McDonnell	Corporal	1934	Monaghan	Married
John McEntee	Corporal	1919	Monaghan	Married
Matthew McGrath	Private	1941	Wexford	Single
Joseph McGuinness	Private	1941	Westmeath	Single
Kevin McLoughlin	Sergeant	1921	Meath	Single
Terence McMahon	Private	1942	Dublin	Single
Francis McManus	Private	1941	Sligo	Single
John McManus	Corporal	1932	Sligo	Married
Anthony McNerney	Private	1927	Longford	Single
Patrick Neville	Quartermaster Sergeant	1918	Clare	Married
James Nicell	Private	1941	Donegal	Single

Name	Rank	Year of Birth	From	Marital Status
John O'Brien	Corporal	1924	Wexford	Married
Peter O'Callaghan	Corporal	1934	Sligo	Married
Michael O'Connor	Corporal	1927	Westmeath	Married
Michael O'Farrell	Private	1941	Galway	Single
James O'Kane	Private	1938	Tyrone	Single
Joseph O'Kane	Private	1936	Tyrone	Single
Robert Orr	Private	1942	Kilkenny	Single
Michael O'Sullivan	Private	1940	Galway	Single
John Peppard	Private	1922	Westmeath	Married
Christopher Powell	Private	1943	Longford	Single
John Prendergast	Company Sergeant	1915	Tipperary	Married
John Purtill	Private	1942	Longford	Single
Martin Quinlan	Private	1943	Longford	Single
Timothy Quinn	Corporal	1942	Limerick	Single
James Rea	Sergeant	1936	Cork	Single
James Redmond	Private	1942	Westmeath	Single
Patrick Rhatigan	Corporal	1941	Westmeath	Single
Daniel Regan	Private	1943	Roscommon	Single
Joseph Relihan	Corporal	1925	Kerry	Married
William Riggs	Private	1932	Westmeath	Single
Christopher Roche	Corporal	1928	Roscommon	Married
Anthony Roper	Private	1942	Westmeath	Single
James Scally	Private	1933	Westmeath	Single
Michael Seery	Private	1932	Westmeath	Single
John Shanagher	Private	1941	Clare	Single
Michael Smith	Corporal	1936	Cavan	Married
John Stanford	Private	1940	Sligo	Single
Noel Stanley	Private	1940	Offaly	Single
Timothy Sullivan	Private	1941	Waterford	Single
Bernard Sweeney	Private	1925	Monaghan	Married
Philip Sweeney	Private	1940	Leitrim	Single
James Tahaney	Private	1942	Sligo	Single
George Tiernan	Sergeant	1925	Roscommon	Married
Sean Tiernan	Corporal	1942	Roscommon	Single
Michael Tighe	Private	1939	Roscommon	Single
Charles Tomkins	Private	1909	Wexford	Married
Patrick Williams	Private	1934	Sligo	Single
Francis Williams	Corporal	1920	Dublin	Married
James Kavanagh	Private	1938	Tipperary	Single
John Dreelin	Private	1943	Kilkenny	Single

The following are members of the Cavalry Group attached to A Company, along with Lieut Kevin Knightly, already listed with the officers. William Ready was attached to A Company as a fitter/mechanic.

Name	Rank	Year of Birth	From	Marital Status
Colman Geary	Sergeant	1935	Kildare	Married
Thomas O'Connor	Corporal	1941	Tipperary	Single
James Lucey	Corporal	1940	Kerry	Single
Patrick McCarton	Private	1939	Dublin	Single
Michael Nolan	Private	1943	Kilkenny	Single
John Shanahan	Private	1922	Limerick	Married
Joseph O'Brien	Private	1920	Wicklow	Married
Michael Dunne	Private	1939	Dublin	Married
William Ready	Private	1941	Cavan	Single

APPENDIX C

PRESENT-DAY NAMES
OF PLACES MENTIONED

The Congo	DR Congo (Democratic Republic of Congo)
Katanga	Katanga
Jadotville	Likasi
Elisabethville	Lubumbashi
Leopoldville	Kinshasa
Albertville	Kalemie
Stanleyville	Kisangani
Kolwezi	Kolwezi
Luluabourg	Kananga
Rhodesia	Zimbabwe

APPENDIX D

[Speech made by Comdt. W. G. Donnelly (Capt. Liam Donnelly in Jadotville) in Custume Barracks, Athlone, on 24 November 2005 at a ceremony unveiling a memorial to commemorate the actions of the officers, NCOs and men of A Company, 35th Infantry Battalion in Jadotville, 1961.]

Today is just Thursday for most people in Ireland. To the survivors of A Company 35th Infantry Battalion who served at Jadotville, it is a day we have longed for, looked forward to and wondered if it would ever take place. This day renews in us pride in our Defence Forces who share with us the justification, reward and recognition of the bravery, devotion to duty and professionalism of every member of the Company, and in particular the leadership and ability of our Company Commander, Comdt. P. Quinlan. I am particularly pleased that Mr Willie O'Dea TD, Minister for Defence, has taken such personal interest in bringing the issues involved in 'The Jadotville Affair' to a satisfactory conclusion. He has been untiring in his support of this project since his appointment as Minister for Defence.

WHY DID IT TAKE SO LONG?
It has taken a long time for all of this to be brought to fruition—44 years. Think of 44 years, what is it? 1900–1944, a period in which two world wars were fought. In the early years of that 44-year period, the myths and fairy tales, carefully quoted half-truths and smokescreens used to airbrush 'Jadotville' out of Irish military history, did not permit, in my opinion, a reasoned, neutral, independent, critical examination of every aspect of what was called 'The Jadotville Affair.' It was therefore 1996 when I made my first submission. It was made to the Chief of Staff of the day, seeking a critical examination and assessment of 'The Jadotville Affair.'

The submission set out the unusual circumstances surrounding A Company's presence at 'Jadotville', and the strategic shortcomings of both military and political decisions. Every statement in the submission was supported by detailed references. The submission was made seeking these requirements:

1. Official recognition of the professionalism and bravery of the Company operating under most unusual circumstances.
2. Recognition of the bravery and professionalism of Comdt. P. Quinlan O/C A Company as expressed in the commendation by General Raja.
3. Commendation of bravery of Personnel as submitted to be re-examined.

My submission in 1996 yielded no fruit. I never received a response in writing as to the result of my submission. I was given a verbal reply, which reflected a lack of interest and a lack of critical examination of the problem. Needless to remark, I was annoyed, amazed and disappointed. How could I inform any member of A Company of that situation? I could not, and bided my time for another opportunity.

I waited eight years, 1996 to 2004, and then resubmitted the exact same submission as I did in 1996. At that stage Lieutenant General Jim Sreenan was Chief of Staff. I estimated that he would take appropriate action, and whatever the outcome I would abide by it. I was delighted when the Chief of Staff informed me that he would select a Board of Officers to critically examine my submission. This was perfect. At that time too Col. Terry O'Neill had two prestigious contributions:

1. International Peacekeeping: The Irish Company at Jadotville, Congo, 1961; Soldiers or Symbols.
2. United Nations Peacekeeping in the post-Cold War era.

RTÉ (Radio 1) had produced the 2004 prize-winning documentary *The Siege of Jadotville*, produced by Tom McGuire. My submission had been mentioned twice in Dáil debates. On reading such debates it was clear that Mr Willie O'Dea TD, Minister for Defence, had a total empathy with the problems and their solution. Not to be overlooked was the contribution of Pte. John O'Gorman, who had approached the situation from a political point of view. My thanks to Noel Carey for his constant help, encouragement and support. When the board had critically examined my submission and delivered their report to Lt. Gen. Sreenan he invited me to a meeting to discuss the outcome. The Board had agreed to two of my three requests: Recognition of the unit's performance, and recognition of the role of the Company Commander, P. Quinlan.

My third request, the awarding of medals for those who had been commended, was not accepted. This request was not granted as the original board's decision was final and re-examination was not permitted in accordance with DFR. While disappointed, I could do no more on this issue, delighted that the personnel of A Company were awarded medals at a later time for other battles – Lt. Tom Quinlan, Cpl. Bill Allan and Sgt. W. Hegarty, to name a few.

This day then is the start of the process of which we will all feel proud. To the Chief of Staff we owe an immense amount of gratitude for his positive attitude, his fortitude and assistance and the methodology selected for resolving the complex issues involved.

To the Board of Officers, I have no idea who they were, I thank them for their independence of thought, their diligence and positive approach. I thank the Minister for Defence, Minister O'Dea, who carried the debate through the Dáil with care and diligence at a time when he was new to the ministry. His constant support of the Irish Defence Forces as the only legitimate armed force in this country is greatly appreciated.

What of this man, Company Commander Pat Quinlan? He has permeated our lives. He was always steadfast. He took enormous pride in the accomplishment of his unit. He could be pugnacious in asserting his beliefs, but he respected those who differed from him. He could be hard, but not petty. His enemies were the slipshod and the second-rate. The alleged consequences of 'Jadotville' were an unspoken and extraordinary burden, which drained him, but he would never have admitted it. One had to know him well to understand the manner in which he communicated. The meanings of the nudges and mumbles by which he conveyed his infinite caring came to be understood over time. Brigadier Gen. Kas Raja's assessment of Comdt. Quinlan: 'I should like to make particular mention of Comdt. Quinlan, who was in command of the Company that had the misfortune to suffer so much in Jadotville. This officer needs little commendation as his performance in maintaining the discipline and high morale of his men during a particularly difficult stage of Katanga operations speaks for itself. I have great personal admiration for the initiative, courage, drive and restraint of this officer, and I believe that he could be held as an example to all soldiers.' If he were here today, he would be so happy. He would tell us, don't look back. The future is full of exciting challenges. BUT WE DO LOOK BACK, AND WE REMEMBER HIM WITH PRIDE.

There are six elements vital to today's ceremony:

1. The survivors who are here, and for one reason or another, those survivors who cannot be.
2. To those who are deceased, we think of and pray for you.
3. To the wives, sweethearts and families who had such trauma during and after 'Jadotville', we acknowledge your role and support.
4. The survivors and deceased of the Relief Column who twice attempted with inadequate strength and support of relieve the situation at Jadotville.
5. The planners and organisers of this excellent occasion, especially O/C 4th Brigade Brigadier Gen. F. Swords.
6. The last element can be quoted as the cornerstone of this day's significance. It is this: the presence of Mr Willie O'Dea TD, Minister for Defence, is of major importance. Why? It is because as we approach the 50th anniversary of Ireland joining the United Nations it was appropriate in the Minister's view to place the deeds and bravery of A Company beside other Irish units who have served in the UN.

This is all history now, but from today it is history with a difference. The 'Jadotville Affair', for so long airbrushed from army history and records, may from today be talked about, written about, studied, and be the basis for real study, so that awful, sickening statement used so glibly today will have real meaning and significance. 'Ensure that such an episode will never be allowed to happen again.'

Thank you.

378